T0344178

Contents

Articles

Didier Debaise and Isabelle Stengers

MONOGRAPH SERIES

The Sociological Review Monographs
2022, Vol. 70(2) 3–17
© The Author(s) 2022
Article reuse guidelines:
sagepub.com/journals-permissions
DOI: 10.1177/00380261221084417
journals.sagepub.com/home/sor

After progress: Experiments in the revaluation of values

Martin Savransky
Department of Sociology, Goldsmiths, University of London, UK

Craig Lundy
School of Social Sciences and Professions, London Metropolitan University, UK

Abstract

What might it take to learn to think and live after progress? The notion of 'progress' is arguably the defining idea of modernity: a civilisational imagery of a boundless, linear and upwards trajectory towards a future that, guided by reason and technology, will be 'better' than the present. It was this notion that placed techno-science at the heart of the modern political culture, and it was the global unevenness of 'progress' that imagined European imperialism as a civilising mission inflicted upon 'backward' others for their own sake. Whilst during the postcolonial era the modern idea of progress and its deleterious consequences on a global scale have deservingly been the object of fierce criticism, 'progress', its promises and its discontents still command global political imaginations, values and policies to this day. In the wake of its devastating social, political and ecological effects, this article argues that the imperative of progress is now one we cannot live with but do not know how to live without. Thinking of progress not as one modern value among others but as the very mode of evaluation from which modern values are derived, this article provides an introductory exploration of the question of what thinking and living after progress might mean. It also provides an overview of the many contributions that compose this monograph, as divergent experiments in the radical revaluation of our values.

Keywords
colonialism, ecology, Nietzsche, progress, values

Outposts of progress

'In a hundred years', said Carlier, 'there will be perhaps a town here. Quays, and warehouses, and barracks, and – and – billiard-rooms. Civilization, my boy, and virtue – and all.

Corresponding author:
Martin Savransky, Department of Sociology, Goldsmiths, University of London, Lewisham Way, London SE14 6NW, UK.
Email: m.savransky@gold.ac.uk

And then, chaps will read that two good fellows, Kayerts and Carlier, were the first civilized men to live in this very spot!' Kayerts, his trading station chief, nodded approvingly: 'Yes', he replied, 'it is a consolation to think of that' (Conrad, 2002, p. 9). Tasked by the Great Trading Company with taking charge of a trading station in a remote part of Africa, the two men instead 'got on well together in the fellowship of their stupidity and laziness. Together they did nothing, absolutely nothing, and enjoyed the sense of the idleness for which they were paid' (2002, p. 7). Indeed, the only reason these 'pioneers of trade and progress' had the conversation from which a sense of consolation derived was that, after several months of doing nothing except looking 'on their empty courtyard in the vibrating brilliance of vertical sunshine', they came across a wreck of novels and some old copies of a home paper left behind by the previous occupant of the post, whose life had withered away after a bout of fever. The print, in particular, extolled the promises of 'Our Colonial Expansion' in the loftiest language, allowing them for a brief moment to forget the death of their predecessor while rendering their purposeless lives the very spearheads of progress, their idle days an exemplar of 'the merits of those who went about bringing light, and faith and commerce to the dark places of the earth'. If the promise of a future modern civilisation looking back at the foundations of its progressive fate served as consolation, therefore, it was because the present that these two white, largely pathetic characters inhabited was nothing if not thoroughly debased, void not only of all the 'virtues' that were the object of Kayerts and Carlier's momentary aspirations, but also of any sense of significance, of purpose, meaning, of a life worth living there and then.

But the consolation was just that – a brief moment of solace and comfort. For indeed, Joseph Conrad's classic story is nothing if not a story of descent: of the plundering and colonial exploitation of Africa, of Kayerts's and Carlier's lives into illness and suicide, of their promises of global trade and profit into slavery and ivory extraction, their colonial dreams of civilisation into the shambles. If widely – and rightly – regarded as an early critique of colonialism, based on Conrad's own experience at Congo, it is especially apposite that the title of this story be none other than 'An Outpost of Progress'. For indeed, while there has been no shortage of consoling thinkers who insist, with sociologist Robert Nisbet (1980, p. 8), that 'the idea of progress . . . has done more good over a twenty-five hundred-year period, led to more creativeness in more spheres, and given more strength to human hope and to individual desire for improvement than any other single idea in Western history', descent too paradoxically accompanies the story of this commanding idea, this all-pervading imagery which promised a boundless moral, social and economic ascent – guided by reason and technology – towards an open-ended but ever 'better' future. And it is from the ruins of some of its multiple ramshackle outposts, in the wake of its often devastating effects, that the contributions to this *Sociological Review* monograph situate themselves: as heterogeneous propositions in a collective experiment to imagine forms of social thought and social life *after* progress.

The idea of progress may, according to Nisbet (1980), have roots in the long Christian tradition. But there is no doubt that it was in the eighteenth century that imperial Europe placed its promise and power at the very heart of the project of Modernity. Animated as much by the extractive activities of its various imperial and colonial 'outposts' as by the scientific, industrial and political revolutions that transformed Europe – and much of the world – in the eighteenth century, 'progress' became the guiding modern philosophy of history ever since, inaugurating a new experience of time that claimed to break with the eschatological temporality of previous absolutist forms of government in which predictions of the coming End of the World and the Final Judgement set limits to human ambition and hope. Instead, progress engendered a new, universal historicity which 'made possible the attribution to history of the latent power of human events and suffering, a power that connected and motivated everything in accordance with a secret or evident plan to which one could feel responsible, or in whose name one could believe oneself to be acting' (Koselleck, 2004, p. 35). It opened up 'a future that transcended the hitherto predictable, natural space of time and experience, and thence – propelled by its own dynamic – provoked new, transnatural, long-term prognoses' (2004, p. 22).

It was this new historicity that, among societies who defined themselves as or aspired to be 'modern' (Chatterjee, 1993), in turn gave rise to a conception of the social as a sphere of autonomy, one capable – by nothing but its own means and aspirations – to work towards an open-ended future in which hopes of desired prosperity and affluence (intellectual, scientific, political, material, moral and cultural) would progressively be fulfilled (Charbonnier, 2021). And if the notion of progress opened up the future, rendered it largely unknown and unimagined – save, perhaps, for science fiction writers and other 'prophets of progress' (Bowler, 2017) – yet filled with hope and promise, this new philosophy of history powered by techno-capitalism and its fossils in turn engendered a new everyday experience at the heart of modern Europe. A mode of experience, in other words, which dramatically distanced collective expectations from all previous experience, introducing a chasm between past and future which was 'fed continually from a number of sources: technical development, the increase of population, the social unfolding of human rights, and the corresponding shift in political systems' (Koselleck, 2004, p. 60).

As such, by the end of the nineteenth century progress had become not merely one idea among others but a settled and almost universal faith betraying the very trajectory of History (Bury, 1920; but see Slaboch, 2018); not a value among others but the very *perspective of evaluation* from which the values of economic growth, civilisation, human development, moral betterment, industrialisation, human rights and technological innovation were derived. Never again, historian Eric Hobsbawm (1996, p. 269) once noted, 'was it to be so easy for blunt common sense, which knew in any case that the triumphal world of liberal capitalist progress was the best of all possible worlds, to mobilise the universe on behalf of its prejudices'. Yet not only was this best of all possible worlds (in Europe) reliant upon the value extraction and appropriation from the colonies and the Earth, shaping the world and its peoples – human and more – and their labour into homogeneous, fungible and scalable monocultures of production, trade and accumulation (Tsing, 2015). In relay and return, this progressive historicity and universal mode of evaluation had as its corollary the creation of a geopolitical 'hierarchy produced through a consideration of the best existing constitution or the state of scientific, technical, or economic development' (Koselleck, 2004, p. 238).

It was such a geography of anachronisms that enabled European colonialism to order, along a single diachronic line of progress and regress, other forms of life and sociality, other forms of knowledge, and other regions of the Earth – effectively conceiving of non-European peoples, like the cosmologies and stories by which they lived, as part of

Europe's past (Fabian, 1983; Hindess, 2008; Savransky, 2021a). Which is why, if the plane of historicity that 'progress' inaugurated served both to justify the imperial world-order and to absolve earth-wide colonial dispossession and devastation as the burden that modern societies had to accept and forcefully impose upon 'backward' peoples for *their* own sake, the decolonisation struggles of the 1950s and 1960s never managed to contest or displace the imperative of progress. In its stead, the march of progress carried on in the form of a world-system of postcolonial dependency and counter-insurgency that, under the aegis of humanitarian aid and the promotion of freedom and rights, established tech-nocratic strategies and programmes of development to 'modernise' and bring about eco-nomic prosperity and social progress to the so-called Third World, progressively seeking to incorporate ever more remote communities into the world capitalist economy whilst turning every corner of the Earth into a 'resource' (Escobar, 1995).

Far from recoiling in the face of seemingly crumbling empires, it was precisely since the mid-twentieth century that the machinic forces of progress truly gathered pace and, with the shift from coal to oil, found a new gear, further entrenching its descent as much into our modes of valuation as into our modes of earthly habitation. Indeed, this is the period that environmental historians and scientists now refer to as 'The Great Acceleration', the period that has seen three-quarters of all anthropogenic emissions of carbon dioxide dumped into the atmosphere, that saw the numbers of motor vehicles around the planet swell by over 800 million, the period of the Cold War and of the nuclear arms race, the period of earth-wide urbanisation, of the three-hundred-fold mul-tiplication of tons of plastic, of synthetic fertilisers and toxic treadmills, of mass dam constructions and exponential water use, of GDP growth and the tripling of the world population, of massive biodiversity loss, crippling global inequalities, of ocean acidifica-tion and rising global temperatures (see McNeill, 2001; McNeill & Engelke, 2014; Steffen et al., 2015).

What's more, even if the increasing alarm at the rising ecological vulnerabilities to which this history has given way makes the cruelties of the modern promise and project of progress perceptible with increasing force, and leads people in Europe and North America to report decreasing confidence in the standards of living of future generations (Pew Research Centre, 2017), it is not to the specious and profoundly questionable prop-ositions of the likes of Steven Pinker and his acolytes that one may turn to find signs of progress's health. While it cannot be denied that the ecological maelstrom has shaken confidence in progress's promises, it cannot be accepted that it has simply withered away. Instead, it is precisely as much in the public sense of dread and loss at the possible inflection of progressive historicity with which the reports by the Intergovernmental Panel on Climate Change (IPCC) are received, as in the ever renewing promises of green reform and revolution (from green growth and the Green Industrial Revolution, to the Green New Deal and proposals for Ecological Civilisation [see Savransky, this issue]), that one may turn to notice that, in spite of all, progress insists and persists in the configu-ration of the present. With relentless insistence, it calls upon our beleaguered present just as it called 'to Kayerts from the river. Progress and civilization and all the virtues. Society . . . calling to its accomplished child to come, to be taken care of, to be instructed, to be judged, to be condemned; it called him to return to that rubbish heap from which he had wandered away, so that justice could be done' (Conrad, 2002, p. 24).

After progress: A revaluation of values

What, in light of the history that has fuelled what is a veritable progressive machine – as much an idea as an experience of historical time, as much a mode of evaluation as a geopolitical project of world-making – might it mean to think and live *after progress*? What might be at stake in affirming the possibility of learning to appraise the present otherwise, to make lives worth living and futures worth living for outside of progressive coordinates? And in one and the same breath: what are the terms of order, the evidences and the disqualifications such possibilities must question before they themselves can become perceptible? Born of the manifold propositions, exchanges and improvisational experiments that were nurtured during a symposium series on the theme of 'After Progress' in 2019 (generously funded by The Sociological Review Foundation) and further multiplied and extended in the digital exhibition of collaborative storytelling that accompanies this monograph (www.afterprogress.com), it is as much with these questions as with the multiple attendant problems and challenges that such questions pose to a variety of different areas, histories and concepts, that the contributions to this monograph seek to grapple, contend and experiment. Bringing together over 12 international scholars from a variety of disciplinary backgrounds and forms of expertise, as well as dozens of attendants and participants who joined in the discussion, the symposium explored the ruinous philosophical, political and ecological histories of modern progress. Together, we discussed the equally vibrant histories of criticism that emerged in response, as well as the manifold experiments, practices, stories, experiences, concepts, challenges and cosmo-visions of collective forms of life and thought in and out of Europe that render thinking and living after progress possible by the very fact that – in upending the historicist, colonial, developmental and extractivist logics of progress – this multitude of practices, stories and propositions have already undertaken it.

Indeed, if the contributions that make up this monograph can be considered divergent experiments in contending with these questions, it is because what they share is a sense that no response to such questions can rest content with a purely critical gesture that would point to the evident flaws in the very *idea* of progress so as to pursue its 'reconstruction' (cf. Wagner, 2016), or to seek critical satisfaction in the reiteration of the important and already well-articulated denunciations of progress's Eurocentric colonialism, impoverished historicism, rationalistic hubris and ecocidal extractivism (Escobar, 1995; Ferguson, 1994; Gudynas, 2021). Such critical connections are vital, and they provide the starting point for many of the pages that follow. But if this briefest of sketches of progress's stranglehold on our political imaginations can teach us anything, it is that progress has never been merely 'ideal', that it has constituted a veritable manner of ploughing the world, of shaping our modes of collective valuation and earthly habitation. Indeed, from the prospects of boundless economic growth, to the slogans of 'Build Back Better' in the wake of the COVID-19 pandemic, through to the promises of reform of what we have come to call 'progressive' politics, the restless promises of progress, the metaphysical optimism with which the modern experience of history has been infused, have come to epitomise that particular kind of 'affectively stunning double bind' the late Lauren Berlant (2011, p. 51) would call 'cruel optimism': one that constitutes, at one and the same time, 'a binding to fantasies that block the satisfactions they offer, and a binding to the promise of optimism as such that the fantasies have come to represent'. And, by itself, mere critique is no cure for that.

As Amy Allen's (2016) recent decolonial study of 'critical theory' and Sanjay Seth's (this issue) problematisation of the circular imbrication between claims to knowledge and promises of progress powerfully suggest, the project of critique – or that project, at least, whose form is most immediately recognisable in the work of those who have advanced the Frankfurt School tradition of critical theory – is by no means immune to such affectively stunning double-binds but rather fuels them whenever the inheritance of the Enlightenment from which 'critique' itself springs does not simultaneously 'deploy critique in the service of criticizing and undermining Enlightenment's own Eurocentrism and thus its ongoing entanglements with the coloniality of power' (Allen, 2016, p. 204). Indeed, when it becomes perceptible that, far from universal, the transcendental appeals to reason and knowledge on which certain critical traditions rest are inextricable from the provincialism of a Western, modern culture that has harboured global aspirations and pursued them through colonial domination and epistemological disqualification (Seth, 2021), the contemporary standard-bearers of critical theory seek at every turn to resist 'the false conclusion that the criteria of reason themselves change with every new context' (Habermas, 2001, pp. 148–149). Which is why they avail themselves of what Seth (this issue) describes as a circular strategy. One that, in connecting 'the superiority of modern western knowledge' to 'the superiority of modernity as a social phenomenon', presupposes what it seeks to explain. Far from emancipating us from the illusions of progress, therefore, critique can often perpetuate a cruel optimism of its own – at once binding itself to fantasies of social and moral progress whose colonial foundations block the satisfactions they offer, and binding the politics of emancipation to the promises of the Enlightenment tradition that such fantasies have come to represent.

The making of critical connections that always bind the imperative of progress to the forces of oppression, domination and extraction remains vital to the multifarious contributions to this monograph. But such connections function less as vehicles for enlightenment than as vectors of conceptual and political indetermination. They seek to upend modern foundations and loosen progress's grip on our imaginations so as to experiment with the possibility of inhabiting the present otherwise; to wager – against all odds – on the chance of rendering ourselves capable of thinking, living and imagining for other times to come, for worlds to be otherwise composed (Savransky, 2021b). Indeed, to say that progress has become not merely a modern value among others but the very perspective of evaluation from which values – of growth, emancipation, civilisation, human development, moral betterment, industrialisation, human rights and technological innovation– are derived, is to recall with Friedrich Nietzsche (1990) that a critique of established values and facts is never enough. That is, critique is never enough unless it also pursues, and seeks to precipitate, a radical transformation of that differential element, that perspective of appraisal and evaluation, from which the very value of those values is derived. After all, the very imperative of progress makes present that, as Gilles Deleuze (2006, p. 2) put it with reference to Nietzsche, 'we always have the beliefs, feelings and thoughts that we deserve given our way of being and our style of life'. And as such, it is never enough to think our way into another way of being, but *we must learn to live our way into other modes of thinking* (Savransky, 2021a, p. 275).

Yet precisely because we always have the beliefs, thoughts and values we deserve given our ways of being and our styles of life, the imperative of progress is one we cannot live with but do not know how to live without. As such, to live one's way into other modes of thinking outside of the modern stories of progress is to confront the fact that, without such stories, the 'ruin glares at us with the horror of its abandonment', that it is 'not easy to know how to make a life, much less avert planetary destruction' (Tsing, 2015, p. 282). Which is why the revaluation of values involved in thinking and living 'after progress' requires not only the critical assessment of established values but also, and above all, a much riskier, uncertain and speculative art of creating and experimenting with other perspectives of evaluation and other modes of habitation, of affirming and nurturing forms of social life at odds with the progressive times. Such, indeed, is the art of those Nietzsche (1990, §211) called 'the philosophical labourers', who are not to be 'confused with philosophers' but are instead those on whose steps the philosopher follows: labourers are the 'critic and sceptic and dogmatist and historian and, in addition, poet and collector and traveller and reader of riddles and moralist and seer and "free spirit" and practically everything'. They are those who traverse 'the whole range of human values and value-feelings' and render themselves able 'to gaze from the heights into every distance, from the depths into every height, from the nook-and-corner into every broad expanse with manifold eyes and a manifold conscience', but do not do so with the purpose of establishing transcendental principles, or to discover universal truths.

The task of those whom Nietzsche calls the philosophical and scientific labourers, rather, is to '*create values*'. They are the ones who 'reach for the future with creative hand, and everything that is or has been becomes for them a means, an instrument, a hammer'. Their labour is the labour of those who refuse, in spite of all, to give to the stories of progress the power to inform even our own stories of ruination. Their art is the art of those who are prepared to take the risk of philosophising with a hammer or a tuning fork, not simply to smash the idols of progress but to affirm that, even at this time of socioecological devastation and perilous political repatternings, there are practical and conceptual propositions, political interstices and social undercurrents, a profusion of minor stories, earthly experiments, speculative propositions, and insistent possibilities, that proffer generative contributions to the questions of how we might understand and effect change, learn to live and die well with others, and make other worlds possible, when we no longer rely on the modern coordinates of progress as either our horizon or our home.

What would it take to refuse the promise of a horizon that renders the devastation of social and environmental ecologies the price freedom, security and prosperity must pay for their own realisation on Earth? What flights of political experimentation might be opened up in the rejection of the consolations proffered by those who find amidst disaster the signs of a universality to come, the solace of a new civilisation, of a good common world to be finally composed? What would be involved in refusing to let the rise of environmental reflexivity become the new name for the progressive imperative? Which improvised forms of organisation might be engendered outside the prospect of redemption, across the line that marks the limit of modern conceptions of justice? Which collective projects of activism and resurgence might be nurtured in the incommensurability between grief and grievance, loss and compensation? What forms of democracy might spring forth in the surrounds of the progressive state, in the unruly appositions of progress and regress, salvation and damnation? What might get underway in the ongoing and unfinished struggles to make lives and worlds on unstable ecological terrain, to learn to live and die well if not always better?

Progress asunder: Knowledges, histories and aesthetics otherwise

The invitation to imagine an 'after' to that which was meant to have no afters, of stepping outside the imperative of progress and experimenting from its ruins rather than labouring reconstructively in its shadow, necessarily calls for a profusion of divergent wagers, of singular attempts, of *essays* in the etymological sense of the word. It is a provocation to grapple with perilous possibilities one faintly envisages but cannot fully understand, creating values whose intensity one savours but whose value remains as yet unsettled, contending with problems one senses but has not yet learned how to pose. It is a radical call for the plural, a gamble on one and many openings to the otherwise and to the outside. And if this is so it is not least because the march of modern progress brought with it nothing short of a 'great singularisation and simplification', seeking to turn the world into a single order by drawing other temporalities of social life into its rhythms, such that 'Freedom took the place of freedoms, Justice that of rights and servitudes, Progress that of progressions (*les progrès*, the plural) and from the diversity of revolutions, "The Revolution" emerged' (Koselleck, 2014, p. 35).

Nurturing the heterogeneous as heterogeneous, the *essays* that compose this monograph do not, therefore, contribute to a would-be collective work of composing a common world in which the spectre of progress would have been reduced to a faint memory, or thrown, like The Revolution once hoped to do, the long progressive present into the dustbin of history. What they instead pursue is a multiplicity of situated openings, of ongoing and unfinished struggles, picking holes in the progressive whole so as to precipitate heterogeneous openings to a profusion of divergent milieus. In some cases, these struggles concern the incisive interrogation of the histories, ideas, evidences and disqualifications that must be questioned for the very possibility of an opening to become perceptible. In this regard, Seth's article provides a backdrop to many other speculative explorations in the monograph by offering a lucid critique of the persistent defences of progress amongst critical theorists. Focusing on the relations between knowledge and progress, mentioned above, he examines the manner in which social and political thinkers like Karl-Otto Apel and Jürgen Habermas, among others, have sought to defend their faith in the universality of modern progress and knowledge in the wake of the many counter-attempts to historicise and provincialise modern epistemic foundations thereby upending the very grounds on which the 'fact' of progress can come to be asserted. What Seth finds in his examination of these and other thinkers is that, despite certain 'concessions' about the necessary 'impurity' of reason, the imperative of progress and the presupposition of the universality of modern knowledge nevertheless insist and persist in their work. Illuminating the pitfalls involved in such attempts at upping the ante of progress and knowledge, Seth instead leads us to confront a present in which 'we are possessed of an acute consciousness of the historicity of our knowledge, but without any compelling argument for its superiority to other knowledges'. And given that modern knowledge has been the means of establishing the fact of progress, he invites us 'to ask what can be thought, and what is to be done, after we have dispensed with the idea of progress'.

It is precisely such dispensation that Andrea Bardin and Marco Ferrari pursue in their attempt to move past the intimate connections between the modern idea of progress and a homeostatic conception of social organisation, one only radicalised by neoliberal forms of social regulation. Engaging with the development of this homeostatic politics of regulation through an examination of the historical importance of cybernetics in modern culture, they seek to problematise the manner in which it has reduced both, reality to a series of 'calculable structures', and science to the very operation of calculation. Interrogating what cybernetics leaves unquestioned in order to push the homeostasic imaginary out of bounds, Bardin and Ferrari draw on the philosophy of Gilbert Simondon, and his concept of metastability, in order to seek an after to cybernetics in the possibility of reclaiming 'progress' in non-teleological and non-deterministic ways, as a politics far from equilibrium where the very openness to social and political invention is at stake.

Submitting the very idea of 'progress' to the understanding of complexity, far-from-equilibrium systems and non-linear dynamics that progressive histories of science would argue were themselves a product of scientific progress is the focus of Craig Lundy's essay. Drilling down into the detail of key complexity terms that are often glossed in the literature, as if their meaning and profundity were self-evident, Lundy seeks to isolate the conceptual elements that are 'doing the work' when it comes to the deviation of the complexity framework from the dominant scientific paradigms complicit in the modern idea of progress. While it is certainly possible for the complexity gambit to be placed under the thumb of modern progress – a fate that some complexity scholars are even fine with – the suggestion here is that if the philosophical implications of a properly complex cosmology are taken seriously, then this should indicate avenues for rethinking the idea of progress, and more specifically the *form* of this idea, enabling in turn an evasion of the presiding modern rendition of progress as 'betterment'.

A shared matter of concern across the essays that compose the monograph is the need to speculatively probe forms of organisation – of organisms, of collectives, of knowledges, of thoughts, of the Earth – that affirm the possibility of flourishing without presupposing the horizon of betterment or reinforcing the imperative progress. It is the immediate urgency of this which becomes particularly poignant in Lara Choksey's socio-literary exploration of and beyond what she calls 'the epidemiological plot', in which 'human powers of causality – and technological dominance over organic processes – are latched to a residual teleological hinge shared across liberal and communitarian futurisms, with progress displacing divine purpose with natural cause, scientism displacing style with fact, and research consortia displacing men of letters'. As Choksey argues, the effects of the epidemiological plot are as much historical as they are scientific, as much political as they are literary – they concern the very forms and genres of organisation by which certain kinds of knowledges, narratives and sociopolitical temporalities are orchestrated. Taking as her starting point the destituitive cry ('I can't breathe!') that in the summer of 2020 conjoined the crises of COVID-19 and police brutality against

Black lives and gave way to a mode of politics and aesthesis of urgency 'that simultane-ously holds and bypasses the possibility of achieving a just end', Choksey develops a pensive and sustained engagement with the epistolary genre as she seeks to attend to the orchestration of non-progressive forms of organisation – in literature as in politics – that flesh out and bypass 'the repeated disappointments of the plot of progress (the possibility of a universal cure) to bring an end to the protracted and deadening distress of the present'.

Unmaking progress: Natures, cultures and the politics of scale

The attempt to sidestep the political and cultural plot progress whilst contending with the protracted disappointments of the present is further addressed and developed, in an eth-nographic key, in the essay by Isaac Marrero-Guillamón. Indeed, focusing on the pro-tracted story of the mountain of Tindaya since its designation as the site for artist Eduardo Chillida's *Monument to Tolerance* that drew it into the anticipatory rhythm of the pros-pect of prosperity that such cultural and touristic development would bring, Marrero-Guillamón's essay is situated precisely in the temporalities of 'limbo' that characterise a present truncated in the hold of a promise of progress that never arrives. Promised in the mid-1990s, the making of *Monument for Tolerance* remains 'suspended, neither in con-struction nor abandoned'. Following the complex tangle of traces conjoining mining, modernist art and heritage preservation that are held in this suspension, Marrero-Guillamón explores how ideas of linear time, endless growth and inexorable advance-ment have shaped the relationship between people, indigeneity and land. But his is also a speculative ethnography, appraising Tindaya itself as an unintended monument to the ruins of modernity whilst affirming the possibility of enacting other, minoritarian futures, connected to the poorly understood indigenous lifeworlds attached to the mountain and its surroundings.

Indeed, Marrero-Guillamón's speculative ethnography also reminds us that the pos-sibility of thinking and living after progress confronts us anew with the concept and poli-tics of scale. And if this is so, it is not least because the quality making 'projects expand without changing their framing assumptions' that Anna Tsing (2015, p. 38) has called 'scalability' has been not only 'a hallmark of modern knowledge' but also one of the defining powers of the progressive machine, promoting 'smooth expansion' by rendering every element 'oblivious to the indeterminacies of encounter' thereby banishing 'mean-ingful diversity, that is, diversity that might change things'. But this is also to say that, while non-progressive forms of organisation and imagination might be – thankfully – unable to smoothly 'scale up', a critique of the notion of scale does not make scalability wither away. The politics of scale makes it frighteningly felt that progress is both some-thing we cannot live with but do not know how to live without, and this becomes remark-ably perceptible in the respective essays by Henrietta Moore and Juan Manuel Moreno, and by Dimitris Papadopoulos. Indeed, the problem that Moore and Moreno seek to grapple with is precisely that of imagining food systems and forms of agriculture after progress. Contemporary food systems, they argue, have been built on the scalable pursuit of productivity and efficiency through the deployment of ever newer technological means, including mechanisation, non-organic fertilisers and chemicals. In the case of modern agricultural systems, the goal is to extract the maximum yield per hectare and to drive down costs. Examining how the march of agricultural progress at once leads to rising levels of toxicity, declining biodiversity, and to the devastation of other agricultural practices and forms of working and inhabiting the land, Moore and Moreno attend to the trials and tribulations of agroecological approaches deployed to remediate these rifts, at once acknowledging its potential and warning against the creeping up of progressive horizons in the very efforts of remediation that much too quickly become 'scalable' thereby ignoring that every agroecological intervention forms 'a specific assemblage of plants, people, soil, fertiliser, technologies, animals, fences, and infrastructures both material and social'.

And if food systems render the imbrications of progress and scales irreducibly problematic, nowhere is this more evident than in the earth-wide suffusion of anthropogenic chemicals. For as Dimitris Papadopoulos reminds us in his essay on the ecological politics of chemical practice, we are all implicated by scale: much like progress itself, anthropogenic chemicals have suffused the Earth to the point where life amidst them, through them, is at once impossible and inevitable. As such, he argues, political ecological struggles after progress are inextricably bound to grapple with the problem of scale, at once as a source of ecological degradation and as a necessary component of many efforts of remediation. Which is why, rather than a dismissal of questions of scale, Papadopoulos seeks an opening for ecological reparation in the possibility of 'scaling out': of commoning social and planetary boundaries through divergently connected experiments implicating amateur scientists, indigenous knowledge practitioners, clandestine chemists, DIY biochemists, university researchers in green and sustainable chemistry, remediation ecologists, biodegradable designs, underground labs and interspecies collaborations. None of these experiments, however, 'make[s] progress'. They do not prefigure the coming about of a global politics of sweeping societal change. Yet perhaps, just perhaps, they might be enough 'to defend and maintain the life of communities facing socio-ecological conflict and destruction'.

After progress, *perhaps*

Perhaps! It is not to the great pronouncements of the coming about of a new epoch, not to the advent of a new global civilisation, that one is given over in the attempt to think and live after progress. It is to a precarious and interstitial *perhaps*, to the irreducible possibility of sensing and trusting the insistence of an indeterminate otherwise, the dim intensity of minor openings that might, just perhaps, inspire in us other sensibilities and other values, other habits and practices sustained in the undercurrents and undersides that manifold stories and experiments make exist (Savransky, 2021a, 2021b). 'But who is willing to concern himself with such dangerous perhapses! For that', Nietzsche (1990, §2) speculated, 'we have to await the arrival of a new species of philosopher, one which possesses tastes and inclinations opposite to and different from those of its predecessors – philosophers of the dangerous "perhaps" in every sense. – And to speak in all seriousness: I see such philosophers arising.' Thinking after progress is labouring in the hold of dangerous perhapses, without warrants or guarantees, risking a revaluation of values in a perilous and precarious present neither destined for a bright future nor certain to be damned, not knowing if such philosophers have, in fact, finally arrived, but labouring regardless to create openings through which one and many perhapses might pass.

And if the dangers of perhaps are perceptible throughout the monograph, their force and power to upend the terms of order only become stronger and louder. For indeed, as Krithika Srinivasan asks in her essay on zoöpolitics after progress, perhaps the socioecological impasse of progress and development to bring about greater prosperity and wellbeing to humankind cannot be disentangled from the profound anthropocentrism and speciesism with which the very concept and value of 'wellbeing' has been inscribed. Even when 'the idea that humankind is ontologically a part of nature is widely accepted', she nevertheless notes that such conceptual acceptance in no way has challenged the human exceptionalism that renders 'unimaginable that humans should live like other animals: with shorter life-spans perhaps, and unsupported by the infrastructures of commercial agriculture, medicine, and engineering that currently insulate many people from the vulnerabilities that are inherent to being a part of nature, including being killed by other animals for food or safety'. Labouring under the possibility of countering the zoöpolitics of progress and development, Srinivasan therefore experiments with a revaluation of what 'being well' might entail were it to become a matter not of anthropocentric exception and protection but of multispecies inception and justice.

Another radical revaluation gets underway in Martin Savransky's essay on what he calls 'ecological uncivilisation'. Responding to the proposition that learning to live in the Anthropocene might require that we learn how to die, Savransky examines the way in which the imperative of progress – and its double, civilisation – persists today in the form of a new ecological reflexivity devoted to the global reorganisation of societies towards just, socioecological transitions beyond the techno-fixes of geoengineering, green growth and their ostensible promises of modern progress. Through a sustained interrogation of the proposal for 'ecological civilisation', developed conceptually by a number of process philosophers and theologians and lately adopted as a guiding policy framework by the Chinese government in its shift to an ecological (geo)politics, Savransky shows that while such a call rejects the substantive values of modern progress, its regulative notion of civilisation retains the modern story of progress as a mode of valuation and therefore reinscribes imperial, colonial values at the heart of ecology. Refusing to submit to a story of progress after progress whilst thinking in the hold of perhaps so as to expand our political imagination, Savransky instead experiments with the possibility that learning to die might well entail learning to live without the concept and ideal of civilisation. Such, indeed, is his plea for 'ecological uncivilisation', a proposal to give oneself over to a permanent experimentation with 'improbable forms of world-making and methodologies of life that are articulated thanks to the earth-wide precariousness that calls them into action and not in spite of them; that are envisaged thanks to ongoing histories of decolonisation and not despite them; that strive to live and die well but not always better'.

Indeed, if such experimentations with inhabiting the Earth after progress, otherwise, are possible at all it is not least because the Earth itself is what Nigel Clark and Bronislaw Szerszynski call a 'planetary multiplicity': a self-differentiating planet with the propensity to shift between multiple operating states, thereby opening up novel possibilities for understanding the many differences discernible in our own species, the many multitudes that compose and inhabit it. Advancing this speculative dialectics of planetary multiplicities and earthly multitudes, they find an unexpected – and surely controversial – motley crew of allies in a certain post-Hegelian tradition that has paid attention to the 'internal disjunctures' that run through both the history of humans and the history of the Earth, thereby disrupting the imperium of modern European thought whilst pursuing the possibility that, perhaps, our interventions, which are 'part of the self-making of the world, are inevitably adventures in asynchronicity – or rather that the judgment of their timeliness is never wholly in our hands'.

It is because the efficacy of any intervention is never in one's hands that any generative experiment in intervening, in getting in between the multifarious forces, dreams, hopes and fears that make up this ongoing and unfinished world, requires to be performed with the trust of a held-out hand. Through a speculative engagement with the pragmatist philosophy of William James, it is precisely this task which Didier Debaise and Isabelle Stengers enjoin us to accept: that of the cultivation of practices that may enable us to participate in a regeneration of ecologies of trust, of ways of living that affirm interdependence in a hostile environment just as they resist the 'thinning down of the world' brought about by progress's homogenising advance. Suggesting that 'the risk of trust, when it bears on interdependence, is not between two individuals, but must take on a meaning that is collectively experienced as such', Debaise and Stengers are concerned with the collective fabrication, after progress, of generative devices which in breaking with the ideal of scalability and with the thinning abstractions of progress can perhaps give way to modes of assembly and assemblage that both presuppose and induce its participants' recursive capacity to make sense in common about situations that concern them. 'We need', they argue, 'to cultivate a fabric of sociality that transforms our claims into practical stories of becoming with each other, thanks to each other and at the risk of each other.'

Together, therefore, the contributions that make up this monograph just as they unmake the workings of progress create neither a blueprint for a post-progressive future nor the contemporary grounds for the kind of impotent attitude and mode of attunement that, Nietzsche would argue, breeds nothing but *ressentiment*: an attunement to the reasons that would justify our contempt for the present, our contempt for the world. Indeed, the challenge of learning to think and live *after* progress is precisely that, because we always have the values we deserve, no after to progress is to be found in its shadows, in the articulation of symmetrically opposed stances, in the designs of blueprints for a future that, finally freed from growth, from techno-scientific advance, from capitalist extraction, would at last be well and truly 'better'. Affirming the inchoate and interstitial character of the 'perhaps', the space without promises that teems with many an insistent otherwise, what they labour towards, what they strive for instead as they once again make an enemy of 'the ideal of today' (Nietzsche, 1990, §212), is to create values, to hazard tools, stories and propositions that may one day open the present up to a multiplicity of becomings, to other tomorrows and to days after tomorrow that – assuming there should be such days – might inspire in us, whoever this 'us' might be, the beliefs, feelings, values, thoughts and imaginations that we would like to deserve according to the divergent styles of life and modes of being that are in the process of making themselves felt on the margins and in the ruins of progress.

Acknowledgements

We are grateful for the continuous support, advice and inspiration of many colleagues and friends who have in different ways contributed to the development of this project, including Steve Brown, Claire Blencowe, Barbara Glowczewski, Elizabeth Povinelli, Iris van der Tuin and Daniela Voss. Our thanks also go to the many participants who attended the *After Progress* symposium series for the thoughtful questions and contributions. Last but not least, our sincere thanks go to *The Sociological Review*, whose ongoing support of this project has made this monograph possible.

Funding

The authors received no financial support for the research, authorship, and/or publication of this article.

References

Allen, A. (2016). *The end of progress: Decolonizing the normative foundations of critical theory*. Columbia University Press.

Berlant, L. (2011). *Cruel optimism*. Duke University Press.

Bury, J. B. (1920). *The idea of progress: An inquiry into its origin and growth*. Macmillan and Co.

Bowler, P. (2017). *A history of the future: Prophets of progress from H.G. Wells to Isaac Asimov*. Cambridge University Press.

Charbonnier, P. (2021). *Affluence and freedom: An environmental history of political ideas*. Polity Press.

Chatterjee, P. (1993). *The nation and its fragments: Colonial and postcolonial histories*. Princeton University Press.

Conrad, J. (2002). *Heart of darkness and other tales*. Oxford University Press.

Deleuze, G. (2006). *Nietzsche and philosophy*. Bloomsbury.

Escobar, A. (1995). *Encountering development: The making and unmaking of the third world*. Princeton University Press.

Fabian, J. (1983). *Time and the other: How anthropology makes its object*. Columbia University Press.

Ferguson, J. (1994). *The anti-politics machine: Development, depoliticization, and bureaucratic power in Lesotho*. University of Minnesota Press.

Gudynas, E. (2021). *Extractivisms: Politics, economy, and ecology*. Columbia University Press.

Habermas, J. (2001). *The postnational constellation*. Polity.

Hindess, B. (2008). Been there, done that. . . . *Postcolonial Studies*, *11*(2), 201–213.

Hobsbawm, E. (1996). *The age of capital: 1848–1875*. Random House.

Koselleck, R. (2004). *Futures past: On the semantics of historical time*. Columbia University Press.

McNeill, J. R. (2001). *Something new under the sun: An environmental history of the twentieth century*. Penguin.

McNeill, J. R., & Engelke, P. (2014). *The great acceleration: An environmental history of the Anthropocene since 1945*. Harvard University Press.

Nietzsche, F. (1990). *Beyond good and evil: Prelude to a philosophy of the future*. Penguin.

Nisbet, R. (1980). *History of the idea of progress*. Heinemann.

Pew Research Centre. (2017, June 5). *Global publics more upbeat about the economy: But many are pessimistic about children's future*. www.pewresearch.org/global/wp-content/uploads/sites/2/2017/06/Pew-Research-Center-Economy-Report-FINAL-June-5-2017-UPDATED.pdf

Savransky, M. (2021a). After progress: Notes for an ecology of perhaps. *Ephemera: Theory & Politics in Organisation*, *21*(1), 267–281.

Savransky, M. (2021b). *Around the day in eighty worlds: Politics of the pluriverse*. Duke University Press.

Seth, S. (2021). *Beyond reason: Postcolonial theory and the social sciences*. Oxford University Press.

Slaboch, M. (2018). *A road to nowhere: The idea of progress and its critics*. University of Pennsylvania Press.

Steffen, W., Broadgate, W., Deutsch, L., Gaffney, O., & Ludwig, C. (2015). The trajectory of the Anthropocene: The great acceleration. *The Anthropocene Review, 2*(1), 81–98.

Tsing, A. L. (2015). *The mushroom at the end of the world: On the possibility of life in capitalist ruins*. Princeton University Press.

Wagner, P. (2016). *Progress: A reconstruction*. Polity Press.

Author biographies

Martin Savransky is Senior Lecturer in the Department of Sociology at Goldsmiths, University of London, where he convenes the MA Ecology, Culture & Society. He is the author of *Around the Day in Eighty Worlds: Politics of the Pluriverse* (Duke University Press, 2021) and *The Adventure of Relevance: An Ethics of Social Inquiry* (Palgrave, 2016), and the co-editor of *Speculative Research: The Lure of Possible Futures* (Routledge, 2017). Working in the interstices between philosophy and the social sciences, his interests include pragmatism, radical pluralism, postcolonial thought, speculative practices, and methodologies of life on unstable ecological terrain.

Craig Lundy is a Reader in Social and Political Thought at London Metropolitan University. The majority of his research has been concerned with exploring the nature of transformational processes, in particular the role that history plays in shaping sociopolitical formations. Much of this research has focused on the work of Gilles Deleuze and the post-Kantian lineage (e.g. Hegel, Marx, Nietzsche, Bergson), however he has also conducted applied research using the principles of complexity theory/science to examine a range of issues including the formation of community identity, the pedagogy of 'service-learning' and the processes of public engagement. Craig is the author of *Deleuze's Bergsonism, History and Becoming: Deleuze's Philosophy of Creativity*, and he co-edited with Daniela Voss the collection *At the Edges of Thought: Deleuze and Post-Kantian Philosophy*, all published by Edinburgh University Press.

Knowledge, progress and the knowledge of progress

The Sociological Review Monographs
2022, Vol. 70(2) 18–33
© The Author(s) 2022
Article reuse guidelines:
sagepub.com/journals-permissions
DOI: 10.1177/00380261221084425
journals.sagepub.com/home/sor

Sanjay Seth
Goldsmiths, University of London, UK

Abstract
Modern societies, and the modern knowledge that was seen to be both an emblem and a precipitating cause of their modernity, have long been seen as marking a great historical advance. Modernity, we have been assured, by the social sciences in general and sociology in particular, is not only different from premodernity and contemporary nonmodern societies, these differences are also signs of intellectual, moral and material progress. In recent times, however, there have been a chorus of criticisms of the core presumptions that undergird modern knowledge. Such criticisms are sufficiently widespread and intellectually serious that the superiority and universality of modern western Reason, which could previously be taken for granted, now have to be argued for. Such defences of the universality of modern knowledge invariably draw on Kant and/or Hegel, as in the case of the two contemporary defenders of modern western knowledge, Karl-Otto Apel and Jürgen Habermas, whose arguments this article will outline and evaluate. It argues that neither convincingly shows that there are transhistorical and transcultural standards by which we can uphold the superiority and universality of modern knowledge, and concludes that there are no grounds to cleave to the idea of 'progress'.

Keywords
Apel, critical theory, Habermas, Kant, modernity, postcolonialism, progress

The narratives of progress that came to dominate and to shape Europe from about the eighteenth century onwards have a curious character. The claim that progress has occurred is a knowledge claim; but the knowledge through which this claim issues serves not only as the instrument via which 'progress' is detected and affirmed, but also doubles up as a cause and emblem of that progress. This is because modern knowledge is at once seen to mark an advance over the medieval and Renaissance knowledges that it supplanted; and also, and relatedly, as playing a crucial role in enabling the moral, material and techno-logical progress that distinguishes modernity from its historical predecessors. What might

Corresponding author:
Sanjay Seth, Department of Politics and International Relations, Goldsmiths, University of London, Lewisham Way, New Cross, London, SE14 6NW, UK.
Email: s.seth@gold.ac.uk

otherwise appear as a circular argument or even as a conjuring trick 'works', to the degree that it works, because this knowledge – modern, western knowledge as I call it, here as elsewhere (Seth, 2007, 2013a, 2020) – is regarded as having transcended its temporal and geocultural origins in the modern West, such that it is 'universal'. It is necessary that this knowledge be seen as universal rather than as merely the knowledge culture of modern Europeans, else its certification that progress has occurred would simply be modern western culture's affirmation of its modes of social organization, now characterized as both different and 'better' than the forms of social organization of others.

This claim to universality was largely accepted for a long historical period, and served to affirm and underpin narratives of progress. As modern western knowledge travelled to new domains in the wake of gunboats, slaveboats, conquest and trade, for many Europeans the fact that they were the conquerors and colonizers, rather than the conquered and colonized, provided irrefutable proof that 'European modes of thought and social organization corresponded much more closely to the underlying realities of the universe than did those of any other people or society, past or present' (Adas, 1989, p. 7). Asking themselves why European military organization, technology and statecraft was superior to their own, non-western elites frequently concurred. Reformers and nationalists began to urge that the knowledge of the foreigner be adopted and disseminated amongst their own peoples, in order that they may avoid being colonized, or emancipate themselves from colonial rule and join the ranks of sovereign, powerful and prosperous nations. These nationalist elites neither accepted European claims to superiority in all areas, nor did they seek to become mirror images of their rulers. As Partha Chatterjee has powerfully and influentially argued, the anti-colonial nationalist project was one to become modern-yet-different, and 'culture' became an increasingly common term for thinking and designating the difference that was to be 'preserved' even as it was being constituted and defined (Chatterjee, 1986, 1993; see also Seth, 2013b). Thus in nineteenth century China, reformers urging changes that would allow China to resist western depredations made a distinction between 'essence' and 'utility' (*ti-yong*); Chinese essence was to be preserved, while knowledges and practices from the West needed to be learned and freely borrowed. The elites who led the Meiji Restoration and implemented a state agenda to 'modernize' Japan, so that it could avoid the fate of India or China, adopted the slogan of *wakan yôsai* (Japanese spirit, western technique), a similar endeavour to acquire western knowledges and techniques precisely as a means to preserve that which was deemed to be at the very heart of Japanese identity. In colonial India most nationalists embraced western knowledge and schooling, while urging that this education be a 'national' education, delivered in the Indian vernaculars rather than in English, such that they inculcated Indian culture and patriotism: as one of their number put it, 'We do not want to be English or German or American or Japanese . . . we want to be Indians, but modern, up-to-date, progressive Indians' (Rai, 1920, p. 75).

The tension between imitation and appropriation, on the one hand, and the assertion of national/cultural difference, on the other, was usually navigated by treating the knowledge in question as western and modern only in origin, but as otherwise 'unmarked'. That modern knowledge first emerged in the West was treated as a matter of mere historical contingency, for this knowledge, it was claimed, was not intrinsically or essentially western. Indeed, in proportion as the colonizer sometimes asserted that their knowledge was intimately tied to uniquely Occidental cultural traits, and was thus intrinsically and not accidentally European, colonized elites insisted all the more stridently that this knowledge belonged to no one and thus to everyone. Embraced and championed by nationalists during the period of colonial rule, once the colonizer was expelled, postcolonial states sought, with varying degrees of success, to disseminate the new knowledge amongst their peoples through schools and universities, and to utilize it to govern their peoples. The globalization of modern western knowledge was thus the joint outcome of the actions of the colonizer, of nationalist elites, and of postcolonial nation-building.

In recent decades, however, both the notion of progress, and the assumed truth and universality of the knowledge that is the measure of progress and one of its causes, have come under sustained challenge from diverse quarters. Today there are many who are deeply sceptical that modern knowledge transcends its time and its place, and its imbrication in power relations; and who suggest instead that far from being universal, it is in fact, and variously, male/patriarchal, heteronormative, or western.[1] Criticism along these lines is sufficiently widespread and influential that the superiority and universality of modern western knowledge, which previously was taken for granted, now has to be argued for and defended. Those who would still defend it, in the words of one of their number, have come to acknowledge 'the intrinsic *impurity* of what we call "reason"' (McCarthy, 1994, p. 8), and to recognize that '"Pure" reason has had to make fundamental and lasting concessions to the impurities of language and culture, temporality and history, practice and interest, body and desire' (McCarthy, 1999, p. 168). That being so, the challenge they face, in the words of Jürgen Habermas, is to acknowledge that 'there is no such thing as a context-transcending reason', whilst at the same time avoiding 'the false conclusion that the criteria of reason themselves change with every new context' (Habermas, 2001a, pp. 148–149).

There is a historical-intellectual precedent to such a refutation of (a different kind of) scepticism; I am referring here to the philosophy of Kant. Kant responded to the scepticism of his time not by 'dogmatically' asserting certain propositions to be true, or by seeking to identify, on empirical grounds, a set of rational principles common to all humans, but by asking instead what sort of conditions had to be satisfied for cognitions and perceptions to occur at all. His answer deduced universal categories of Reason which were not derived from human experience (which was acknowledged to be varied), but were the grounds for our having any experience in the first place. This 'transcendental' move yielded a powerful argument for a Reason that was universal, because notwithstanding the immense variety of human experience, moralities and notions of beauty, it was the precondition for humans having *any* sort of experience, morality or conception of beauty in the first place (Allison, 1983). Modern knowledge, as elaborated and defended by Kant, could now stake a claim to having discovered and defined rational principles which had of necessity to be presupposed, and which were independent of social, cultural and historical particularities. This argument was not without its problems, but it is testimony to the vitality of the line of argument initiated by Kant that many of the most sophisticated contemporary attempts to salvage or retrieve the idea of a singular and universal Reason, while acknowledging that Reason is of this world, do so by returning to Kant. It is usually a Kant stripped of much of the metaphysics, but some version or other of a transcendental argument has been the chief resource for contemporary defenders of Reason, including John Rawls, Karl-Otto Apel, Hilary Putnam and Rainer Forst, who in different ways seek to show that there are inescapable presuppositions of thought and of argumentation that are, therefore, universal and 'true'.

Recognising that Kantian-derived arguments are insufficient, some of the defenders of modern knowledge and 'progress', such as Jürgen Habermas and Axel Honneth, additionally draw upon Hegel. Working with the tradition begun by Kant, Hegel's strategy for overcoming Kant's aporia was to acknowledge that there is no knockdown transcendental argument that will establish the truth of certain categories once and for all; there are only the categories through which historical communities know their world and organize their place in it. However, though the standards of modern morality are specific to modernity, modernity is itself an expression, and a higher working out, of a rationality immanent in social institutions, the most basic content of which is autonomy and free self-determination. Collective life always rests upon shared conceptions of what constitutes and legitimates the institutions of society, but these invariably present themselves as 'givens', as norms and conceptions that are a limit upon, rather than products of, human making. Social institutions and ways of life break down because these conceptions come into contradiction with the social forms with which they are associated, and the resolution of this crisis advances to the next logical/historical stage. There is teleology or progress in all this, inasmuch as each breakdown and reconstitution progresses to a 'higher' level, one where the autonomy of subjectivity/spirit is more fully (if still only partially) recognized, and comes to underlie social institutions and practices. Modernity most fully 'realizes' or lives out and instantiates the autonomy which is presupposed by all collective life; modernity's self-understanding is the self-consciousness of this fact, and this is what makes it superior to other forms of knowledge. This argument treats modernity as a privileged historical moment and a privileged site, one where the facts and processes that have always governed human history finally became discernible, and reveal what has always been true but could not be fully grasped till now. Reason and its discovery are here historicized, and Reason, though universal, only becomes available with the advent of the modern (Kolb, 1986; Pippin, 1991, 1997) .

If such Kant-based or Hegel-influenced arguments are persuasive, it would follow that contemporary challenges to a singular and universal Reason, and to the narrative of progress it underwrites, can be refuted – or at least, accommodated and neutralized. Engaging with Apel's Kantian derived defence of modern knowledge and progress, and at greater length, with Habermas's Hegelian inspired and historicist defence of a singular and universal Reason, I argue that their intellectual sophistication notwithstanding, these defences are not persuasive; and that therefore we must dispense with the idea of 'progress' which they underwrite.

Apel and discourse ethics

The work of the eminent philosopher and social theorist Karl-Otto Apel (1922–2017) seeks to show that, even after we recognize that what is regarded as moral or ethical is always shaped by historical and cultural differences, we still find that there is a universal core beneath all the differences. This is to be found not in some area of overlap, as in a Venn diagram, but rather in certain formal conditions that must be present (and actively or tacitly accepted by all parties) for conversation, including disagreement, to occur at all. Though 'formal' rather than substantive, these unavoidable and shared rules have broader implications that can be shown to derive from the formal requirements. The structure of the argument is indebted to Kant, and Apel describes his efforts at being directed at a 'transcendental-pragmatic transformation of Kantian ethics', designed to take into account (as Kant did not) the historical and cultural 'dependency' of all concrete forms of morality, but 'without giving up the moral universalism of Kantian provenance and falling a victim to historical-relativism' (Apel, 2001, p. 50).[2] Apel additionally seeks to show that these transcendentally derived rules have important real-world implications, providing guidelines for what are and are not morally and politically acceptable positions on a range of important and controversial issues.

It is true, Apel acknowledges, that we always reason out of specific contexts and communities, and thus that our reasoning is always grounded in the historical and cultural presuppositions of determinate lifeworlds. Nonetheless, all public argumentation, because it makes validity/truth/rightness claims for which acceptance is sought from others, also has a transcendental horizon in addition to its historical one; each 'real' communication community presupposes an 'ideal communication community'. Any validity claim, irrespective of its historically and culturally specific content, also has a form that is not historically contingent, because it is a transcendental feature of argument as such. The very performance of moral argumentation thus has certain necessary and inescapable presuppositions built into it, and these provide us with a context-independent standard by which to judge whether a specific claim comes into contradiction with the necessary entailments of making a validity claim. The 'undeniable presuppositions of arguing', as Apel describes them (2000, p. 145), are: any effort to argue and persuade cannot legitimately exercise coercion, or make use of authority; everyone has an equal right to participate in debate and present an argument; and the consensus of everyone who is potentially affected (and not only the active parties in a debate) must be sought. These are the 'a priori' presuppositions that ground all public argument and disagreement, and they cannot be denied without 'performative self-contradiction'. Apel's discourse ethics arrives, in his words, at 'an equivalent to Kant's universalization principle of the "categorical imperative"', providing us with 'an ideal yardstick of a possible examination of all rightness claims,' (Apel, 2001, pp. 59, 72). This can then be drawn upon to provide us with guidelines for arriving at rational and incontrovertible (hence universal) moral judgements on contemporary political issues, including multiculturalism, globalization and international law (see Apel, 1999, 2000, 2007).

According to Apel, what is moral is something that is always the subject of intersubjective argument and agreement, rather than (as for Kant) a question a solitary consciousness poses to itself. This means that moral arguments are always embedded in, and shaped by, historical circumstances and cultural presumptions. But what seems to be a problem for universalist claims also provides the solution to that problem: for in arguing about what is moral, in inevitably particularistic ways, we also and inescapably invoke (now thinking with Kant) the transcendental presuppositions of any and *all* discourse. Reflection upon these allows us to see that whatever the merits or otherwise of the moral issue in question, there are certain parameters, part substantive and part procedural, that we simply cannot deny without 'performative self-contradiction', the knockout phrase at the heart of his argument, and one that Apel repeats again and again. These inescapable and hence universal presuppositions of argument cannot be rationally denied because 'the very attempt to do so brings them into play' (Apel, 1992, p. 140), thereby unwittingly affirming the universal presuppositions underlying argumentation in general.

This 'transcendental-pragmatic' reformulation of Kant is ingenious, but the problems with it are also numerous. Apel seeks to preserve the force of Kant's transcendental argument while making it intersubjective, social and historical. But once (self-)consciousness is replaced by discourse – that is, once the point of departure is not an abstract consciousness but intersubjectivity – attempts at finding a 'form' or 'procedure' that is implicit in every context (and is thus context independent or transcending) will in fact always, wittingly or unwittingly, make presumptions that are not 'merely' formal, procedural or minimal. As Alasdair MacIntyre points out, Kant himself addressed a very specific reading public, 'with its own stock of shared assumptions, expectations and focus of attention'; and as with Kant's public, so with others: 'What is regarded as obvious or taken for granted, what is treated as problematic, which considerations have more weight and which less, which rhetorical modes are acceptable and which not, vary from reading public to reading public' (MacIntyre, 1999, p. 248). That is, what counts as an argument, who the legitimate participants in public argumentation are (everyone? only those over 18? only men? only community elders?), what form a valid argument must take, and so on, will vary according to time and place. The claim that truth or validity claims necessarily entail the free, equal and uncoerced participation of all affected is the presupposition of discourse only in liberal communities, not a feature of discourse as such. As Michael Walzer notes of theories that seek to abstract form from content, or procedure from substance, 'The procedural minimum turns out to be rather more than minimal. . . . The [procedural] rules of engagement constitute in fact a way of life . . . the minimal morality prescribed by these theories is simply abstracted from, and not very far from, contemporary democratic culture' (Walzer, 1994, pp. 12–13).

The 'knockdown' character and the polemical force of Apel's argument derives from the claim that the presumptions underlying public argumentation cannot be denied without self-refutation; to dispute these presumptions is unwittingly to affirm them. But it does not take too much imagination to think of communities possessed of conceptual traditions and idioms in which the act of assertion does not posit that all members are party to the debate, and in which the rules by which debate is conducted and resolved are not those of a liberal democratic culture. Such communities exist – that is precisely why debates over universalism occur, else they would be redundant. If the aim is to persuade those who do not already reason out of our conceptual tradition, then smuggling in presuppositions that are necessarily those of historically particular communities, while claiming 'unavoidable' or 'inescapable' status for them, is far from convincing. As Barbara Herrnstein Smith pithily puts it, the 're-grounding of transcendental rationalism centers on the demonstration of the inescapable necessity of (its conception of) reason as validated by the exposure of the inescapable performative contradiction of anyone denying it'; but as the argument depends 'on the prior acceptance of just the system of ideas, claims and definitions at issue . . . the supposed re-grounding is thoroughly circular' (1997, p. 118). A transcendental argument 'works', if at all, with a solitary and abstract consciousness. Once it is made intersubjective and empirical, as in Apel's case, transcendental arguments become circular, assuming what they are meant to 'ground', and thus cannot 'rescue' the universality of Reason and the belief in progress from contemporary critiques.

If an intellectual strategy indebted to Kant fails to 'rescue' Reason from the now common criticism that what is illegitimately claimed to be 'universal' Reason is in fact always someone's reason – that it is male, or heteronormative or western – then perhaps a strategy that draws upon Hegelian historicism will fare better?

Habermas and 'Occidental rationalism'

Heir to the Frankfurt School of critical theory, and thus to a tradition of thinking in which Kant, Hegel, Weber and Marx loom large, Habermas has been engaged in a project – one pursued with remarkable consistency over many decades – that seeks to show that post-Enlightenment knowledge marks an advance over all knowledges that preceded it, while denying that the dominance of instrumental rationality and a disastrous 'dialectic of Enlightenment' is an inevitable correlate of Reason. Related to this, Habermas grants that there is no context-independent knowledge, while denying that this leads to the conclusion that all knowledges are creatures of their time and place. Habermas agrees that it is necessary to historicize and thus 'detranscendentalize' Reason, but the question, as he poses it, is 'whether the traces of a transcending reason vanish in the sands of historicism and contextualism or whether a reason embodied in historical contexts preserves the power of immanent transcendence' (Habermas, 2008, p. 25). As the rhetorical nature of the question indicates, Habermas thinks that Reason can be historicized and yet transcend its historical contexts, and provide an immanent basis for criticism and emancipation. He seeks to show that modern Occidental knowledge is of this type; that is, it transcends its contexts and is universal, and as such, that it both embodies progress (vis-a-vis earlier knowledges), and that its affirmation that modern times are marked by cognitive and social progress can be taken as objective and authoritative.

Habermas co-produced, with Apel, the claim that discourse necessarily and inescapably involves context-transcending presumptions that cannot be denied without self-contradiction, and he continues to advance this claim in subsequent works. However he also came to recognize that it is not possible to extrapolate from discourse theory to 'ground' or legitimate institutions and practices (Habermas, 1990a, pp. 85–86; 1990b), and thus that 'discourse ethics' cannot, by itself, provide a compelling justification for the truth and universality of modern knowledge. He further acknowledges that since discourse is always embedded in institutions and practices, any Kantian defence of Reason must also be a defence of the modernity within which it is enmeshed (Habermas, 1996). Habermas's defence of modern knowledge and of progress is thus indebted to Kant, but he additionally draws upon Hegel. In McCarthy's characterization of his project, Habermas wants to deploy 'Kant's claim that there are universal and unavoidable presuppositions of theoretical and practical reason', but 'he also wants, thinking now more with Hegel, to present a reconstructed conception of the Bildungsprozesse, the self-formative process of the individual and the species that have rational autonomy as their telos – a kind of systematic history of reason' (McCarthy, 1982, p. 59). Habermas seeks a defence of modern knowledge that is also a defence of modernity, and one that very explicitly and unapologetically seeks, in his words, to connect 'a claim to *universality* with our *Occidental understanding of the world*' (Habermas, 1984, p. 44). Such an Occidental understanding is not merely one of many traditions of reasoning, as is suggested by 'contextualists', who 'maintain that the transition to post-metaphysical concepts of nature, to post-traditional ideas of law and morality [i.e. to what I have been calling modern, western knowledge], only characterizes one tradition amongst others'; against this, Habermas declares in an interview, 'I don't see how this thesis can be seriously defended. I think that Max Weber was right . . . [about] the general cultural significance of Western rationalism' (Habermas, 1992, p. 254). Whereas Apel's work seeks to show that modern knowledge is true and universal *even* though it first arose in the West, Habermas argues that this knowledge is rational and universal *because*, not despite the fact that, it is modern and western.

Why should we privilege modern western knowledge? Habermas suggests that it is possible to 'reconstruct the empirical succession of worldviews as a series of steps in learning', and that such a history displays 'an internally reconstructible growth of knowledge' (Habermas, 1984, pp. 67, 66). Habermas provides such a reconstruction, by means of a contrast between the mythical worldview of non-moderns (specifically, the 'savages' studied by anthropologists) and modern knowledge, and concludes that the most striking feature of savage, mythological thought is that it is 'totalizing', relating everything to everything else; and that as a consequence it is marked by a 'confusion between nature and culture', and between 'culture and internal nature or the subjective world' (Habermas, 1984, p. 51). Because culture and nature have not been separated out from one another, the mythological worldview is not even aware that it is a worldview; that, for instance, animism and magic are superimpositons or projections of culture onto nature. For this reason, as well as the fact that intellectual traditions are accepted on authority, savage thought is not open to questioning or to revision.

With the transition from 'archaic' to 'developed civilizations' – in later works Habermas will borrow Jasper's concept of an 'Axial Age' to characterize this allegedly world-historical shift – mythological thought is replaced by argument and reflection, though the first and highest principles, the foundations of this worldview, 'are themselves removed from argumentation and immunized against objections' (Habermas, 1979, p. 105). With the advent of modern thought, even the highest principles or foundations of the modern worldview lost their unquestioned character, and 'a growing decentration of interpretive systems . . . [led] to an ever-clearer categorical demarcation of the subjectivity of internal nature from the objectivity of external nature, as well as from the normativity of social reality and the intersubjectivity of linguistic reality' (Habermas, 1979, p. 106). That is, modern thought came to recognize that the objective, social and subjective worlds fundamentally differ from one another, and that propositional truth, normative rightness and subjective expressiveness belong to different domains and require different attitudes and protocols of reasoning. This allowed for development within each of these spheres – for example, natural scientific enquiries were no longer constrained by religious requirements, and art become an exploration of subjectivity, rather than being subordinated to exiguous concerns. Borrowing a distinction from Karl Popper and Robin Horton, Habermas concludes that mythological and premodern worldviews are 'closed'; that is, are not capable of reflecting upon and correcting (rather than taking as pre-given) their own presuppositions, whereas modern thought is reflexive and 'open'.

This is a rather standard whiggish account of why we moderns are right whereas our historical predecessors were wrong, and why modern western societies are reflexive whereas other, 'savage' and 'traditional' societies immunize their deepest beliefs from criticism. It is, moreover, drawn from a highly selective reading of the anthropological literature of the 1960s and 1970s (principally Robin Horton, Ernest Gellner, Maurice Godelier, Malinowski, and the debate in Wilson [1970]), containing presumptions and arguments that would be repudiated by many, perhaps even most, anthropologists today. What, in any case, are the *arguments* behind the reiteration of these by now rather shop-worn and self-congratulatory Enlightenment distinctions?

One argument is that the development of worldviews parallels the cognitive and moral development of individual humans from childhood to adulthood: the ways in which peoples understand and engage with their world display 'developmental-logical correlations with ontogenesis', because 'the reproduction of society and the socialization of its members are two aspects of the same process', 'dependent on the same structures' (Habermas, 1979, pp. 104, 99). In *The Theory of Communicative Action* and the earlier *Communication and the Evolution of Society* Habermas draws upon the work of Jean Piaget and Lawrence Kohlberg on the cognitive and moral development of children in order to establish such homologies. At the centre of a child's development is not this or that content of knowledge, but rather 'the decentration of an egocentric understanding of the world' (Habermas, 1984, p. 69). A baby cannot distinguish between itself and the world; there are no boundaries between its corporeal body and the world. Later the child learns to differentiate itself from nature, and from society, and then as a youth, learns that social principles and norms are humanly created, and thus criticizable and revisable. Later still, the 'competent adult' now distinguishes between the external world of nature, the social world and their subjective world, and recognizes that statements or 'validity claims' in each of these has its own protocols. All this, Habermas asserts – albeit with qualifications – roughly corresponds to the progression of mythical, axial and modern worldviews. And just as once we are adult we cannot go 'backwards' to a child's point of view, so too with worldviews: 'With the transition to a new stage the interpretations of the superseded stage are . . . *categorially devalued*. It is not this or that reason, but the *kind* of reason, which is no longer convincing. . . . These devaluative shifts appear to be connected with socio-evolutionary transitions to new levels of learning' (Habermas, 1984, p. 68).

This argument can be dispensed with fairly briefly, for it is a very poor one. There is no reason to believe that individual learning and growth can be correlated with social phenomena (or even what would count as empirical evidence for such a claim), and indeed, every reason to believe that the analogy is a bad one, as are most attempts to map individual, semi-biological processes onto social and historical ones. This analogy certainly has antecedents, but they are not ones that inspire confidence – the claim that there are 'childlike' peoples and mature ones long served as one of the justifications for slavery, colonialism and the dispossession of First Peoples. And because this argument begins with the premise that some societies are rational and mature, and then seeks correlations with ontogenesis, its conclusions are already present in its premise. Those sympathetic to and sharing in Habermas's project have been unwilling to fully endorse his argument (see for example McCarthy, 1982, pp. 69ff.) and in later writings Habermas has ceased to invoke it, although the claim that modern worldviews are the culmination of a 'learning process' remains central to his theory.

Habermas's second and stronger argument is one that ascribes intellectual and cognitive advances to material and sociological developments; progress in the cognitive realm is 'a historical result' that 'arose . . . in the midst of a specific society that possessed corresponding features' (Habermas, 1990b, p. 208). This 'specific society' is a modern society, a form of social organization and collective life that comes about as result of capitalism and industrialization. In this second argument the emphasis is placed on sociological factors; here, the distinctions between the external world (the domain of theoretical reason), the moral and political world (the domain of morality, law and politics) and subjective inwardness (the domain of the arts) only become possible in their fully developed form with modernity, when each of these becomes systemically differentiated from the others, such that they appear as distinct 'subsystems' of the modern lifeworld: it is the advent of modern society that '*objectively* affords contemporaries a privileged access to the general structures of the lifeworld' (Habermas, 1987, p. 403). In premodern societies these distinctions are not institutionalized, and cannot be; modernity lies at the end of a long process of historical development, one that makes it possible to now see that making such distinctions represents a cognitive advance; indeed, marks the culmination of the process of the rationalization of worldviews. In this argument, the superiority of modern western knowledge is connected to the superiority of modernity as a social phenomenon. More so than in the case of Apel, Habermas's thought is conducted not only in a 'social' but more specifically in a 'sociological' register, for his account of what is distinctive about modern society is deeply indebted to a discipline that conceives of itself as the self-consciousness of modern society, as 'emerg[ing] out of the conditions of modern society as well as being a distinctively modern form of explanation of that society' (Bhambra, 2007, p. 47). The philosophical architecture of Habermas's account and defence of modernity is accompanied by sociological cladding.

Modernity is moreover a product of Occidental history, which is why Habermas concurs with Weber on 'the general cultural significance of Western rationalism'. Once this historical process has occurred, it must constitute the 'horizon' for all thinking; no one is exempt, and there is no 'going back'. Non-western societies may continue to be different in some cultural ways, but the social and institutional changes that characterize modernity, and the modern western knowledge which accompanies it – with its divisions between science, law and morality, and aesthetics – are inescapable, and furthermore, mark progress. Or as Habermas puts it, in the form of a rhetorical question to which he provides an answer, 'Are or are not the structures of scientific thought, posttraditional legal and moral representations, and autonomous art, as they have developed in the framework of Western culture, the possession of that "community of civilized men" that is present as a regulative idea? The universalist position does not have to deny the pluralism and the incompatibility of historical versions of "civilized humanity"; but it regards this multiplicity of forms of life as limited to *cultural contents*, and it asserts that every culture must share certain *formal properties* of the modern understanding of the world. . . . Thus the universalist assumption refers to a few necessary structural properties of modern life forms as such' (Habermas, 1984, p. 180).

This second argument, one where the emphasis is now on historical-social changes rather than on cognitive advances, is however subject to the same objection as the first, namely that it assumes what needs to be shown, this time in the context of social evolution rather than on 'learning'. Even a sympathetic interlocutor like Apel wonders whether seeking to ground the claims for Reason in such an empirical and historical manner runs the risk of 'giving the impression of a dogmatically posited teleological philosophy of history' (Apel, 1992, p. 147). And Habermas's project is indeed underpinned by a notion of 'progress' that is asserted rather than convincingly argued, and one that is highly contestable. Moreover it *has* been contested, by legions of anti-colonial and indigenous thinkers and activists, and by the many scholars who have drawn attention to the ways in which 'modernity' was not something that developed autochthonously in the West, but was from the beginning a global process, and one that was heavily dependent on the conquest, colonization and exploitation of the non-western world. As Amy Allen puts it, parsing the arguments of scores of anti-colonial thinkers, past and present, 'the notion of historical progress as a "fact" is bound up with complex relations of domination, exclusion and silencing of colonized and racialized subjects' (Allen, 2016, p. 19), and there is every reason to doubt the claim that there has been progress in history. Centuries of slavery and colonialism, two world wars and a Holocaust, surely call into question the presumption that the modern age has been marked by learning and progress in social, moral and political matters? If they do not, it is hard to imagine what would do so!

Habermas's two arguments – namely, that modern knowledge represents a cognitive advance, and that modernity represents historical evolution and progress – are clearly meant to reinforce each other. The division of reason into three autonomous spheres (corresponding exactly, we may note, with Kant's three critiques) marks progress, and therefore also shows that modernity, the historical 'stage' in which these divisions become possible and then institutionalized, is a more advanced socio-historical form. Conversely, modernity is a historically advanced form of social organization, and since it is characterized by a division of knowledge into three spheres, such an organization of knowledge is also an advance, and also a marker of progress. The two arguments certainly imply each other, but they do not ground each other: rather, each presupposes the validity of the other. The entire edifice of his argument, as some others have also noted (Allen, 2016; Warnke, 1987, pp. 133–134), is circular.

In later works, Habermas acknowledges that 'The suspicion that mechanisms of exclusion are often embedded within the hidden presumptions of universalistic discourses is well-founded – up to a point' (Habermas, 2001a, p. 147). He even concedes that this well-founded suspicion means that the West 'must be only one voice amongst many, in the hermeneutical conversation between cultures' (Habermas, 2002, p. 154). The Olympian insouciance with which he previously affirmed the superiority of modern western knowledge has come to be supplemented, though not replaced, by the (very different) claim that as modernity has come to encompass the entire world, so that no premodern societies are left, the knowledges and institutions that accompany and characterize modernity are *unavoidable* (Habermas, 2001b). But even in the 'conversation between cultures' to which Habermas passingly refers, it is clear that modern western knowledge will be a privileged interlocutor. Since one of the greatest cultural achievements of 'Occidental rationalism' lies in 'the capacity for decentring one's own perspectives, self-reflection, and a self-critical distancing from one's own traditions', even 'overcoming Eurocentrism demands that the West make proper use of its own cognitive resources' (Habermas, 2002, p. 154).[3] Moreover, adds Habermas – without the slightest sense of irony – the critics of Occidental rationalism inadvertently confirm this, for the distance from their own tradition that is the condition of their critique is 'one of the advantages of occidental rationalism' (Habermas, 2001b, p. 119)!

Habermas's minor 'concessions' to critics do not mark any substantial departure from his argumentative strategy, which remains unchanged in essentials – and remains unpersuasive. Claims to truth and universality, whether on the grounds of a cognitive learning process or on the grounds that modernity enabled progress in knowledge, presuppose what they are meant to establish; and in concert they are circular, rather than mutually validating.

After progress

In a contemporary intellectual, political and ethical scene where the truth and universality of a knowledge born in Europe can no longer be blithely assumed and celebrated, defenders of that knowledge and of the narrative of progress that it underpins have frequently returned to Kant for inspiration. A historically and socially grounded version of the transcendental argument is used by Apel to argue that public argumentation has necessary and inescapable presuppositions, and that these provide standards – independent of historical context and cultural and other variation – that are universal, and that ground/ prove that some fundamental liberal values are binding on all rational beings. Ingenious as this argument is, I have sought to show that it is circular and thus unconvincing. Some other Kantians engaged in a similar project have come to a similar conclusion – in his later work Rawls came to abandon his highly influential attempt, in *A Theory of Justice*, to draw upon Kant to arrive at a quasi-transcendental grounding and defence of a liberal conception of justice (see Seth, 2020, pp. 60–67).

Recognizing some of the insufficiencies and problems of Kantian-derived arguments, Habermas defends modern knowledge and 'progress' by additionally drawing upon Hegel. Hegel produced the first and the most important version of an argument/ narrative, which, however, has many different versions, and has been at the heart of modern understandings of modernity and its knowledge. In all versions of this historicizing and teleological narrative, premodern or 'traditional' cultures (including those of the West) are presented as being in thrall to enchantments and cosmologies, whereas we moderns are regarded as having grasped (or having been forced to grasp) the bedrock truths that underpinned these misperceptions all along. This is an account, as Charles Taylor describes it, according to which 'modernity involves our "coming to see" certain kernel truths about the human condition' (Taylor, 1999, p. 170); or as David Kolb puts it, it is one in which modern knowledge is 'not just another in a sequence of historic constructions', but rather 'the unveiling of what has been at the root of these constructions' (Kolb, 1986, pp. 9–10). In all versions of this account – Weberian, Hegelian, Marxist, Habermasian and other – the core presumptions of modern knowledge are not yet another set of parochial assumptions claiming universal validity, like a proselytizing religion, but rather embedded in a narrative that purports to explain both why we humans were once bound to get things wrong, and how it became possible to get them right. This is what I have elsewhere called the 'once was blind, but now can see' account and defence of modern knowledge (Seth, 2013a).

However, once knowledges are acknowledged to be historical, as they are in the above narrative – that is, once the transcendental argument is not the sole or chief argument – assertions of the superiority of modern knowledge rest upon the claim that transitions between worldviews mark some sort of progress. Such privileging of the modern and of modern knowledge – and thus of the modern West, which until recently was regarded as the site and source of modernity and its self-knowledge – may have once seemed self-evident, but it has ceased to be so. Feminist, postmodern, postcolonial, decolonial and other critiques signal a changed intellectual scene. It is precisely in this new context of growing criticism and challenges, that defences of modern knowledge, and of its universality, became necessary. If these defences 'work', then our belief in progress, and in modern knowledge as that which assures us of it and continually delivers it, can be salvaged. An acknowledgement of the socially and historically embedded character of Reason, and a few concessions to feminist, postcolonial and decolonial and 'postmodern' critiques of modern knowledge, will suffice; and even if modern knowledge is conceded to be part of the problem that has led to a grotesquely unequal world and looming environmental catastrophe, we can and must treat it as a necessary part of the solution.

This essay has shown, however, that these defences are not persuasive; and moreover, that once we acknowledge the Hegelian-historicist point that the presuppositions of thought are fundamentally related to time and culture, but can no longer plausibly claim that there is a teleology at work in transitions between worldviews, then 'the legacy of Hegel's historical radicalisation of Kantian modernism' (Pippin, 1997, p. 172) can only be a recognition of the historical specificity of *all* forms of reasoning, including 'Occidental rationalism'. This, I suggest, best characterizes the contemporary intellectual scene: we are possessed of an acute consciousness of the historicity of our knowledge, but now without any compelling argument for its superiority to other knowledges. Since this knowledge has served at once the measure of progress, and one of the foremost evidences of it, it is now possible, and indeed pressingly necessary, to ask what can be thought – and what is to be done – after we have dispensed with the idea of progress.

Acknowledgements

I am grateful to Rajyashree Pandey, Suman Seth and Vanita Seth for their comments and suggestions on an earlier version of this essay; and to Martin Savransky, Craig Lundy and the anonymous reviewers for *The Sociological Review* for their comments on the penultimate version.

Funding

The author received no financial support for the research, authorship, and/or publication of this article.

Notes

1. The literature is too vast to list, but for critiques of the innate maleness of 'Reason' see Lloyd (1984), Irigary (1985) and Keller (1985); on the heteronormalizing presumptions of our knowledge see Sedgwick (1990); and on the parochial and western nature of modern knowledge, see de Sousa Santos (2014, 2018) and Seth (2020).
2. Here as in subsequent quotes from Apel, I eliminate the frequent italicizations/emphases that occur in the original text.
3. Quoting this passage, Amy Allen observes – with great understatement – that 'There's a certain irony involved in saying that the way to avoid Eurocentrism is for the West to celebrate its own cultural achievements, to be even more like itself: even more reflexive and self-critical than it already is' (Allen, 2013, p. 152).

References

Adas, M. (1989). *Machines as the measure of men*. Cornell University Press.

Allen, A. (2013). Having one's cake and eating it too: Habermas's genealogy of postsecular reason. In C. Calhoun, E. Mendieta, & J. VanAntwerpen (Eds.), *Habermas and religion* (pp. 132–153). Polity Press.

Allen, A. (2016). *The end of progress: Decolonizing the normative foundations of critical theory*. Columbia University Press.

Allison, H. E. (1983). *Kant's transcendental idealism: An interpretation and defence*. Yale University Press.

Apel, K.-O. (1992). Normatively grounding 'critical theory' through recourse to the lifeworld? A transcendental-pragmatic attempt to think with Habermas against Habermas. In A. Honneth, T. McCarthy, C. Offe, & A. Wellmer (Eds.), *Philosophical interventions in the unfinished project of Enlightenment*. MIT Press.

Apel, K.-O. (1999). The problem of justice in a multicultural society. In R. Kearney & M. Dooley (Eds.), *Questioning ethics: Contemporary debates in philosophy* (pp. 145–163). Routledge.

Apel, K.-O. (2000). Globalisation and the need for universal ethics. *European Journal of Social Theory, 3*(2), 137–155.

Apel, K.-O. (2001). *The response of discourse ethics*. Peeters.

Apel, K.-O. (2007). Discourse ethics, democracy, and international law: Towards a globalization of practical reason. In S. V. Hicks & D. E. Shannon (Eds.), *The challenges of globalization: Rethinking nature, culture, and freedom*. Blackwell.

Bhambra, G. (2007). *Rethinking modernity: Postcolonialism and the sociological imagination*. Palgrave Macmillan.

Chatterjee, P. (1986). *Nationalist thought and the colonial world: A derivative discourse?* Oxford University Press.

Chatterjee, P. (1993). *The nation and its fragments: Colonial and postcolonial histories*. Princeton University Press.

de Sousa Santos, B. (2014). *Epistemologies of the south: Justice against epistemicide*. Routledge.

de Sousa Santos, B. (2018). *The end of the cognitive empire: The coming of age of epistemologies of the south*. Duke University Press.

Habermas, J. (1979). *Communication and the evolution of society* (T. McCarthy, Trans.). Heinemann.

Habermas, J. (1984). *The theory of communicative action* (Vol. 1, T. McCarthy, Trans.). Beacon Press.

Habermas, J. (1987). *The theory of communicative action* (Vol. 2, T. McCarthy, Trans.). Polity Press.

Habermas, J. (1990a). Discourse ethics: Notes on a program of philosophical justification. In *Moral consciousness and communicative action* (pp. 43–115), (C. Lenhardt & S. Weber Nicholsen, Trans.). Polity.

Habermas, J. (1990b). Morality and ethical life: Does Hegel's critique of Kant apply to discourse ethics? In *Moral consciousness and communicative action* (pp. 192–216), (C. Lenhardt & S. Weber Nicholsen, Trans.). Polity.

Habermas, J. (1992). Discourse, ethics, law and *Sittlichkeit* [interview with T. Huiid Nielsen, January 1990]. In P. Dews (Ed.), *Autonomy and solidarity: Interviews with Jurgen Habermas* (rev. ed.). Verso.

Habermas, J. (1996). Modernity: An unfinished project. In M. Passerin d'Entreves & S. Benhabib (Eds.), *Habermas and the unfinished project of modernity* (pp. 38–58). Polity.

Habermas, J. (2001a). Conceptions of modernity: A look back at two traditions. In *The postnational constellation: Political essays* (pp. 130–156), (M. Pensky, Trans.). Polity.

Habermas, J. (2001b). Remarks on legitimation through human rights. In *The postnational constellation: Political essays* (pp. 113–129), (M. Pensky, Trans.). Polity.

Habermas, J. (2002). A conversation about God and the world: Interview with Eduardo Mendieta. In *Religion and rationality: Essays on reason, God, and modernity* (pp. 147–167). Polity.

Habermas, J. (2008). Communicative action and the detranscendentalized 'use of Reason'. In *Between naturalism and religion: Philosophical essays* (pp. 24–76), (C. Cronin, Trans.). Polity.

Irigary, L. (1985). *Speculum of the other woman* (G. C. Gill, Trans.). Cornell University Press.

Keller, E. F. (1985). *Reflections on gender and science.* Yale University Press.

Kolb, D. (1986). *The critique of pure modernity: Hegel, Heidegger, and after.* University of Chicago Press.

Lloyd, G. (1984). *The man of reason: 'Male' and 'female' in western philosophy.* Methuen.

MacIntyre, A. (1999). Some Enlightenment projects reconsidered. In R. Kearney & M. Dooley (Eds.), *Questioning ethics: Contemporary debates in philosophy* (pp. 57–78). Routledge.

McCarthy, T. (1982). Rationality and relativism: Habermas's 'overcoming' of hermeneutics. In J. B. Thompson & D. Held (Eds.), *Habermas: Critical debates.* Macmillan.

McCarthy, T. (1994). Part 1: Philosophy and critical theory: A reprise. In D. C. Hoy & T. McCarthy (Eds.), *Critical theory.* Blackwell.

McCarthy, T. (1999). Enlightenment and the idea of public reason. In R. Kearney & M. Dooley (Eds.), *Questioning ethics: Contemporary debates in philosophy* (pp. 164–180). Routledge.

Pippin, R. (1991). *Modernism as a philosophical problem.* Basil Blackwell

Pippin, R. (1997). *Idealism as modernism: Hegelian variations.* Cambridge University Press.

Rai, L. (1920). *The problem of national education in India.* Allen and Unwin.

Sedgwick, E. K. (1990). *Epistemology of the closet.* University of California Press.

Seth, S. (2007). *Subject lessons: The western education of colonial India.* Duke University Press.

Seth, S. (2013a). 'Once was blind but now can see': Modernity and the social sciences. *International Political Sociology, 7*(2), 136–151.

Seth, S. (2013b). Nationalism, modernity and the 'woman question' in India and China. *Journal of Asian Studies, 72*(2), 273–297.

Seth, S. (2020). *Beyond reason: Postcolonial theory and the social sciences.* Oxford University Press.

Smith, B. H. (1997). *Belief and resistance: Dynamics of contemporary intellectual controversy.* Harvard University Press.

Taylor, C. (1999). Two theories of modernity. *Public Culture, 11*(1), 153–174.

Walzer, M. (1994). *Thick and thin: Moral argument at home and abroad.* University of Notre Dame Press.

Warnke, G. (1987). *Gadamer: Hermeneutics, tradition and reason.* Polity.

Wilson, B. R. (Ed.). (1970). *Rationality.* Basil Blackwell.

Author biography

Sanjay Seth has written extensively on postcolonial theory, social and political theory, and modern Indian history, including *Beyond Reason: Postcolonial Theory and the Social Sciences* (Oxford University Press, 2020), *Subject Lessons: The Western Education of Colonial India* (Duke University Press, 2007), *Marxist Theory and Nationalist Politics: Colonial India* (Sage, 1995), and essays in a variety of journals including *The American Historical Review, Comparative Studies in Society and History, Social Text, Positions, Cultural Sociology, International Political Sociology* and *Journal of Asian Studies. Humanidades, Universalismo e Diferença Histórica,* a collection of his essays in Portuguese translation, was recently published in Brazil and *História e Pós-colonialismo,* another translated collection, has just been published in Lisbon by Imprensa de História Contemporânea. Seth was a founding co-editor of the journal *Postcolonial Studies* (1998–2020).

Article

MONOGRAPH SERIES

The Sociological Review Monographs
2022, Vol. 70(2) 34–49
© The Author(s) 2022

Article reuse guidelines:
sagepub.com/journals-permissions
DOI: 10.1177/00380261221084426
journals.sagepub.com/home/sor

Governing progress: From cybernetic homeostasis to Simondon's politics of metastability

Andrea Bardin
Oxford Brookes University, UK

Marco Ferrari
Universita degli Studi di Padova, Italy

Abstract
In this article we analyse the idea of progress and show that, since its early-modern inception, it has relied on a twofold commitment. On the one hand, it rests on a project of mathematical modelisation of natural and social reality, deterministically conceived. On the other hand, it requires the production of a stable social order capable of implementing that model. This stance, we argue, is still dominant and defines the '(hyper-)modern condition'. Following Gilbert Simondon, we take the cybernetic notion of dynamic stability ('homeostasis') as paradigmatic of the hyper-modern condition. As we explain, this core notion has covered multiple epistemic domains, including the social sciences, and contributed to reformulate the modern idea of progress within the terms dictated by neoliberal governmentality. The connection we establish between cybernetics and neoliberalism will eventually allow us to use Simondon's theory against both. In our view, Simondon's concept of 'metastability' supports an alternative understanding of progress based on the ideas of social change and the government of normative invention, which includes the opening of social systems to a future beyond their own preservation.

Keywords
cybernetics, homeostasis, metastability, progress, Simondon, Wiener

Introduction

In the theory of the artificial body politic Hobbes elaborated relying on modern mechanics, the idea of progress signalled a path for human beings that required a safe space of

Corresponding author:
Andrea Bardin, Oxford Brookes University, Oxford, OX3 0BP, UK.
Email: abardin@brookes.ac.uk

social stability, security and happiness, to be granted by his political *automaton*: 'Felicity is a continual progress of the desire, from one object to another. . . . The cause whereof is, that the object of man's desire, is not to enjoy once only, and for one instant of time; but to assure for ever, the way of his future desire' (Hobbes, 2012, p. 150). Three centuries later, this time inspired by cybernetics (Oliva, 2016), Hayek imagined a similar automatic system in which 'the correspondence of expectations that makes it possible for all parties to achieve what they are striving for . . . is brought about by a process of learning by trial and error' operating through 'what cybernetics has taught us to call negative feedback' (Hayek, 1982, II, pp. 124–125). In our view, both these statements rely on an onto-epistemological stance that assumes the 'primacy of being over becoming' (Koyré, 1966, p. 13, n.5). This stance implies a commitment to reducing natural and social reality (ontology) to the mathematisable structures that are used to explain it (epistemology), and calls for political power to grant the progressive implementation of scientific models of order. The concept of progress is – such is our claim here – based on the idea of a dynamic but 'stable' order as both its condition of possibility and goal.

The article will support this claim relying on the French philosopher Gilbert Simondon's radical attempt to critique the cybernetic notion of dynamic stability ('homeostasis') and develop the concept of 'metastability'. Simondon, most known as a philosopher of technics for his *Of the Mode of Existence of Technical Objects* (1958/2017), carries on the lifetime project of reform of the social sciences inspired by a critical 'reform' of the cybernetic paradigm (Simondon, 1958/2020, pp. 674–699; Simondon, 2019). In his main work, *Individuation in Light of Notions of Form and Information* (1958/2020), he provides a full onto-epistemology of systemic processes of 'individuation' that he conceives as alternative to both the accounts provided by the Aristotelian and Gestalt notions of form, and the cybernetic notion of information. Simondon deems a 'reform' of cybernetic concepts as fundamental to his project and, as we are going to explain, a critique of the notion of progress plays a crucial role in it.

In several instances Simondon challenges the 'mythical' idea of progress born in early modernity out of an 'illusion of simultaneity', which ultimately reduces all apparent development to 'a fixed state'. For Simondon this idea of progress is 'mythical' for two reasons. Firstly, because it implies an idea of unidirectional change ('false entelechy') that hides all the alternative futures ('rich virtualities') potentially present at each 'stage' of development. Secondly, because it relies on a misguided conception of a universal chain of causes and effects that 'masks the very reality of invention' (Simondon, 1958/2017, p. 122). The idea of progress is, in short, as teleological and deterministic as the mechanical world picture it is rooted in: it depicts a fixed development towards a prescribed end-state which excludes the possibility of any radical change and invention. In this article, we are going to explore such a claim following Simondon's own suggestion that this misplaced understanding of progress – rooted in the scientific depiction of the natural order as 'uniform, necessary, universal and analytical' first elaborated in the 'deterministic age' (Simondon, 2015, p. 274) – was still present in the cybernetic sciences of his time, along with an updated attempt to combine determinism and teleology. Highlighting a substantial continuity among these stances, we shall refer, beyond Lyotard, to a '(hyper-)modern condition', thus preferring the prefix hyper- to post- and stressing the connections between the early modern and contemporary 'condition'.

What we see at work in the (hyper-)modern condition is the same twofold onto-epistemological *reduction* that was operating in early modernity: the reduction of reality to calculable structures (either conceived in deterministic or probabilistic terms) and the reduction of science to an operation of calculation (either algebraic or statistical). On the one hand, reality is deterministically conceived in terms of structured elements developing over time according to fixed 'laws' that predetermine the outcome of such development. On the other hand, this whole process is conceived as, in principle, entirely describable in terms of a combinatory of elements within a pre-given syntax. Thus, the production of scientific knowledge is a process of verification and decision that takes place within a field of research entirely mapped on the basis of a set of pre-established 'proof principles' (Bailly & Longo, 2011). This twofold onto-epistemological reduction creates a system entirely formalisable, whether in logical or mathematical terms, which mirrors the uninterrupted chains of causes and effects connecting every single element or event to the deterministic whole they belong to. The idea of progress as continuous development of human knowledge and society relies, in short, on an imagination of nature, human nature included, in the shape of a world of 'realised' geometry (Koyré, 1966, p. 301). The kind of scientific knowledge that sustains such a vision can only be formalised on the basis of the assumption that a calculability of the whole is possible, at least in principle, with no exceptions. This generates an idea of progress conceived as the development of a predetermined order – an initially given set of elements and rules (or natural 'laws') – determining the unrolling of natural and human history. The principle directing this development is one of preservation and expansion of the initial order, and each moment in time is the necessary result of every preceding moment and the condition of the future.

In this article we take cybernetics as paradigmatic of a crisis in the (hyper-)modern condition and the idea of progress it entails. In several epistemic domains, paradigms originally derived from cybernetics are currently being reconsidered if not dismissed. The idea of living being propounded by molecular biology which opened the century of the genome (Kay, 2000) is being criticised by 'organismal' biology in the light of the inherent 'historicity' and variability of the organism (Soto et al., 2016). Against the hardware/software model that has dominated neurosciences for a few decades, a tendency of studying the brain and neurosynaptic structures through the concept of plasticity is gaining pace (Malabou, 2008). In mathematics, a rethinking of modelling practices is being elaborated that shifts the focus from 'dynamical structuralism' (Thom, 1972/1975) to the 'heterogenous virtual' (Sarti et al., 2019). In all these examples what is being challenged is the very idea of a dynamic development aimed at delivering more and more complex forms of homeostatic equilibrium. We believe that a step forward beyond this idea of progress should critically point out what cybernetics left unquestioned, namely radical transformation and invention, also in the social field. Our suggestion is therefore to start from Simondon's critique to cybernetics and reconceptualise the concept of progress as the emergence of social invention from a metastable system full of potentials. The two sections of the article are thus devoted to the two different understandings of progress implicit in Wiener's concept of homeostasis and in Simondon's concept of metastability.

The first part of the article focuses on the concept of homeostasis, and notably on the way this was elaborated by Norbert Wiener. We do not intend to overlook the variety of theoretical positions testified by the complex history of the cybernetic institutions and canon (Kline, 2015; Le Roux, 2018; Scott, 2004), but our focus allows us to pinpoint the elements through which the cybernetic project has contributed to the idea of progress as a developing order that heavily influenced conceptions of government widespread in the social sciences (Heyck, 2015; Rodríguez, 2019; Tiqqun, 2020). We will claim that this is a model of government still based on the 'mythical' idea of progress as teleological and deterministic attacked by Simondon. It prescribes homeostasis, that is the dynamic preservation of a stable equilibrium which, when breaking down, is set to be restructured according to the same invariant principles – an idea also fully in place, as we aim to explain, in neoliberal governmentality. Such a hyper-modern art of government is well captured by Rouvroy as the 'art not to change the world' (Rouvroy, 2016).

The second part studies Simondon's concept of metastability – a 'stability far from equilibrium' opposed to the idea of 'dynamic stability' implied by Wiener's concept of homeostasis – against both the cybernetic and neoliberal understanding of government. Many scholars have analysed and elaborated on Simondon's attempt to 'reform' the cybernetic concept of information (Hui, 2015; Iliadis, 2013; Mills, 2016), but fewer studies have stressed the political relevance of his attempt to provide an 'axiomatic of the human sciences' alternative to the version promoted by cybernetics (Bardin, 2015; Guchet, 2010), which will allow us to stress the (hyper-)modern roots of the latter. Simondon's concept of 'metastability' drives our critique to the hyper-modern idea of government and the very concept of progress it is based on, thus indicating a path *after progress*. In our view, this path does not prescribe the abandonment of the concept of progress as such, which would restate the relativist stigma of the postmodern age. It rather invites us to rethink progress in non-teleological and non-deterministic terms, as something that requires a new idea of the government of political and social invention.

The cybernetic order: Progress and homeostasis

Cybernetics has been differently qualified by its interpreters. It has been classified as the archaeology of a specific epistemic domain – whether of the cognitive sciences (Dupuy, 2009), informatics (Breton, 1990) or automata theory and artificial intelligence (Dertouzos & Moses, 1980). It has been more widely conceived as the techno-scientific (Segal, 2003; Triclot, 2008) and cultural (Breton, 1997; Day, 2001) context in which the concepts of, and discourses on, information and communication originated and circulated (Kline, 2015; Sfez, 1992). It has been valorised as an attempt to question anthropological categories and challenge the human/machine dualism (Haraway, 1991; Hayles, 1999). Last but not least, it has been classified as a science drawing its worldview from the military technology and research it was rooted in and the actualisation of technocratic thinking (Edwards, 1996; Galison, 1994; Geoghegan, 2012). All these studies fail to question the elements of continuity that bind cybernetics to the onto-epistemological stance inaugurated by classical mechanics and its political implications. A brief historical excursus will allow us to make this explicit, and hence to interrogate cybernetics as an attempt that, despite its original features, does not exit the hyper-modern condition and reproduces the conceptions of progress and political order embedded in it, especially via the concept of homeostasis.

From the mind of Descartes' benign God to Newton and Leibniz's clockwork universe, through Laplace's demon, and up to the ideal worlds depicted in Hilbert and Frege's logical formalisations, we recognise the tracts of the same onto-epistemological stance, elegantly criticised by Bachelard as based on 'philosophical factors of easy unification such as the creator's unity of action, nature's unity of plan, or logical unity' (Bachelard, 2002, p. 26). This onto-epistemological stance includes a narrative about the interconnection of scientific and social progress exemplarily displayed in the following passage from Laplace:

> All these efforts in the search for truth tend to lead it [*l'esprit humain*] back continually to the vast intelligence which we have just mentioned, but from which it will always remain infinitely removed. This tendency, peculiar to the human race, is that which renders it superior to animals; and their progress in this respect distinguishes nations and ages and constitutes their true glory. (Laplace, 1814/1986, pp. 3–4)

This framework meets its crisis in the nineteenth century, when thermodynamics and statistical mechanics serve as a prelude to the twentieth-century attacks on the early-modern worldview later carried forward by the biological and evolutionary sciences, as well as by the theories of relativity and quantum mechanics (Prigogine & Stengers, 1985). Since its inception, and even before Wiener had given it its name, cybernetics was openly challenging the ontology established by modern science – mechanicism, stable equilibrium, linear development – by rehabilitating the very category of finality to describe homeostatic equilibrium as non-mechanistic, dynamic and adaptive (Ashby, 1940; Rosenblueth et al., 1943). This is not to say cybernetics ever aimed at a rehabilitation of the classical idea of final cause. It rather complicated the radical opposition between determinism and teleology that had marked the emergence of the mechanical world picture in the first place. In fact, cybernetics aimed at explaining teleological behaviour as an emergent property of deterministic systems in what we will call a 'mechanistic teleology'.

In Wiener's mind, the advent of cybernetics was meant to break with the clockwork universe of classical mechanics 'in which everything happened precisely according to law, a compact, tightly organized universe in which the whole future depends strictly upon the whole past'. Defining information as 'measure of order', cybernetics could conceive developing systems as constantly recalibrating the variables and functions they relied upon. The image of 'a rigid deterministic world' was to be wiped out thanks to statistical mechanics – 'the first great revolution of twentieth century physics' – and the idea of a contingent universe would strike back in the agenda of science (Wiener, 1954/1988, pp. 7–12). The concept of feedback was formed by rethinking concepts such as behaviour, purpose and teleology (Rosenblueth et al., 1943) in order to explain the capacity of a system to adapt its functioning and 'goals' on the basis of new information gathered from the environment. This new idea of organisation was initially applied by cyberneticians to machines, but it was 'intimately connected' with the concept of homeostasis elaborated by the American physiologist Walter Cannon (1926), via the French physician Claude Bernard's (1878) notion of an organism's 'internal milieu' (Wiener, 1953/1985b, p. 391; 1951/1985a). Homeostasis described the mechanisms of automatic regulation through which an organism could maintain a healthy state of equilibrium in its internal milieu by balancing reactions to and actions on the 'external milieu'. As Canguilhem summarised, it was 'Claude Bernard who generated Cannon, who generated Rosenblueth next to Wiener' (Canguilhem, 2000, p. 82). Arturo Rosenblueth, a student of Cannon's and close to Wiener (to the point of being the dedicatee of *Cybernetics*), indeed represented 'the intellectual bridge' between the physiological concept of homeostasis and the cybernetic concept of feedback (Cooper, 2008, p. 425). Homeostasis and feedback were thus indissolubly embedded in the interdisciplinary ambitions of cybernetics, which included covering biological, technical as well as social systems.

However, Wiener's cybernetics hardly abandoned the framework inaugurated by modern science and its epistemological attempt to provide knowledge and command over an objective natural field. The stable functioning of all 'teleological' systems endowed with a feedback mechanism was driven by the same kind of determinism that characterised non-teleological systems. The general theory of information pursued by cybernetics was meant to provide the same formal description of the functioning of all systems (Ashby, 1956). In short, cybernetics continued with other means the twofold onto-epistemological reduction carried on by modern science. From this perspective, the Galilean-Cartesian revolution can be considered not only the dawn of modern science, but also of a narrative of science connected to an onto-epistemological stance that finds in the cybernetic revolution a displacement, a reformulation on the same formalistic and deterministic grounds. As Simondon nicely put it, cybernetics aimed at drafting 'a new *Discourse on the Method*' (Simondon, 2016, p. 197), in what was perhaps the last formidable, systematic attempt to preserve the onto-epistemological stance inaugurated by modern science. Wiener's non-deterministic ontology was in fact mechanical determinism in disguise, still implying a twofold onto-epistemological *reduction*: the reduction of reality to calculable structures and the reduction of science to an operation of (statistical) calculation. This reduction, we are claiming, is a hyper-modern variation of the early-modern ideas of progress as 'stable' development and government as the production of order sustained by the concept of homeostasis.

The concept of homeostasis offers a dynamic description of the functioning of all kinds of systems that seriously challenges a 'static' understanding of equilibrium. A homeostatic system does develop its initial state, and its organisation is subject to a variety of modifications resulting from the feedback signals collected through its mechanisms of regulation. Examples of feedback mechanisms span a variety of fields, such as technology (thermostats, steam engines, anti-aircraft gun servo-mechanisms following their targets), physiology (blood pressure or body temperature regulation in a changing milieu) and economics (price variation related to financial fluctuations). However dynamic, such systems' development is oriented by invariant 'laws' and the overall necessity to preserve a degree of internal stability and equilibrium, and it is, in principle, mathematically foreseeable – if statistically, that is, within a defined margin of error. The concept of homeostasis thus does not allow *any* questioning of a system's conditions of stability and goals, it only allows for a 'dynamic' preservation of stability within the given conditions of possibility and established goals. In this sense Ashby's claims that 'there is no such thing as "good organization" in any absolute sense' and yet to any system 'its own organization will always, by definition be good' (Ashby, 1962, pp. 262, 273) expose a tension that is at the very core of the cybernetic concepts of homeostasis and organisation. Homeostasis represents thus a 'mechanistic teleology' which is descriptive and normative at the same time. Defining organisation as (dynamic) stability, implies assuming homeostasis as both a scientific model describing the functioning of all systems, and the actual norm prescribing their immanent telos.

We believe this 'mechanistic teleology' is rooted in a hyper-modern version of the same old onto-epistemological reduction, which pertains to first-order cybernetics' concern with 'observed systems', as well as to second-order cybernetics' focus on 'observing systems' (Von Foerster, 1979). In first-order cybernetics, the functioning of regulatory mechanisms can only be optimal when aleatory phenomena – classified as 'noise' – are adequately kept under control and ideally eliminated by the system. Second-order cybernetics is perhaps more refined in recognising the beneficial role played by 'noise' in system self-organisation processes (Ashby, 1962; Atlan, 2011; Von Foerster, 1960) and the importance of the amplification or even radical reconfiguration of the system's functions. However, the whole theory is still focused on the system's conditions of existence, for the purpose of which the system is only allowed to 'choose the form of determinism that guarantees its continued existence' (De Latil, 1956, p. 313). This is why we are claiming that cybernetics does not exit the deterministic horizon of the hyper-modern condition and the conception of progress therein. Rather, it reinforces the idea of progress as a development of more and more complex forms of order granting stability, and recruits 'the uncertainty and the contingency of events' within its 'incomplete determinism' (Wiener, 1954/1988, pp. 8, 11) as allies in the defence of the 'dynamic' order of things.

Such a concept of organisation was mainly formulated in terms of information and communication theory applied to neurophysiology, but it rapidly expanded over several epistemic domains, the social sciences included. The colonisation of the latter by cybernetic concepts was not at all immediate, as one might think looking at the great number of social scientists (Gregory Bateson and Margaret Mead above all) who participated in the Macy conferences on cybernetics that took place in New York between 1946 and 1953 (Heims, 1991). However cautious not to take this analogy at face value, and wary of the risks this would entail (Wiener, 1961/2019, pp. 39–41, 226–228), Wiener himself acknowledged that 'the social system' is 'an organization . . . bound together by a system of communication, and that it has dynamics in which circular processes of a feedback nature play an important part' (Wiener, 1961/2019, p. 35). Following Wiener's intuition in disregard of his own warning, multiple attempts were carried out by social scientists (within institutions and associations more or less openly inspired by cybernetics) to apply cybernetic concepts to their specific epistemic domains. Psychology, anthropology, economy and sociology were the loci of a variety of such attempts. Rodríguez (2019) refers, for instance, to structural anthropology, systemic psychology, symbolic interactionism, as well as Luhmann's functionalism. Many of these approaches have drawn on cybernetic concepts and terminology, which in itself would justify our aim to trace a theoretical link between cybernetics and social theory. Our polemic target in this piece is, however, the theoretical core of what Michel Foucault (2008) called neoliberal governmentality. By this we understand the contemporary form of political rationality we see as emblematic of the hyper-modern condition formerly embodied in cybernetics and in its attempt to govern progress.

In our view, the cybernetic concept of organisation enlightens the theoretical and practical shift from state sovereignty and classical liberalism to neoliberal governmentality. The crisis of the modern state's sovereignty becomes evident in the inability of state institutions to reduce to a unitary and stable order the proliferation of local and global conflicts in complex societies. Cybernetics offers instead the model of a constructivist conception of government capable of regulating the network of automatic mechanisms present in society. This should not be taken as a straightforward identification of cybernetics and neoliberalism, but rather as the mark of a deeper onto-epistemological connection that went beyond Wiener's own intentions. Wiener was indeed highly critical of any 'faith' in free competition as 'homeostatic process' (Wiener, 1961/2019, p. 220). Nevertheless, when neoliberals looked for a remedy to the state of permanent crisis of liberalism, what they aimed at was an 'epistemic revolution' (Mirowski & Nik-Khah, 2017; Ouellet, 2016) whose premises resonated strongly with the cybernetic diagnosis concerning the crisis of modern science. At the very origins of neoliberalism, before cybernetics was even born, Hayek claimed that the growing complexity of social reality had made all neoclassical theories of equilibrium inadequate and any deterministic political planning an impossible and potentially dangerous task (Hayek, 1937/2014). A few years later, he explicitly invited the study of self-organising systems through 'what cybernetics has taught us to call negative feedback' (Hayek, 1982, II, p. 125). Far from fully exploring the genealogy of the concept of homeostasis, our intention here is to show that the cybernetic understanding of organisation *as* homeostasis can offer a key to the dynamic but ultimately stable conception of social systems and progress implicit in neoliberal governmentality.

The point of government in a neoliberal perspective is neither to limit the freedom of initiative, nor to assume that social stability depends on an invisible hand, but rather to carry on a detailed regulation of liberties for the sake of the 'spontaneous' equilibrium of the markets. An incessant work of data extraction through ever perfected algorithms sets the conditions of possibility of the subjects' behaviour – economic actors, ideally self-employees – and orients it towards the preservation of the system's dynamic stability. Social change is thus governed and reduced to the hyper-modern idea of progress, conceived as a variation within the parameters deemed necessary for the reproduction and survival of the system. All the 'irrational' noise that is not immediately reducible to progress thus conceived is either silenced or – once neutralised – included in the pattern as a risky and unforeseen opportunity to perfect the system's survival (Castel, 1991; Dean, 1998; Ewald, 1991). More radically, these elements are normatively integrated in the system's core dynamics in the form of an ethics of flexibility (Fraser, 2003) establishing the 'good' functioning of governmentality.

The government of progress is thus resolved in the incessant operation of protection, management and promotion of homeostatic mechanisms deemed capable of self-regulation, but in fact selected and – if necessary – substituted with others, offering a more inclusive and complex capacity of adaptation to the macro-mechanism of the market. This macro-mechanism is the undisputed horizon that imposes to political power the task of providing a homeostatic equilibrium functional to its progressive implementation. With its 'soft' determinism and immanent teleology the market thus appears to be a hyper-modern version of the clockwork universe theorised in early-modern mechanical science, and the vector of a similar onto-epistemological reduction of social reality to a mathematical form. And this reduction still relies on a 'mythical' concept of progress alimenting an 'illusion of simultaneity' that hides a plurality of paths by projecting the 'eternal present' of the market on all possible futures.

Simondon: Progress and metastability

The connection we have established between cybernetics and neoliberalism will allow us to use Simondon's concept of 'metastability' against both of them. Although acknowledging Wiener's invention of the term (Simondon, 2014, p. 236), Simondon elaborated the concept of metastability drawing on Canguilhem's work and in explicit contrast to the cybernetic concept of homeostasis. Metastability describes systems macroscopically stable but internally characterised by an uneven distribution of potentials and hosting processes that make that stability only apparent. Metastable systems enjoy a 'stability far from equilibrium' in which the aleatory 'encounter' with a minimal quantity of energy or information can trigger a brusque alteration of equilibrium, and lead to the invention of new structures and hence to a new 'metastable state'. The notion of metastable equilibrium marks the project of an 'axiomatic of human sciences' Simondon presents in explicit opposition to the cybernetic theory of society, questioning at the same time the notion of homeostasis and the deterministic ontology the latter relies upon (Simondon, 1958/2020, pp. 697ff.). Briefly sketching Simondon's project will allow us to outline the theory of government he elaborates in contrast to Wiener's, and explain how this may be used as an antidote to the neoliberal conception of government and the hyper-modern condition it shares with cybernetics. Simondon's concept of 'metastability', we will argue, can support an alternative understanding of progress based on the idea of government as the facilitation of normative invention.

In his social theory, Simondon expands on Canguilhem's study of social normativity. Canguilhem's starting point is a critical reading of the biological modelling of society adopted within the French sociological tradition. In that paradigm the sociologist is asked to define the 'normal type' and provide the politician, the social physician, with the task of re-establishing the 'normal state', independently of the way society 'appears to itself' (Durkheim, 1924, p. 54). Canguilhem provides a decisive critique to the organic model and a radical turn to its political implications. What he considers socially 'pathological' is not the deviation from normality, but, on the contrary, the very normalisation of a 'stable' form of equilibrium. Relying on the work of the German neurologist and thinker Kurt Goldstein, he assumes that, both organically and socially, 'the healthy state, much more than the normal state . . . is the state which allows transition to new norms', while 'pathological constants' are 'repulsive and strictly conservative' (Canguilhem, 1991, p. 228) and in fact typical of a form of life stuck in its own 'narrowed milieu' and incapable of further normative invention (Goldstein, 1995, p. 188). Simondon welcomes Canguilhem's advice to consider society in its own terms, as 'neither machine nor life' (Canguilhem, 2002), and takes it a step further, also attacking the technological modelling of society theorised by cybernetics.

Simondon detects in Wiener's cybernetic theory of society an attempt to reduce the complexity of social systems to the technological model of the 'automaton'. For

Simondon automata are emblematic of the hyper-modern condition – they represent a rigidly deterministic understanding of change that *de facto* cancels it: 'the automaton is entirely given in its initial state, it functions but does not become' (Simondon, 2016, p. 401). 'Direct adaptation' and 'structural stability' are the hallmarks of 'the perfect automaton', and ultimately rely on the same normative assumptions implicit in the concept of 'homeostasis' that Wiener's technological model implicitly sets as the ultimate goal of social organisation. Simondon reverses this value judgement while questioning the epistemic value of the model itself. The very study of technical objects shows that 'automatism' describes 'a rather low degree of technical perfection' and its idea is in fact a myth rooted in 'economic or social' thinking rather than in technical knowledge (Simondon, 1958/2017, p. 17). In social theory, the ideas of automatism and homeostasis, although describing a crucial aspect of social dynamics – that is the closure within 'a stereotypical, hypertelic and inevolutive adaptation' – fail to grasp the 'constructive and creative adaptation' of societies. While for Wiener homeostatic stabilisation defines both the core functioning and the goal of social systems, for Simondon a degree of social homeostasis is both a prerequisite of society – the 'rate of automatism' that grants 'stability and cohesion' – and a problem (Simondon, 1958/2020, pp. 422–423).

Wiener's hyper-modern renewal of the Hobbesian myth of a political 'automaton' is, from Simondon's perspective, an epistemological mistake and a political danger. Statistical mechanics hinders a proper understanding of processes harbouring a 'margin of indeterminacy' (Simondon, 1958/2017, pp. 147–159) that can only be understood through a 'non-probabilistic method' (Simondon, 1958/2020, p. 697), and the myth of the automaton surreptitiously becomes a goal whose actual realisation would destroy the very system it was supposed to save. A perfect 'automatic' homeostasis, far from solving the problem of social regulation would substitute the social system's 'tense' metastability with the kind of dynamic stability that ultimately leads the system to exhaustion. The self-destructive goal of automatism is in fact the cancellation of any 'margin of indeterminacy' with the result that 'there is no longer any possible variation; the functioning repeats indefinitely' (Simondon, 1958/2017, p. 152) until entropy consumes all the residual potentials, leading to the 'resolution of all tensions', that is 'death'. For Simondon, on the contrary, a system only keeps working and developing as long as it 'conserves the tensions in the equilibrium of metastability instead of nullifying them in the equilibrium of stability' (Simondon, 1958/2020, p. 226).

It is on this basis that Simondon sketches his theory of government as an alternative to Wiener's. Playing a biological model against Wiener's normative assumption that 'a good homeostatic regulation is the ultimate purpose of societies, the ideal that must animate every act of government' (Simondon, 1958/2017, p. 162) Simondon theorises government as an act of normative invention relying on existing social automatisms but exceeding them. An 'act of government' for Simondon should be 'grounded in homeostases so as to develop itself and to continue its coming-into-being, rather than remaining perpetually in the same state' (p. 162). Governing is 'inventing' solutions aimed at making the system 'metastable', that is open to further invention, rather than contributing to reproduce the ideal order imagined by social theory and imposed by politics as a goal.

Many critics of neoliberal governmentality, and in particular of its 'algorithmic' version, have been inspired by Simondon. This is evident in their stressing the importance

of creating spaces of political conflict in which social invention – the 'transindividual
. . . coupling between the inventive and organisational capacities of several subjects'
(Simondon, 1958/2017, p. 258) – can take place against the dominant neoliberal neutrali-
sation of subjectivity and conflict (Rouvroy & Berns, 2013; Stiegler, 2016). The idea of
'progress' may appear to be embedded in precisely the stance these theorists are criticis-
ing, but we believe that Simondon's concept of metastability allows for a different idea
of progress. In neoliberalism, the market's 'spontaneous' continuation is paradoxically
assumed as the goal of politics, which entails the reduction of progress to a sequence of
preventive social adaptations to ever-emerging 'local' risks within the naturalised framework of the market. Thus, the neoliberal promotion of risk-management ethics – a lifestyle informed by constant planning, resource management, etc. – is one of the most
powerful ideological tools for the preservation of social homeostasis within the market
economy. This government of behaviour is capable of de-activating the potential reinvention of social forms. 'Governmentality' thus conceived is not simply a matter of preventing the risk of a radically disruptive event, it is about governing its possibility as
such. The 'progressive' mechanisms of social reproduction governed by the market's
open dynamics thus entirely absorbs what is a completely different kind of 'risk' represented by human inventiveness and imagination, which Simondon theorises under the
label of metastability.

The 'risky' politics of metastability theorised by Simondon is based on the assumption that progress conceived as the 'invention of new goals' makes radical novelty possible. This concept of progress is based on an understanding of social systems as
inherently metastable because of the 'fairly dangerous' automatism characterising the
human being, who 'always risks inventing and equipping new structures' (Simondon,
1958/2020, p. 423). This is not to say that Simondon resorts to a vitalist view on the
exceptionality of life over matter or some sort of social evolutionism. Rather, he theorises 'invention' as an emergent property of the bio-technical nature of human beings and
societies. This tendency towards invention is for Simondon embedded in the partial indeterminacy or 'historicity' that, in his ontology, defines all systems and processes (Bardin,
2021, pp. 36–37). At the level of human natural and social (i.e. 'transindividual') 'historicity', technical activity is not a mere vector of technological progress, it is an actual
challenge to existing social norms. Human 'progress' takes place at the scale of the 'metastable' system formed by 'human beings and the world' and mediated by technical
objects whose functioning exceeds all efforts of symbolisation (Simondon, 1958/2017,
p. 168). Progress thus conceived is not a triumphal march, it is the result of a disharmoni-
ous relationship between biological patterns that vary in the very long term of natural
history, the quick accumulation of technoscientific innovations, and the social rhythm of
culture that attempts to render these processes compatible with its institutional present
(Simondon, 2010). This is neither 'progress conceived as a march in a direction fixed in
advance', nor a process of 'humanisation of nature', but rather an aleatory process of
'naturalisation of humans' mediated by the 'techno-geographical milieu' they keep
inventing (Simondon, 1958/2017, p. 58).

This notion of progress entails a political risk because it leaves political practice without a safety net. In this open dynamic, the emergence of finality and hence of social
invention is grounded on the structural lack of control of technical reality that nurtures

the very possibility of human freedom: 'Man [*sic*] frees himself from his situation of being enslaved by the finality of the whole, by learning how to create finality . . . as not to have to be passively subjected to a *de facto* integration' (Simondon, 1958/2017, p. 119). This is what, according to Simondon, cybernetics itself teaches us, but crucially missing the point that risk cannot be recaptured within the existing social norms and mode of production. On the contrary, risk conceived as a structural margin of indeterminacy ('historicity') is embedded in technical activity, and a constant challenge to the whole 'system of values' (Simondon, 1958/2020, pp. 414–415). We believe Simondon's concept of metastability opens in this sense to the possibility of moving beyond the paradoxical conflation of determinism and teleology theorised within the hyper-modern idea of progress, ultimately shared by cybernetics and neoliberalism, and allows to 'think together nature and excess, technology and revolution' (Toscano, 2012, pp. 107–108). It thus calls for an alternative theory of government.

Governing progress, in Simondon's sense, is part of the collective effort of inventing mediations and solutions in which science and politics can play a crucial role if they do not reduce the reality of non-symbolic processes to their – also scientific – imagination. This kind of government will have more to do with the 'invention' of new technical and cultural possibilities than with the dreamed regulation of the existent by a philosopher-king (Simondon, 1958/2017, pp. 161–163). Such inventions run, of course, the risk of failure, but this is precisely where their political value lies. Simondon's concept of progress does not allow acts of government a safety net offered by social theory predictions. On the contrary, Simondon's social theory certifies that not running the risk of normative invention is equal to suffering a different kind of defeat, the defeat of accepting an allegedly 'progressive' politics that, as a matter of fact, reaffirms the norms codified by the theory and resists radical change. This is precisely how Wiener sees progress grounded on the idea of the dynamic stability (homeostasis) of 'local and temporary islands of decreasing entropy', which 'enables some of us to assert the existence of progress' (Wiener, 1954/1988, p. 36). Instead, Simondon's vision is condensed in an ethical formula that critically mirrors Wiener's statement by reversing it, and postulates that 'there are no lost islands in becoming, no domains eternally closed in themselves' and 'each gesture' is an act of invention within a (metastable) network that connects past and future (Simondon, 1958/2020, p. 377). This ethical gesture is inherently political, it requires the active consideration of entropy and death as part of a system's functioning, and the assumption of social invention as the core of an idea of progress to be formulated *beyond* the hyper-modern condition.

Conclusion: Governing progress

If one assumes the exhaustion of the (hyper-)modern idea of progress, one is also deprived of the theoretical background that has long informed the mechanical understanding of social dynamics, an understanding that still informs neoliberal governmentality. A critique of the concept of homeostasis that grounds this idea of progress, we have claimed, allows for a different approach. In this sense, our article firstly offers a historical contribution by exposing the onto-epistemological stance that underpins much theorisation of early modern science and cybernetics, liberalism and neoliberalism.

Secondly, it aims to show that Simondon's concept of metastability opens the path for a reformulation of the idea of progress within a framework that sees partial indeterminacy (or 'historicity') at the core of social dynamics and their government. From this perspective, knowing the social and acting politically means favouring the 'metastable' tension that enables scientific *and* political invention, defying the automatic defence of a mythically established social order. Governing progress therefore requires the radical endorsement of change, which includes the contemplation of death and failure as a necessary part of it, and therefore the opening of social systems to a future beyond the mere preservation of their own existence.

Funding

The authors received no financial support for the research, authorship, and/or publication of this article.

References

Ashby, W. R. (1940). Adaptiveness and equilibrium. *Journal of Mental Science, 86*, 478–483.
Ashby, W. R. (1956). *Introduction to cybernetics*. Chapman & Hall.
Ashby, W. R. (1962). Principles of the self-organizing system. In H. Von Foerster & Zopf, G. W., Jr. (Eds.), *Principles of self-organization* (pp. 255–278). Pergamon Press.
Atlan, H. (2011). Noise as a principle of self-organization. In S. Geroulanos & T. Meyers (Eds.), *Selected writings: On self-organization, philosophy, bioethics, and Judaism* (pp. 95–113). Fordham University Press.
Bachelard, G. (2002). *The formation of the scientific mind: A contribution to a psychoanalysis of objective knowledge*. Clinamen.
Bailly, F., & Longo, G. (2011). *Mathematics and the natural sciences: The physical singularity of life*. Imperial College Press.
Bardin, A. (2015). *Epistemology and political philosophy in Gilbert Simondon: Individuation, technics, social systems*. Springer.
Bardin, A. (2021). Simondon contra new materialism: Political anthropology reloaded. *Theory, Culture & Society, 38*(5), 25–44.
Bernard, C. (1878). *Leçons sur les phénomènes de la vie communs aux animaux et aux végétaux* [Lessons on the phenomena of life common to animals and plants]. Bailliere.
Breton, P. (1990). *La tribu informatique. Enquête sur une passion moderne* [The computer tribe: Investigating a modern passion]. Seuil.
Breton, P. (1997). *L'utopie de la communication. Le mythe du «village planétaire»* [The communication utopia. The myth of the 'global village']. La Découverte.
Canguilhem, G. (1991). *The normal and the pathological*. Zone Books.
Canguilhem, G. (2000). La formation du concept de régulation biologique aux XVIIIe et XIXe siècles [The formation of the concept of biological regulation in the 18th and 19th centuries]. In *Idéologie et rationalité dans l'histoire des sciences de la vie* [Ideology and rationality in the history of the life sciences] (pp. 81–100). Vrin.
Canguilhem, G. (2002). Le problème des régulations dans l'organisme et dans la société [The problem of regulations in the organism and in society]. In *Écrits sur la médecine* [Writings on medicine] (pp. 101–125). Seuil.
Cannon, W. (1926). Physiological regulation of normal states: some tentative postulates concerning biological homeostatics. In A. Petit (Ed.), *À Charles Richet, ses amis, ses collègues, ses élèves* [To Charles Richet, his friends, colleagues and students] (pp. 91–93). Les Éditions Medicales.

Castel, R. (1991). From dangerous to risk. In G. Burchell, C. Gordon, & P. Miller (Eds.), *The Foucault effect: Studies in governmentality* (pp. 281–298). Harvester Wheatsheaf.

Cooper, S. J. (2008). From Claude Bernard to Walter Cannon: Emergence of the concept of homeostasis. *Appetite, 51*(33), 419–427.

Day, R. E. (2001). *The modern invention of information: Discourse, history and power.* Southern Illinois University Press.

De Latil, P. (1956). *Thinking by machine: A study of cybernetics.* Sidgwick and Jackson.

Dean, M. (1998). Risk, calculable and incalculable. *Soziale Welt, 49*(1), 25–42.

Dertouzos, M. L., & Moses, J. (Eds.). (1980). *The computer age: A twenty-year view.* The MIT Press.

Dupuy, J. P. (2009). *On the origins of cognitive science: The mechanization of the mind.* The MIT Press.

Durkheim, É. (1924). *Sociologie et philosophie* [Sociology and philosophy]. Alcan.

Edwards, P. (1996). *The closed world: Computers and the politics of discourse in Cold War America.* The MIT Press.

Ewald, F. (1991). Insurance and risk. In G. Burchell, C. Gordon, & P. Miller (Eds.), *The Foucault effect: Studies in governmentality* (pp. 197–210). Harvester Wheatsheaf.

Foucault, M. (2008). *The birth of biopolitics: Lectures at the Collège de France 1978–79.* Palgrave Macmillan.

Fraser, N. (2003). From discipline to flexibilization? Rereading Foucault in the shadow of globalization. *Constellations, 10*(2), 160–171.

Galison, P. (1994). The ontology of the enemy: Norbert Wiener and the cybernetic vision. *Critical Inquiry, 21*(1), 228–266.

Geoghegan, B. D. (2012). *The cybernetic apparatus: Media, liberalism, and the reform of the human society* [PhD thesis, Northwestern University, Evanston, Illinois].

Goldstein, K. (1995). *The organism: A holistic approach to biology derived from pathological data in man.* Zone Books.

Guchet, X. (2010). *Pour un humanisme technologique. Culture, technique et société dans la philosophie de Gilbert Simondon* [For a technological humanism: Culture, technique and society in the philosophy of Gilbert Simondon]. PUF.

Haraway, D. (1991). *Simians, cyborgs, and women: The reinvention of nature.* Routledge.

Hayek, F. A. (1982). *Law, legislation and liberty: A new statement of the liberal principles of justice and political economy.* Routledge.

Hayek, F. A. (2014). Economics and knowledge. In *The market and other orders* (B. Caldwell, Ed., pp. 57–77). University of Chicago Press (Original work published 1937).

Hayles, K. N. (1999). *How we became posthuman: Virtual bodies in cybernetics, literature, and informatics.* University of Chicago Press.

Heims, S. (1991). *The cybernetics group: Constructing a social science for postwar America.* The MIT Press.

Heyck, H. (2015). *Age of system: Understanding the development of modern social science.* Johns Hopkins University Press.

Hobbes, T. (2012). *Leviathan: The English and Latin texts (2 vols.).* Oxford University Press.

Hui, Y. (2015). Simondon et la Question de l'information [Simondon and the question of information]. *Cahiers Simondon, 6*, 29–47.

Iliadis, A. (2013). Informational ontology: The meaning of Gilbert Simondon's concept of individuation. *Communication+1, 2*(1), 1–19.

Kay, L. E. (2000). *Who wrote the book of life? A history of the genetic code.* Stanford University Press.

Kline, R. R. (2015). *The cybernetics moment. Or why we call our age the information age.* Johns Hopkins University Press.

Koyré, A. (1966). *Études Galiléennes* [Galileo studies]. Hermann.

Kupiec, J.-J. (2000). *Ni Dieu ni gène. Pour une autre théorie de l'hérédité* [Neither God nor genes. For a different heredity theory]. Seuil.

Laplace, P.-S. (1986). *Essai philosophique sur les probabilités* [A philosophical essay on probabilities]. Bourgois (Original work published 1814).

Le Roux, R. (2018). *Une histoire de la cybernétique en France (1948.1975)* [History of cybernetics in France, 1948–1975]. Garnier.

Malabou, C. (2008). *What should we do with our brain?* Fordham University Press.

Mills, S. (2016). *Gilbert Simondon: Information, technology and media.* Rowman & Littlefield.

Mirowski, P., & Nik-Khah, E. (2017). *The knowledge we have lost in information: The history of information in modern economics.* Oxford University Press.

Oliva, G. (2016). The road to servomechanisms: The influence of cybernetics on Hayek from *The Sensory Order* to the social order. *Research in the History of Economic Thought and Methodology, 34A,* 161–198.

Ouellet, M. (2016). *La revolution culturelle du capital. Le capitalisme cybernétique dans la société globale de l'information* [Capital's cultural revolution. Cybernetic capitalism in the global information society]. Écosociété.

Prigogine, I., & Stengers, I. (1985). *Order out of chaos: Man's new dialogue with nature.* Fontana.

Rodríguez, P. M. (2019). *Las palabras en las cosas. Saber, poder y subjetivación entre algoritmos y biomoléculas* [The Order within things. Knowledge, power and subjectivation between algorithms and biomolecules]. Cactus.

Rosenblueth, A., Wiener, N., & Bigelow, J. (1943). Behavior, purpose and teleology. *Philosophy of Science, 10*(1), 18–24.

Rouvroy, A., & Berns, T. (2013). Gouvernementalité algorithmique et perspectives d'émancipation. Le disparate comme condition d'individuation par la relation? [Algorithmic governmentality and prospects for emancipation. The disparate as a condition of individuation through relationship?] *Réseaux, 177*(1), 163–196.

Rouvroy, A. (2016). L'art de ne pas changer le monde [The art of not changing the world]. *La Revue Nouvelle, 8,* 44–50.

Sarti, A., Citti, G., & Piotrowski, D. (2019). Differential heterogenesis and the emergence of semiotic function. *Semiotica, 230,* 1–34.

Segal, J. (2003). *Le Zéro et le un. Histoire de la notion scientifique d'information au XXe siècle* [Zero and one. History of the notion of information in the 20th century]. Syllepse.

Scott, B. (2004). Second-order cybernetics: An historical introduction. *Kybernetes, 33*(9–10), 1365–1378.

Sfez, L. (1992). *Critique de la communication* [Critique of communication]. Seuil.

Simondon, G. (2010). The limits of human progress: A critical study. *Cultural Politics, 6*(2), 229–236.

Simondon, G. (2014). *Sur la technique (1953–1983)* [On technics. 1953–1983]. PUF.

Simondon, G. (2015). *Sur la psychologie (1956–1967)* [On psychology. 1956–1967]. PUF.

Simondon, G. (2016). *Sur la philosophie (1950–1980)* [On philosophy. 1950–1980]. PUF.

Simondon, G. (2017). *Of the mode of existence of technical objects.* Univocal Publishing (Original work published 1958).

Simondon, G. (2019). Form, information, and potentials (summary and debate). *Philosophy Today, 63*(3), 573–585.

Simondon, G. (2020). *Individuation in light of notions of form and information.* University of Minnesota Press (Original work published 1958).

Soto, A. M., Longo, G., & Noble, D. (Eds.). (2016). From the century of the genome to the century of the organism: New theoretical approaches [Special Issue]. *Progress in Biophysics and Molecular Biology, 122*(1).

Stiegler, B. (2016). *Automatic society: The future of work.* Polity Press.

Thom, R. (1975). *Structural stability and morphogenesis: An outline of a general theory of models*. W. A. Benjamin, Inc.

Tiqqun (2020). *The cybernetic hypothesis*. Semiotext(e).

Toscano, A. (2012). The disparate: Ontology and politics in Simondon [Special issue: Deleuze and Simondon]. *Pli. The Warwick Journal of Philosophy*, 107–117.

Triclot, M. (2008). *Le moment cybernétique. La constitution de la notion d'information* [The cybernetic moment. The constitution of the notion of information]. Éditions Champ Vallon.

Von Foerster, H. (1960). On self-organizing systems and their environments. In M. C. Yovits & S. Cameron (Eds.), *Self-organizing systems* (pp. 31–50). Pergamon Press.

Von Foerster, H. (1979). Cybernetics of cybernetics. In K. Krippendorff (Ed.), *Communication and control* (pp. 5–8). Gordon and Breach.

Wiener, N. (1985a). Homeostasis in the individual and society. In *Collected works with commentaries. Volume IV. Cybernetics, science, and society; ethics, aesthetics, and literary criticism; book reviews and obituaries* (P. Masani, Ed., pp. 380–383). The MIT Press (Original work published 1951).

Wiener, N. (1985b). Problems of organization. In *Collected works with commentaries. Volume IV. Cybernetics, science, and society; ethics, aesthetics, and literary criticism; book reviews and obituaries* (P. Masani, Ed., pp. 391–399). The MIT Press (Original work published 1953).

Wiener, N. (1988). *The human use of human beings: Cybernetics and society*. Da Capo Press (Original work published 1954).

Wiener, N. (2019). *Cybernetics, or control and communication in the animal and the machine*. The MIT Press (Original work published 1961).

Author biographies

Andrea Bardin is Senior Lecturer in Politics at Oxford Brookes University. He works on the relationship between science and political thought from early modernity to the present, and has written extensively on Thomas Hobbes and Gilbert Simondon.

Marco Ferrari is Research Fellow in Political Philosophy at the University of Padua, he has explored the connection between science and political thought through German idealism, psychoanalysis and contemporary French philosophy. He has published several works on Jacques Lacan and Alain Badiou.

MONOGRAPH SERIES

The Sociological Review Monographs
2022, Vol. 70(2) 50–66
© The Author(s) 2022
Article reuse guidelines:
sagepub.com/journals-permissions
DOI: 10.1177/00380261221084429
journals.sagepub.com/home/sor

Towards a complex conception of progress

Craig Lundy
School of Social Sciences and Professions, London Metropolitan University, UK

Abstract
For many decades, scholars working within the broad paradigm of complexity studies/theory have explored the nonlinear dynamics that contour physical and social systems. In doing so, radical theories that contest both Newtonian and neo-Darwinian understandings of reality have been posited, augmenting how we think about processes of change. But throughout these developments, the modern idea of progress has arguably remained insufficiently contested. This article seeks to show how the framework of complexity can offer conceptual resources for rethinking progress. Key characteristics of complexity are articulated and critically examined with the aim of pinpointing how they might contribute to a conception of progress that is worthy of the name yet divergent from its dominant 'modern' form.

Keywords
attractors, complexity, contingency, emergence, nonlinear, path-dependence, progress

Introduction

The world of quantum physics is full of wacky and wonderful theories: 'Schrödinger's cat', 'Wigner's friend' and 'the uncertainty principle' are just some of the infamous experiments and ideas that challenge common sense notions of causation, stretching the limits of credulity. But despite successes in shaking up the classical framework of physics, how many quantum scholars *live their lives* according to these findings? How many have changed the way that they view the course of human history, the narrative of their career, or their plans for the future due to the revelations of quantum physics? I would hazard to say not many. When it comes to the way that human beings project into the future and reflect on the journey of their lives and society, conventional 'common sense' notions of cause/effect and the mantra of progress still reign supreme. But what if we were to allow developments in contemporary science about the nature of change and causation to influence our understanding of human affairs, and in particular the manner

Corresponding author:
Craig Lundy, School of Social Sciences and Professions, London Metropolitan University, London, N7 8DB, UK.
Email: c.lundy@londonmet.ac.uk

of their transformation over time? Throughout history many of the great explanations of human society and its vicissitudes have been wedded to and/or inspired by theories of the physical cosmos. It would appear, though, that the notion of progress bequeathed by modernity remains largely intact despite major shifts in scientific understanding since the Enlightenment. Could a reappraisal of progress in light of these developments lead to a more widespread alteration in how this idea is viewed and used?

For the past several decades there have been some attempts to do just this in the field of 'complexity studies'. Drawing on findings in biology, physics and mathematics that contest the orthodoxies of Newtonian and Darwinian science, scholars in the humanities and social sciences have explored how these 'complex' and 'nonlinear' alternatives can inform our appreciation of social and social-physical systems. Insofar as the 'complexity' paradigm provides an alternative way of thinking about and understanding processes of change, one would assume that these implications would – or at least could – extend to the framework of 'progress' that underlies much human sense-making. Efforts to explicitly articulate what a properly complex conception of progress might look like, however, have been arguably underdone. This article aims to address the lacuna by exploring how progress might be reconceived according to key principles and findings of complexity theory. The purpose of doing this will not be to convince the reader that a complex conception of progress is 'correct' or 'true', with other conceptions 'incorrect' or 'false'; my intention is to merely explore how the complexity paradigm can contribute to challenging and evading the conventional understanding of progress and progression. Complexity theory no doubt has its own flaws and weaknesses, some of which I will touch on, but it would still seem to me that there is mileage to be gained from mining the resources of complexity in order to gesture towards a new notion of progress that goes beyond its modern form, simultaneously sidestepping the interminable critique and defence of this modern idea.

The focus for much of this article will be on processual aspects of progress in a technical sense, such as 'nonlinear' trajectories of change, the dynamics of 'emergence' and the nature of 'attractors'. As a consequence, the ethical dimensions of progress will be downplayed in favour of examining the relation of elements in a system and/or series. Like many scientific theories of nature, complexity theory is often presented in an a-ethical fashion – the dynamics and principles are neither 'good' nor 'bad', they simply are.[1] Although this position is naïve, since all scientific theories are based on and sometimes produce their own cultural myths, it would seem to me that complexity theory has the capacity to give us a way of thinking about progress and progression that diverges from the modern ethic of 'betterment'. Rephrasing this suggestion in the form of an open question: to the extent that complexity theory offers a cosmology detached from the classical Newtonian and Darwinian frameworks, which are themselves shot through with the modern idea of progress and its ethic of betterment, what ramifications might this alternative have for reconfiguring progress? I will speak to this question after outlining the nonlinear, emergent, attracted and path-dependent characteristics of complex progress.

Nonlinear progress

The 'modern' idea of progress is often characterised as giving a 'linear' account of history, in which progress proceeds in a line – more specifically, a 'straight' line, heading 'upwards', which is to say in the direction of 'betterment'. Seen this way, progress is a linear sequence of gradual unerring betterment, the diagonal line heading from bottom left to top right. It is important to note, however, that the 'modern' idea of progress need not be understood as linear. To take one paradigmatic case, Sofie Møller (2021) has argued that Kant's philosophy of progress, contrary to conventional wisdom (Allen, 2016, p. 8; Koselleck, 2002, p. 227), is built on a notion of *nonlinear* progress. According to Møller, progress for Kant refers to the 'way in which humanity . . . reaches its full potential' (2021, pp. 130–131). This journey, though, is by no means smooth: periods of progress are followed by regression, after which a leftover 'germ of enlightenment' is taken up, facilitating the next 'stage of improvement' (Kant, 1995, 8:30). Insofar as Kant's position allows for periods of regression, and as such departs from the 'linear' account described above, it is understandable why Møller describes Kant's philosophy of progress as 'non-linear'. But this raises the question: does anyone *really* believe in a vision of historical progress that is entirely devoid of any deviations or periods of stagnation whatsoever? I suspect that even evangelists of progress would baulk at this 'straw man' figure, and in fact Møller's own definition of linear progress allows for 'minor setbacks' (2021, p. 128). Seen from this perspective, practically every account of progress is a nonlinear account. If the terms linear/nonlinear are to have any meaning, therefore, it would seem that they must refer to more than the mere existence of regression or unevenness. Kant's philosophy of progress, to be sure, is not nonlinear simply because there are periods of regression; more significantly, it is because these regressions are a 'contingent occurrence' (Kant, 1995, 7:88). From this we can see that nonlinearity refers not merely to the fact that regressions occur, but furthermore that they are contingent and unpredictable. To borrow an example from sports, some defeats are occasionally characterised as 'good' or 'productive' if they spark a reaction that leads to victory. However, what makes this journey nonlinear is not simply that such defeats/reactions happen, but that they cannot be predicted in advance and could have happened differently or not at all. At this point it is customary for analysis to move on to an investigation of what 'causes' this line to meander and whether we can 'know' its direction in advance. But before we jump to these questions, let us turn to complexity theory to see how nonlinearity is defined there.

Nonlinearity is a key feature of complex systems, referred to in practically all of the literature in this field. Whilst there are some recurring descriptions of nonlinearity amongst this literature, there is also no small amount of discrepancy. According to most experts, the term 'nonlinearity' refers first and foremost to *relational proportionality*, or more exactly the lack of it (Durie & Wyatt, 2007, pp. 1930–1931). At a technical (mathematical) level, a nonlinear system does not satisfy the 'superposition principle', where $f(x + y) = f(x) + f(y)$. Re-worded in prose:

> [In a linear system] the sum of two solutions is again a solution, which makes linear equations relatively easy to solve. They are called 'linear' because they can be represented on a graph by a straight line. Nonlinear equations, by contrast, are represented by graphs that are curved, are very difficult to solve, and display a host of unusual properties. (Capra, 2005, p. 35)

Astill and Cairney make the point in slightly different language, stating that linearity is where 'the change in the dependent variable is always the same amount for any given amount of change in the independent variable' (2015, p. 133). Nonlinearity, on the other hand, is where 'small changes may lead to large consequences', and vice versa (DeLanda, 2002, p. 52; see also Preiser, 2019, pp. 708–711; Walby, 2003, p. 12; Walby, 2007, pp. 455–456, 464–465).[2] This characteristic has been commonly referred to as the 'butterfly effect', where the flap of a butterfly's wings in one part of the world leads to a tornado in another part of the world. However, if this example is significant, it is not only due to the illustration of disproportionality. More profoundly, the causal chain between the butterfly and the tornado cannot be reliably predicted.

This difficultly of prediction and modelling, it should be said, does not apply to all nonlinear relationships, some of which can be easily 'transformed' or disaggregated into linear relationships. In fact, a significant section of complexity scientists/mathematicians specialise in 'solving' difficult nonlinear equations by replacing them with a number of smaller linear approximations (Capra, 2005, p. 35; see also Gare, 2000, pp. 329–340). The advent of high-powered computers has made this line of work much more successful than previously imagined, but several complexity scholars argue that there remains a qualitative difference between 'complicated' problems/systems, which may be 'big' but can be broken down into numerous 'small', 'non-complicated' problems/systems, and properly 'complex' problems/systems that cannot be 'linearised' in the same fashion. For such scholars, there is an irreducible uncertainty inherent in complex systems, regardless of the prevailing capacity for calculation (Kernick, 2006; Thrift, 1999). Again in the words of Astill and Cairney: 'The very essence of the "butterfly effect" of complex systems and non-linearity is that, as we vary some independent variable(s) consistently, we cannot hope to find a recognizable, or even necessarily repeatable, pattern emerging in the dependent variable that we can express in any reductive way' (2015, p. 135). In this respect, the disproportional nature of nonlinear relationships is of less importance than the claim that such disproportionality is difficult if not impossible to map into the future (Astill & Cairney, 2015, pp. 132–135; Cilliers, 2005, p. 258; Clark, 2005, p. 173; Durie & Wyatt, 2007, p. 1931; Eppel & Rhodes, 2018, pp. 949–950). If small changes *may* lead to large consequences in a nonlinear system, why does this happen only sometimes, and why can't we predict when it will? We thus return to the task of explaining why the nonlinear line meanders, and in an unpredictable way.

Some complexity scholars have suggested that the uncertainty is a result of the 'high connectivity' in a nonlinear system (Van Uden et al., 2001), or what Clark calls 'the density of interconnections and the multitude of possible combinations' (2000, p. 21; see also DeLanda, 1997, pp. 109, 273). Such responses, however, seem inadequate, for they imply that the impasse could be merely due to the present limits of our computational power. If we presume that nonlinear systems are fundamentally irreducible – i.e. cannot be fully predicted in principle, not simply because they are 'really complicated' and beyond our current computational means – it would appear that some other explanation for this is needed.

A common candidate for this within the complexity literature is 'feedback loops', of which there are two kinds: *negative* feedback loops that 'dampen' the propensity for change and maintain the status quo of a system, and *positive* feedback loops that 'amplify' perturbations leading to systemic change (Kernick, 2006, p. 386; Preiser, 2019, p. 711; Richardson et al., 2001, p. 7). Once again, though, it is not entirely clear how feedback loops render a nonlinear system unpredictable. Presumably it is because these feedback loops are themselves unpredictable, as a result of 'small random events' that 'happen' (Arthur, 1999, pp. 107–109), but what makes them random, and what makes them happen or not happen? Even more worryingly, feedback loops are often pointed to as a self-evident illustration of nonlinearity, but what about them is actually nonlinear? Consider DeLanda's example of a (negative) feedback loop: the regulating thermostat. DeLanda says that when the effector (heating-cooling element) changes the room temperature 'it thereby affects the subsequent behavior of the sensor' (1997, p. 67). From this he concludes that 'the causal relation does not form a straight arrow but folds back on itself, forming a closed loop' (1997, p. 67). This loop, 'in which the effects react back on their causes' (DeLanda, 1999, p. 9), is furthermore said to be an example of 'circular causality' (1997, p. 67) and 'reverse causality' (1997, p. 293). From this description we can see why feedback loops would be associated with nonlinearity as opposed to linearity (see also DeLanda, 1997, p. 55; 2002, p. 53). On closer inspection, however, the characterisation of these relations as a 'loop' is little more than a play on words. This is because the events must surely occur *in time*, which continues to unfold asymmetrically and does not repeat or go backwards. When the sensor tells the heating-cooling element to turn on for the second time, it does so for a second time, not the first or the third. There may be resemblance between iterations, but history does not *actually* repeat itself. The history of the First and Second World War, for example, might be said to involve a 'back and forth' set of reactions between the protagonists, but this does not mean it cannot be explained by conventional causal-linear mechanisms. If you say something to me and my response to you influences what you next say to me, this is hardly an example of reverse causality that undermines the classical understanding of cause and effect; far from being a radical paradigm-shattering illustration of causality, this 'back and forth' exchange or so-called 'loop' could hardly be more ordinary.[3]

The nonlinearity of feedback loops is thus only achieved by placing them *outside of time* – it relies upon the abstraction of a temporal series into a spatial loop. Or in the words of Smith and Jenks (2005, p. 152): ' "recursive causality" – a characteristic of complexity, implied in "bringing forth worlds" – still has a temporal direction, which makes that particular expression questionable'. If feedback loops are not even suitable for explaining nonlinearity, there is little hope that they will be able to explain the unpredictability of nonlinear systems for us. We should not be surprised by this, for if Ilya Prigogine has taught us nothing else about complex systems it is that they are composed of *irreversible processes*.[4] And herein lies the clue to explaining the unpredictability of nonlinear progressions: to say that nothing truly repeats itself is to say that reality is continually being created, becoming. If the future is unpredictable, this is because it is not entirely reducible to the present or past. Nonlinearity may be suitable for describing the disproportionality of progressions, but it would appear that it does not provide a sufficient reason for the uncertainty and unpredictability of complex progressions. For that we will need to turn to another key principle of complexity theory: *emergence*.

Emergent progress

As we have now seen, the distinction between linear and nonlinear progressions could refer to the quality of the line that is unfolding – i.e. its directionality or disproportionality

– but regardless of this distinction the more significant consideration is whether the progression is contingent or necessary, predictable or unpredictable. To illustrate the point, most scholars who speak about nonlinear processes do so in order to indicate the element of randomness or uncertainty, they do not have in mind those nonlinear equations that can be completely reduced to determinant linear subsets. By the same token, linearity for these scholars refers to a set of relations characterised by necessity, uni-directionality, direct proportionality and uniqueness (where the same cause always leads to the same effect [DeLanda, 2002, pp. 138–139]). Although it is doubtful whether anyone actually believes that this strict definition of linearity is an accurate description of reality, especially in the realm of human affairs, the purpose of the straight line motif is to counterpose a vision of progression devoid of uncertainty in every respect – a far-fetched vision, which emphasises and advocates the contingency of its nonlinear alternative.

At this point it is worth reflecting on another giant of modernity that is frequently associated with the European philosophy of progress, Hegel. In recent years there has been an attempt to recuperate Hegel's reputation when it comes to his theory of world history and the progress it entails. In contrast to the portrayal of Hegel's philosophy of history as a form of historicism that universalises history by virtue of a unitary and totalising force, some have argued that creativity and contingency lies at the core of his vision. As we already saw with Kant, for Hegel the progression of history is far from smooth and measured; instead, history proceeds by way of struggle and contradiction, with progressions resulting from various contingent circumstances and unpredictable events. Indeed, this is what history is: the progress from one level of freedom and self-consciousness to the next that is instigated by the dialectical resolution of contingent occurrences. Contingency, in this respect, is *required* for historical progress to occur (see De Boer, 2009; Macdonald, 2006; Maker, 2009). So what we have here is a theory of how new social formations emerge, one of the most influential theories of emergence ever articulated, which features contingency prominently. All this said, it must be remembered that Hegel's aim is not to celebrate the contingent and insist on its irreducibility. Far from it:

> The sole aim of philosophical enquiry is to eliminate the contingent. Contingency is the same as external necessity, that is, a necessity which originates in causes which are themselves no more than external circumstances. In history, we must look for a general design, the ultimate end of the world, and not a particular end of the subjective spirit or mind; and we must comprehend it by means of reason, which cannot concern itself with particular or finite ends, but only with the absolute. (Hegel, 1975, p. 28)

Thus while there may be 'setbacks', 'accidents' and 'unexpected events' in history, these are all retrospectively understood and determined via the dialectic of reason, which ultimately moves in the direction of becoming progressively 'free' and self-determining. Contingency is ultimately reducible to a necessity-making-mechanism that functions according to the principles of dialectics (contradiction/antagonism) – e.g. x and y are contingent or accidental *with respect to the totalising power that makes them so* – a power and process that is by no means random and devoid of direction, even if this is only retrospectively revealed. Hence the significance of the retrospectivity at the heart of

Hegelian historicism, which orders externalities according to an internal(ising) mechanism. Malabou and Zizek are right to focus on this aspect of retrospection (see Clark & Szersynski, 2022), but who or what is it that retrospectively projects, and how? All roads lead back to Geist and the dialectical mechanism of contradiction/antagonism. This mechanism may be thought of as creative or productive in a certain sense, but as pointed out by Deleuze, this sense is more exactly *creation by negation* (Deleuze, 1962/1983, pp. 8–10). The mechanism might also rely on difference and in a certain sense produce it, but it is a difference reducible to the identity of Geist (even if this identity is never 'finished'/ fully understood and we never actually reach the 'end of history').[5]

What, then, would a theory of emergent progression look like that is worthy of the name? Let us consider the example from complexity theory. Like nonlinearity, emergence is a touchstone term of complexity scholarship that is frequently referred to but often left unexplained. At its most basic, a phenomenon is said to *emerge* from an interaction of elements. In its more prosaic formulation, emergence is regularly used in complexity scholarship to refer to the emergence of 'order out of chaos' (Prigogine & Stengers, 2017), or using slightly different language, the emergence of new 'patterns' (Urry, 2005, p. 239). Walby prefers to conceive of this using the terminology of 'levels', in which each level has a different pattern and 'one level is emergent from other' (Walby, 2007, pp. 460, 463; see also Walby, 2003, pp. 2, 4, 10–11). But far more common amongst the literature is a discussion of how a large number of small interactions, acting/reacting in response to 'local stimuli', produces a collective order (Trenholm & Ferlie, 2013). The pattern or order of flocking birds, for example, is said to emerge from three rules: maintaining a minimum distance from objects, matching one's speed with adjacent birds, and moving towards the perceived centre. As another example, Goodwin explains how when the density of an ant colony reaches a 'critical value', there is a transition from a 'chaotic pattern' to a 'dynamic order': 'The group behaves in a collective mode that could not be predicted from the behaviour of individuals', which Goodwin takes to be 'a clear example of emergent behaviour' (Goodwin, 1994, pp. 65–66). As these examples suggest, a crucial feature of emergence in complexity theory is that the emergent order does not reside 'in' the individual components, but *between* them. In the words of Human, the emergent phenomena 'cannot be found inside the individual properties of the components but [are] a result of their interaction' (Human, 2016, p. 428).[6] The examples also do a good job at indicating how order and chaos are not dialectically opposed or antagonistic, but are instead part of the same continuum or spectrum. Prigogine's work on 'dissipative structures' can help us here. Similar to Goodwin's ant colonies, Prigogine's research shows that an increase in the flow of energy in a system can lead to a point of instability that results in the emergence of new structures and forms of order (Capra, 2005, p. 37). The increase in energy flow is said to push the system 'far from equilibrium' or 'to the edge of chaos', and in order to '"cope" with the excess energy better' the system reorganises itself (Smith & Jenks, 2005, p. 145) – a process referred to by others as adaptive self-organisation (Anderson et al., 2005). As such, 'life exists at the edge of chaos, moving from chaos into order and back again in a perpetual exploration of emergent order' (Goodwin, 1994, p. 169).

We can already see some important distinctions between the complex version of emergence and that of Hegel – notably the absence of a dialectical mechanism and the preference for a more fluid continuum of change. What we haven't yet been given, however, is an explanation of why the emergent patterns are qualitatively contingent, indeterminate and/or unpredictable. For instance, while it may be difficult for us humans with our limited brain-power and computing capacity to calculate all of the micro-interactions that occur in the flocking of birds, is this the reason why we cannot predict in advance the exact patterns that emerge, or is there some deeper ontological impediment?

There is no consensus on this amongst the complexity theory community – while some complexity scholars are preoccupied with reducing (if not eliminating) unpredictability for the purposes of modelling the future, others argue that the whole point of complexity thinking is to break free of the classical reductionist framework and liberate the future from certainty. Those in the latter camp invariably remark that complex systems are *open*, and it is this simple word that would appear to be doing much of the heavy lifting. The characteristic of emergence in complexity theory depends upon the existence of openness, otherwise that which emerged would have been foreclosed. As with nonlinearity, openness is conceptually defined by what it is not: closed. In a closed system all behaviour can be predicted from the outset, at least in principle. If complex systems retain a kernel of uncertainty or unpredictability, if they are 'non-totalizable' (Human & Cilliers, 2013, p. 36), it is because the system is open to the outside, to external influences that precipitate the emergence of new patterns (Boulton et al., 2015). When a system is open in this manner, it becomes impossible to 'know' all of the elements at play. We cannot even be certain that the same input will have the same effect, since other changes in the surrounding context could influence the outcome (Cilliers, 2000). It is the openness of complex systems, in other words, which affirms the basic insight that history never repeats itself.

But does the element of openness merely displace and not dissolve the promise of certainty? When we say that a system is open, are we not just saying that it is part of a larger system, which might itself be determined and predictable if one had the capacity? And to what extent are the demarcations of inside/outside arbitrary and relative to the projecting subject (Cilliers, 2005, p. 258; Kernick, 2006; Van Uden et al., 2001, p. 63)? It may be convenient for the sake of analysis to demarcate a system that can be grasped by the human mind and then add the addendum that the system is 'open' to the things that we left outside it in our act of demarcating, but is this anything more than an exercise in mental gymnastics? What do the birds care if we happen to 'see' a pattern in the outline shape they form when flying? In this respect, the characteristic of openness is itself a product of the determination of inside/outside – a determination that creates the system that can then be said to be open to things outside it. If a complex system is un-totalisable due to its ability to affect and be affected by the surrounding environment, this may assure the complexity of one system, but this doesn't explain why the universe as a totality is complex. Acknowledging this, however, does not make the activity meaningless. On the contrary, it emphases how demarcated systems are projected entities whose meaning is produced by and from the perspective of a subject. As stated by Deleuze: 'The interior is only a selected interior, and the exterior, a projected interior' (Deleuze, 1970/1988, p. 125). We will return to this crucial point in the final section of the article. For the moment, however, it should be noted that the activity of individuation being referred to here – the selection process in which a shape or order is carved out of chaos

– is not a purely subjective determination, for even if everything is ultimately connected with everything this does not preclude the existence of corporeal subsets that have a certain systematicity or privileged set of relations. Hence Prigogine's term 'dissipative structures': the physical phenomena being examined and described do indeed form a 'structure', albeit one that changes or dissipates over time through interactions both internal and external. The terminology of open/closed and inside/outside is therefore a subjective convenience, but it is not an arbitrary fantasy and it is employed for a good reason: to better understand and describe reality.

What, then, does all this mean for a complex conception of emergent progress? To remind, part of the reason we have gone to complexity theory is to see whether it has useful conceptual resources for taking us beyond the modern idea of progress and its conventional views on the nature of emergence such as we find in Kant, Hegel and related thinkers (e.g. Marx, Habermas). In particular, it was hoped that this complex theory of progress would provide a compelling alternative to those theories of emergence that are based on necessity. In the work of scientists such as Goodwin and Prigogine we can find revealing accounts of how new patterns emerge in the natural world, 'order out of chaos'. Their theories are of *asymmetrical* or *irreversible* progressions, but they retain the characteristic of contingency by virtue of their openness. In one respect, the determination of open/closed and inside/outside of complex systems could be said to depend on the perspective of the observer, but this hardly means that the behaviour of an ant colony or a dissipative structure will change if it is observed by a human subject (or not). Rather, it is the *description* of patterns that depends on the subject. In describing a sequence of systemic change, complexity theory provides an explanation of how new phenomena emerge through interactions in a 'world of becoming', to borrow Connolly's phrase (2011). It would be misleading, however, to imply that complexity theory proposes a vision of the future as 'radically open', as if anything could happen and everything is equally likely. Similarly, coming from the other direction, it would be a mistake to presume that in complexity theory the past bears no impact on the present. Quite the opposite: emergent progress in complexity theory is both 'path-dependent' and influenced by 'attractors'. In what respect, we might then ask, is the complex conception of progress different from the mechanistic and teleological accounts that it aims to distance itself from?

Attracted and path-dependent progress

In his book *Creative Evolution*, Henri Bergson criticises those accounts of evolution that fall foul of what he calls 'radical mechanism' or 'radical finalism'. Describing the former he says:

> The essence of mechanical explanation, in fact, is to regard the future and the past as calculable functions of the present, and thus to claim that *all is given*. On this hypothesis, past, present and future would be open at a glance to a super-human intellect capable of making the calculation. (Bergson, 1907/1998, p. 37, emphasis in original)

As Bergson elaborates, the mechanistic vision of causation, in which nature is conceived as 'an immense machine regulated by mathematical laws' (Bergson, 1907/1998, p. 45), overly valorises the past by suggesting that the coordinates of the present (and future) reside within it. Bergson does not deny that the past contours the present and future – indeed, his concepts of duration and memory are essentially an attempt to describe their continuity, as a 'heterogeneous multiplicity'. But his point here is that if a new emergence is to be worthy of the name, then it must be more than a mere rearrangement of the old. According to Bergson, genuine emergence is an impossibility in radical mechanism, for it 'implies a metaphysic in which the totality of the real is postulated complete in eternity' (Bergson, 1907/1998, p. 39).

Unlike radical mechanism, radical finalism does not rely on a 'billiard balls' vision of cause and effect; instead, it is a teleological doctrine that posits the programme to be realised. But as with radical mechanism, radical finalism operates by extrapolating from the known and the datum of the past forward into the future. For this reason Bergson says that radical finalism is nothing more than an inversion of radical mechanism: 'it holds in front of us the light with which it claims to guide us, instead of putting it behind. It substitutes the attraction of the future for the impulsion of the past' (Bergson, 1907/1998, p. 39). It is important to note that Bergson is not against all theories of finalism – in fact, his theory about the individuation of the *élan vital* is itself a form of finalism, but as Deleuze summarises in his book on Bergson: 'There is finality because life does not operate without directions; but there is no "goal", because these directions do not pre-exist ready-made, and are themselves created "along with" the act that runs through them' (Deleuze, 1966/1991, p. 106).

Complexity theory offers another way of navigating between radical mechanism and radical finalism, between determinism and teleology. Perhaps the most important accomplishment of complexity science has been its critique of the classical Newtonian framework – to bring about 'the end of certainty' (Prigogine, 1997). As this phrase suggests, complexity liberates the future, but this does not mean that the future is a blank canvas. On the contrary, complexity theory has a lot to say about how processes unfold, influenced by so-called 'attractors'. As Capra explains, when mathematicians 'solve' a nonlinear equation, 'the result is not a formula but a visual shape, a pattern traced by the computer, known as an "attractor"' (Capra, 2005, p. 35). The attractor is a representation of the system's long-term dynamics. A nonlinear system can have several attractors (which is to say, multiple solutions). Depending on where a trajectory commences it will eventually gravitate towards the attractor that organises that particular region of the system, what is referred to as the 'basin of attraction'. Drawing on the ontology of Deleuze, DeLanda describes the alternative states or basins of attraction as *virtually coexistent*. Although one attractor may be 'actualised' at a particular point in time, 'All one has to do to reveal their virtual presence is to give a large enough shock to the system to push it out of one basin of attraction and into another' (DeLanda, 2002, p. 66–67). From this description of attractors it is clear that the manner in which complex systems undergo change is not a free-for-all; phase spaces are each characterised by distinct dynamics, which are visually represented by the various attractor patterns. Being nothing more than visual representations, it would be wrong to say that the attractors themselves exude an active pulling power of the system towards it, like a magnet. But at a more general level it would also be a mistake to equate mathematics with reality. As Gare remarks: 'Dynamical systems are not systems in the world but mathematical models of systems'

(Gare, 2000, p. 329). If there is one obvious difference between the two it is that the mathematical models are *of space* and exist *outside of real time.*

As it happens, Bergson's critique of radical mechanism and radical finalism turns on just this point. If mechanistic explanations seem convincing, it is because they 'hold good for the systems that our thought artificially detaches from the whole' (Bergson, 1907/1998, p. 37), systems that are 'withdrawn, by hypothesis, from the action of real time' (Bergson, 1907/1998, p. 29). So too with radical finalism, in which 'succession remains none the less a mere appearance, as indeed does movement itself' (Bergson, 1907/1998, p. 39). Complexity theory, it would seem, is well placed to avoid the trap of spatialising time, due to its emphasis on irreversible and asymmetrical temporal processes. As Prigogine and Stengers say, 'reality is embedded in the flow of time' (2017, p. xxix). In this vein, complexity scholars often remark that in complex systems 'history matters'. This phrase, however, could refer to several things. To start with, it could mean that unlike 'ahistorical' sciences that are devoid of temporality, complex systems each have a unique story. In the words of Clark, 'each complex system acquires its own individual and singular history' (Clark, 2005, p. 177), or as he says elsewhere, '[life] evolves through a succession of time-irreversible events which are in turn entwined in the no-less-irrevocable movements of the world around it, all the way up to the level of the universe' (Clark, 2005, p. 165). This motif of nothing happening twice suggests that 'history matters' because it never repeats itself.

Distinct from but related to this point is a second sense in which the phrase is used, whereby 'history matters' because it informs what comes next. As a complex system undergoes change, it becomes faced with 'bifurcation points' where it must 'choose' between alternatives. The path chosen in turn has consequences for what happens next; or seen from the other end, outcomes are 'subject to the historical path taken' (Arthur, 1999). The development of the QWERTY typewriter keyboard is an oft-cited example of this, in which the initial path 'chosen' guides future developments (Waldrop, 1993, p. 40).[7] Such examples illustrate how complex systems are 'path dependent' and can experience 'lock-in', as the momentum of their trajectory influences the direction of their development. Using slightly different language, Richardson et al. say that a complex system 'has a memory' (2001, pp. 7–8). But these sorts of statements lead us back to the delicate dance of necessity and contingency. On the one hand, the phrase 'history matters' is uttered to affirm contingency and reject the reduction of emergent progress to the mechanics of the past or the telos of the future. For Urry, the phrase 'history matters' means that 'different paths could have been taken' (Urry, 2005, p. 239); and for DeLanda, 'with multiple possible outcomes *the details of the history followed do matter*' (DeLanda, 2005, p. 83, emphasis added). But on the other hand, 'history matters' because it *constrains* emergence. History might not repeat itself, but it quite often *informs* what happens next. This is not to say that all paths are predetermined, but neither are they entirely open. What complexity theory gives us is a way of understanding how the dynamics of a system guides and constrains the nature of its development, from both a spatial perspective (i.e. basins of attraction) and temporal (i.e. its history), whilst retaining an element of contingency and indetermination.

Although this process differs fundamentally from the Newtonian framework and the modern idea of progress, it is nonetheless a form of development that clearly involves *progression*. One moment does not simply come after the next, each one *builds* on the last. As Bergson says of duration, it 'is the continuous progress of the past which gnaws into the future and which swells as it advances' (Bergson, 1907/1998, p. 4). And again: 'Real duration is that duration which gnaws on things, and leaves on them the mark of its tooth' (Bergson, 1907/1998, p. 46). The process of change described by complexity could be said to similarly constitute an 'advance', insofar as it involves an incessant moving forward – there is no going back, because time is irreversible. This is why the word 'history' is completely appropriate: what we are dealing with here is not time in the abstract, but *real duration*, which bites and bleeds and scars. This is also why 'history matters' in complexity, in a way that it doesn't in deterministic and teleological accounts of progress. But most importantly, the advance of complexity is not one of 'betterment'. Unlike Darwinian and neo-Darwinian renditions of evolution, the process of development described by complexity does not necessarily involve an underlying sense of 'improvement' or 'better fit'. Indeed, some complexity biologists, such as Brian Goodwin, claim that one of the best things about complexity is its ability to evade the Christian ethic of striving and betterment that is endemic in much evolutionary theory (Goodwin, 1994, pp. 28–32). As he demonstrates by outlining key developments in Darwin's theory and comparing the Darwinian principles of evolution with the central ethical tenets of Christianity, Darwinism 'has its metaphorical roots in one of our deepest cultural myths, the story of the fall and redemption of humanity' (Goodwin, 1994, p. 30). Darwin no doubt commits heresy, by toppling God from His position, but the story, for the most part, 'remained much the same as before in terms of competition, struggle, work and progress' (1994, p. 30). There has been no shortage of attempts to distance the Great Man and his 'dangerous idea' from the more unpalatable instances of 'social Darwinism', but as Goodwin points out, Darwin was an adherent to the myth of progress and its underlying ethic of betterment, and this myth most certainly informed his theory of evolution and his view of humanity.[8] It would appear that complexity does not participate in perpetuating this myth of progress; or perhaps more modestly, it would appear that inasmuch as complexity offers a way of understanding processes of change that departs from the Newtonian and Darwinian frameworks, it potentially gives us a way of conceiving progression without the baggage that the modern version of this idea lugs around. All that being said, it must be admitted, as Goodwin does, that complexity theory is also riddled with anthropomorphism and the overlaying of cultural predilections on natural phenomena – a characteristic it shares with all other theories of naturalism. What, then, is its worth?

Conceptualising progress with complexity

The conception of progress is to a large degree an epistemological concern, a matter of perspective. As Frantz Fanon would say, what the colonisers call progress and Enlightenment goes by other names according to the colonised, such as oppression and injustice.[9] This was already apparent in Kant's schema, and most obviously in Hegel's, where nonlinearity is a byproduct of the particular way in which 'setbacks' are identified by an observer who privileges certain end points. In the case of Kant, progress may be 'epistemically unwarranted', as Møller confesses, but it is a 'necessary presupposition' that should be assumed 'for practical purposes' – namely, *for the purpose of achieving progress* (2021, pp. 138–139). Kant's nonlinear progress, it would therefore seem, is circular as well as subjective.

Can the same be said of complexity theory? In some respects yes. As we saw above, 'circular causality' and the celebrated 'feedback loops' of complexity theory are only circular loops at the level of appearance. It is obviously useful for humans to find patterns in nature and the social world, including what appear to us as 'loops', but a different being would extract different patterns. The patterns are *of* nature, they are *really* there, but it is us that place the pattern *on* nature, that *patternise*. When humans find images in the clouds, or look at the night sky and see the outline of a zodiac constellation, it is not as if this activity creates the clouds or the stars themselves, but the pattern identified nonetheless belongs to and comes from the subject projecting it. If three stars appear to align in a straight line to an observer then this is indeed a fact of reality, but it is a fact that belongs to the projecting subject. And when this subject stops projecting then the line will vanish, though the stars involved certainly won't. Thus with each emerging pattern identified by the complexity scholar, the question must be posed: to whom is that a pattern, and who is to say there wasn't a pattern there before, which you simply couldn't see and mistook for chaos? As Bergson teaches us, 'disorder is simply the order we are not looking for' (Bergson, 1934/2007, p. 80). So too with nonlinearity: who is to say it is nothing more than the linearity we weren't expecting or are incapable of seeing? While this comment applies to nonlinearity in general, Gare points out that it is especially true of nonlinear dynamical systems, which 'are capable of revealing the world to be unpredictable and capable of generating macroscopic patterns with their own dynamics; but this is at the level of appearance' (2000, p. 333). As he continues: 'The underlying dynamics are deterministic and would appear to rule out anything but the appearance of emergence.' Because of this we should not get overly excited about the pretty patterns that appear in our computer models: 'Since computers can simulate virtually anything, that a simulation appears life-like is of no great significance' (2000, p. 333).

There is a difference, however, between acknowledging the deterministic aspect of nonlinear dynamics and projecting idealised forms into the future. Bergson makes a similar point when critiquing the conventional understanding of 'possibility', in which future possibles are posed as ideal options 'out there', one of which is selected or 'realised'. This way of thinking, whereby possibilities pre-exist 'under the form of an idea' (Bergson, 1934/2007, p. 83), is based on the same reductive reasoning that guides 'radical mechanism' and 'radical finalism' – a reductionism that makes genuine emergence impossible: 'This is why the idea of reading in a present state of the material universe the future of living forms, and of unfolding now their history yet to come, involves a veritable absurdity' (Bergson, 1907/1998, p. 341). If complexity theory is good at undermining presumptions of the classical model, it is because it avoids positing the inverse: the future is no longer closed, but neither is it radically open; 'history matters', but it is not a straightjacket; there is no progress as betterment, but time does 'move on', it advances and accumulates. And it is to be expected that complexity will have its own fair share of myths, metaphors and analogies – after all, it is a theory concocted by humans to try and *make sense* of reality. As Goodwin reminds us:

> All theories have metaphorical dimensions which I regard as not only inevitable but also as extremely important. For it is these dimensions that give depth and meaning to scientific ideas,

that add to their persuasiveness and colour the way we see reality. Science, after all, is not a culture-free activity. The point of recognizing this . . . is simply to help us to stand back, to take stock, to contemplate alternative ways of describing biological reality. (Goodwin, 1994, p. 32)

Complexity theory will never rid itself of this epistemological constraint, but this doesn't mean it is marked for the scrap heap: its use is that it 'tells a rather different story' (Goodwin, 1994, p. 32). Goodwin is here referring to the story of life at the biological level, but it just may be that the story also helps us to reimagine progress and take us beyond its modern coordinates.

Conclusion

It is hardly novel to point out that progress has been one of the most ubiquitous and ethically suspect ideas from modernity to the present. Few are the 'critically minded' academics that would defend this idea, or at least the Eurocentric version complicit in colonialism and environmental destruction. This is because the intellectual critique of progress – from postcolonial scholars, existential philosophers and numerous other fields – has been convincingly and repeatedly made. And yet the conventional idea of progress depressingly remains as strong as ever. It is vital that the critique and deconstruction of progress goes on, even if the effects that we seek from it remain elusive, but perhaps what demands even more attention are *constructive* attempts to engender alternatives – by which I mean both *alternatives to* progress and alternative *notions of* progress. This article has been preoccupied with the latter. All notions of progress are underpinned by a particular onto-epistemological theory of process and a cosmology of change, many of which draw from and/or connect to scientific frameworks. The task of this article has been to explore how insights from complexity studies/theory might prompt us to *think and apply progress differently*. This has not been straightforward, for isolating exactly where and how complexity diverges from conventional accounts of change and progress is not as self-evident as some scholars suggest. Nonetheless, by articulating what is meant by complexity terms such as 'nonlinearity', 'emergence', 'open', 'attractors' and 'path-dependence' in contradistinction from the classical scientific framework that is coordinate with the modern idea of progress, this exercise has hopefully offered some leads on how we might move beyond the status quo of progress to a more complex understanding and experience of it.

Funding

The author received no financial support for the research, authorship, and/or publication of this article.

Notes

1. For more on this see Burton et al. (2019, pp. 99–101).
2. Expanding on this point, some argue that the same input can lead to different outputs (Astill & Cairney, 2015, p. 132; Smith & Jenks, 2005, p. 155).
3. For a distinct but related critique of 'homeostasis' and 'feedback' in Weiner's cybernetics see Bardin and Ferrari's chapter in this collection. As they argue, Weiner uses these concepts in

order to challenge static understandings of equilibrium and the 'clockwork' universe of modern science, but he ultimately replicates the same epistemological reductions, to the extent that 'Weiner's non-deterministic ontology was in fact mechanical determinism in disguise' (Bardin & Ferrari, 2022, p. 253).

4. In the first paragraph of their Preface to *Order out of Chaos* (2017, p. xxvii), Prigogine and Stengers offer two examples of phenomena that might 'appear to us' to be reversible, in the sense of a cycle/circuit or loop: the motion of a frictionless pendulum and the motion of the earth around the sun – but their point here is that this is merely an *appearance*, and more specifically an appearance *to us*.

5. For more on this see Lundy (2016).

6. Human goes on to equate this with 'the old adage that the whole is more than the sum of its parts' (Human, 2016, p. 428); however according to others such as John Urry, 'It is not that the sum is greater than the size of its parts but that there are system effects that are different from its parts' (Urry, 2006, p. 113).

7. For other examples in the social sciences see Durie and Wyatt (2007, p. 1936) and Van Uden et al. (2001).

8. In commenting on the native inhabitants of Tierra del Fuego, Darwin says that 'The perfect equality of all the inhabitants will for many years prevent their civilization. [Until this changes] there must be an end to all hopes of bettering their condition' (see Goodwin, 1994, p. 31).

9. 'All the Mediterranean values, the triumph of the individual, of enlightenment and Beauty turn into pale, lifeless trinkets. All those discourses appear a jumble of dead words. Those values which seemed to ennoble the soul prove worthless because they have nothing in common with the real-life struggle in which the people are engaged' (Fanon, 2004, p. 11).

References

Allen, A. (2016). *The end of progress: Decolonizing the normative foundations of critical theory.* Columbia University Press.

Anderson, R. A., Crabtree, B. F., Steele, D. J., & McDaniel, R. R., Jr. (2005). Case study research: The view from complexity science. *Qualitative Health Research, 5*(5), 669–685.

Arthur, W. B. (1999). Complexity and the economy. *Science, 284,* 107–109.

Astill, S., & Cairney, P. (2015). Complexity theory and political science: Do new theories require new methods? In R. Geyer & P. Cairney (Eds.), *Handbook on complexity and public policy* (pp. 131–149). Edward Elgar.

Bardin, A., & Ferrari, M. (2022). Governing progress: From cybernetic homeostasis to Simondon's politics of metastability. In C. Lundy & M. Savransky (Eds.), pp. 248–263. Sociological Review Monograph Series.

Bergson, H. (1998). *Creative evolution.* Dover (Original work published 1907).

Bergson, H. (2007). *The creative mind: An introduction to metaphysics.* Dover (Original work published 1934).

Boulton, J. B., Allen, P. M., & Bowman, C. (2015). *Embracing complexity: Strategic perspectives for an age of turbulence.* Oxford University Press.

Burton, S., Hutchings, S., Lundy, C., & Lyons-Lewis, A. (2019). Evaluation the complexity of service-learning practices: Lessons from and for complex systems theory. *Journal of Higher Education Outreach and Engagement, 23*(3), 89–103.

Capra, F. (2005). Complexity and life. *Theory, Culture and Society, 22*(5), 33–44.

Cilliers, P. (2000). What can we learn from a theory of complexity? *Emergence, 2*(1), 23–33.

Cilliers, P. (2005). Complexity, deconstruction and relativism. *Theory, Culture and Society, 22*(5), 255–267.

Clark, N. (2000). 'Botanizing on the asphalt'? The complex life of cosmopolitan bodies. *Body & Society, 6*(3–4), 12–33.

Clark, N. (2005). Ex-orbitant globality. *Theory, Culture and Society, 22*(5), 165–185.

Clark, N., & Szersynski, B. (2022). Earthly multitudes: Dialectics, universality and progress in wounded worlds. In C. Lundy & M. Savransky (Eds.), p. XX. Sociological Review Monograph Series.

Connolly, W. E. (2011). *A world of becoming.* Duke University Press.

De Boer, K. (2009). Hegel's account of the present: An open-ended history. In W. Dudley (Ed.), *Hegel and history* (pp. 51–67). SUNY Press.

DeLanda, M. (1997). *A thousand years of nonlinear history.* Zone Books.

DeLanda, M. (1999). Deleuze and the open-ended becoming of the world. *Dialogues.* www.cddc. vt.edu/host/delanda/pages/becoming.htm (accessed 18 October 2021).

DeLanda, M. (2002). *Intensive science and virtual philosophy.* Continuum.

DeLanda, M. (2005). Space: Extensive and intensive, actual and virtual. In I. Buchanan & L. Gregg (Eds.), *Deleuze and space* (pp. 80–88). Edinburgh University Press.

Deleuze, G. (1983). *Nietzsche and philosophy.* Continuum (Original work published 1962).

Deleuze, G. (1991). *Bergsonism.* Zone Books (Original work published 1966).

Deleuze, G. (1988). *Spinoza: Practical philosophy.* City Lights Books (Original work published 1970).

Durie, R., & Wyatt, K. (2007). New communities, new relations: The impact of community organization on health outcomes. *Social Science & Medicine, 65*(9), 1928–1941.

Eppel, E. A., & Rhodes, M. L. (2018). Complexity theory and public management: A 'becoming' field. *Public Management Review, 20*(7), 949–959.

Fanon, F. (2004). *The wretched of the earth.* Grove Press.

Gare, A. (2000). Systems theory and complexity. *Democracy and Nature, 6*(3), 327–339.

Goodwin, B. (1994). *How the leopard changed its spots: The evolution of complexity* (new ed.). Phoenix.

Hegel, G. W. F. (1975). *Lectures on the philosophy of world history* (H. B. Nisbet, Trans.). Cambridge University Press.

Human, O. (2016). Complexity: E-special introduction. *Theory, Culture and Society, 33*(7–8), 421–440.

Human, O, & Cilliers, P. (2013). Towards and economy of complexity: Derrida, Morin and Bataille. *Theory, Culture and Society, 30*(5), 24–44.

Kant, I. (1995). *The Cambridge edition of the works of Immanuel Kant* (P. Guyer & A. W. Wood, Ed.). Cambridge University Press.

Kernick, D. (2006). Wanted – new methodologies for health service research. Is complexity theory the answer? *Family Practice, 23*, 385–390.

Koselleck, R. (2002). *The practice of conceptual history: Timing history, spacing concepts.* Stanford University Press.

Lundy, C. (2016). The necessity and contingency of university history: Deleuze and Guattari contra Hegel. *Journal of the Philosophy of History, 10*(1), 51–75.

Macdonald, I. (2006). What is conceptual history? In K. Deligiorgi (Ed.), *Hegel: New directions* (pp. 207–226). Acumen.

Maker, W. (2009). The end of history and the nihilism of becoming. In W. Dudley (Ed.), *Hegel and history* (pp. 15–34). SUNY Press.

Møller, S. (2021). Kant on non-linear progress. *Ethics and Politics, 23*(2), 127–147.

Preiser, R. (2019). Identifying general trends and patterns in complex systems research: An overview of theoretical and practical implications. *Systems Research and Behavioral Science, 36*, 706–714.

Prigogine, I. (1997). *The end of certainty: Time, chaos and the new laws of nature*. The Free Press.

Prigogine, I., & Stengers, I. (2017). *Order out of chaos*. Verso.

Richardson, K. A., Cilliers, P., & Lissack, M. (2001). Complexity science: A 'gray' science for the 'stuff in between'. *Emergence*, *3*(2), 6–18.

Smith, J., & Jenks, C. (2005). Complexity, ecology and the materiality of information. *Theory, Culture and Society*, *22*(5), 141–163.

Thrift, N. (1999). The place of complexity. *Theory, Culture and Society*, *16*(3), 31–69.

Trenholm, S., & Ferlie, E. (2013). Using complexity theory to analyse the organisational response to resurgent tuberculosis across London. *Social Science & Medicine*, *93*, 229–237.

Urry, J. (2005). The complexities of the global. *Theory, Culture and Society*, *22*(5), 235–254.

Urry, J. (2006). Complexity. *Theory, Culture and Society*, *23*(2–3), 111–117.

Van Uden, J., Richardson, K. A., & Cilliers, P. (2001). Postmodernism revisited? Complexity science and the study of organisations. *Tamara: Journal of Critical Postmodern Organization Science*, *1*(3), 53–67.

Walby, S. (2003, April). *Complexity theory, globalisation and diversity*. Paper presented to the British Sociological Association, University of York.

Walby, S. (2007). Complexity theory, systems theory, and multiple intersecting social inequalities. *Philosophy of the Social Sciences*, *37*(4), 449–470.

Waldrop, M. M. (1993). *Complexity: The emerging science at the edge of order and chaos*. Touchstone.

Author biography

Craig Lundy is a Reader in Social and Political Thought at London Metropolitan University. The majority of his research has been concerned with exploring the nature of transformational processes, in particular the role that history plays in shaping socio-political formations. Much of this research has focused on the work of Gilles Deleuze and the post-Kantian lineage (e.g. Hegel, Marx, Nietzsche, Bergson), however he has also conducted applied research using the principles of complexity theory/science to examine a range of issues including the formation of community identity, the pedagogy of 'service-learning' and the processes of public engagement. Craig is the author of *Deleuze's Bergsonism, History and Becoming: Deleuze's Philosophy of Creativity*, and he co-edited with Daniela Voss the collection *At the Edges of Thought: Deleuze and Post-Kantian Philosophy*, all published by Edinburgh University Press.

MONOGRAPH SERIES

Epidemiological plots and the national syndrome

The Sociological Review Monographs
2022, Vol. 70(2) 67–81
© The Author(s) 2022

Article reuse guidelines:
sagepub.com/journals-permissions
DOI: 10.1177/00380261221084430
journals.sagepub.com/home/sor

Lara Choksey
University College London, UK

Abstract

When mass demonstrations against state-sanctioned violence 'play dead', they deliver collective judgements on the failure of justice. In this article, I discuss the epidemiological plot, a crisis genre motivated by the idea that the state can be cured through its own processes. This plot is preoccupied with defending the state against viral invasion, moral and medical, and by coercing consensus around what and whom can be included within it. I expand on this in a reading of Bram Stoker's *Dracula* (1897), where a medical-sociological consortium forms to annihilate a foreign threat to national health: vampirism. I suggest that *Dracula*'s exhaustion of its compliant reader through its proliferation of data offers an analogy for a normative and mainstream socio-scientific literacy that serves, increasingly, as a condition for full participation in public life. I move from this to consider entanglements with the time of judgement in Ashon Crawley's *The Lonely Letters* (2020), arguing that these circumvent the progressive historicism of national timekeeping.

Keywords

crisis management, epidemiology, judgement, nationalism, postcolonial justice

Introduction

In June 2020, twinned experiences of mass death joined up in international demonstrations against state-sanctioned violence. COVID-19 had underscored domestic and international fault-lines of crisis management, and Black Lives Matter centred anti-black brutality as the common and founding history of Euro-US imperialism. After the murder of George Floyd, 'I can't breathe' ricocheted from a North American semi-periphery into global demonstrations of playing dead. 'I can't breathe' became the bending of a bent note: the preservation of names, the care taken with final words, and the freezing of time, repeating what Elizabeth Freeman calls a 'performance [that] turns toward rather than away from the timelessness' (2019, p. 85). These coexisting and overlapping crisis responses saw congregations playing dead in an aesthesis of urgency that exceeded the

Corresponding author:
Lara Choksey, Department of English Language and Literature, University College London, Gower Street, London WC1E 6BT, UK.
Email: L.Choksey@ucl.ac.uk

possibility of achieving a just end within existing legal structures. 'I can't breathe' is a protracted, collective judgement on the failure to find, invent, or implement a cure. Where else is there to go, when the time of justice is exhausted?

These demonstrations confound institutional forms of narrative-making, conservatively understood as the assembly of documentation and the promise of a just resolution that adheres to existing laws, within the limited continuum of international justice and national civil rights. Against this, solidarity across multiple vectors of discontent has forced a confrontation with the continuities of the present – not as a crisis, but as business as usual. This solidarity asks what sense of shared life is possible in this situation. It challenges the common sense of public reality made permissible by the nation's professional practitioners: not just its government and military leaders, but its congress of expert opinions – lawyers and doctors, judges and scientists, and corporate interlopers. It is not so much that these demonstrations say that there is no progress to be made; rather, they challenge the temporal parameters of balancing the scales in national scenes of justice-making. In these demonstrations, the emphasis on justice is suspended for the sake of spectacular, temporary and prosaic forms of judgement. They make visible the limits of justice in demonstrations of judgement that exceed what is possible in the arbitration of the present. These limits exceed the national; this moment of solidarity took on the world-system and its local manifestations, and refused to concede to an image of the national as a syndrome that might be managed through its own processes. This articulates a difference between management and cure: between the limitations of what can be done within these processes, which hold off delivering a cure.

The scale of this refusal matters because in the situation of mass contagion, the possibility of justice is held in the promise of cure; in lieu of a cure, crisis management buys time. This play-off between management and cure has its own plot, couched in a genre that emerged in the early nineteenth century, between literary fiction as a trustworthy site for documenting human experience and the development of sociological enquiry that borrowed empirical methods from the natural sciences. I call this genre the epidemiological plot, and I give a sense of what I mean by this through a reading of Bram Stoker's *Dracula* (1897/2003). Stoker's version of the vampire myth converts the English aristocrat of John Polidori's 'The Vampyre' (1819/2008) into Transylvanian nobility, and closes the distance of Polidori's third-person gaze into a claustrophobic collection of documentation, where the reader is asked to participate directly and laboriously in the stitching together of plot. The novel is held together by phonograph transcripts, newspaper cuttings, legal letters and personal correspondence. Unlike Polidori's short story, the subject of Stoker's novel is not the vampire, but the formation of a consortium of professionals that work together to defend a breached national border against an invasive, mysterious syndrome: vampir*ism*. The plot is generated by the efforts of this group to convert this unknown monster from a syndrome of national decline to a success story of collaborative rehabilitation. In doing this, the consortium reaffirms a consensus around who and what can be included in a healthy national community. The quest to manage vampirism is a proxy negotiation over the state's terms of citizenship and belonging through the identification of a threat, and the professionalisation of crisis response.

Here, I propose reading these responses as epidemiological plots to show how measures taken to manage the spread of contagion grant emergency powers to consortia of experts. This extension of emergency powers centres the institutional time of the state as the prerogative of national progress in plots where national values determine the scale and distribution of justice, and permits civic violence on behalf of national interests. The epidemiological plot also recruits its own public by cultivating the reader as a fellow member of the consortium. It assumes compliance with its terms: the protection and defence of national borders by any means necessary. It also highlights the dissonance between the partiality of national interests (which need to be managed) and the abstract promise of the state as a general cure.

While it is true that crisis responses expose both the narrowness of national interests and the mechanisms of disaster capitalism – as well as how this combination upholds the abstraction and mythologising of state power – I will not rehearse this well-trodden ground here. I am more curious about moments that interrupt the nation's continued reinvention of itself as a body to be rehabilitated. These moments do not happen in the legal machinery of justice, which always routes its imagined community back to the protection and defence of national interests. Instead, these moments disturb the processes of professional truth-making dramatised in *Dracula*. In the second part of this article, I move from *Dracula* to Ashon Crawley's *The Lonely Letters* (2020a) as an example of a cure without a plot, made up of whatever can be seized in moments of exhaustion. In Crawley's 'agnosticostal' rendering of Pentecostal spaces and Blackpentecostal practices, moving through flesh and spirit and speaking in tongues, there is not much to follow and no figure or structure to venerate (2020b). Nor is there an embodied contagion. Time might be the problem, or at least a persistent anxiety to record its passing. Crawley's quasi-fictional letters to a silent interlocutor whose responses are never shown demonstrate a practice of being 'caught up in the cause of justice' without cultivating a relation of dependency with the law, or by appealing to the strength of the state (Crawley, 2016, p. 2).

Instead, Crawley foregrounds the power of everyday judgement. Judgement comprises a different entanglement with ordinary time, but one that encounters this time as already unnatural and halfway on its way to somewhere else, stuck between zones, dead time, slow time, time that is frenzied and time at tempo, languid and compromised. Judgement not only takes place in these disjunctions; it can mediate their association. If demonstrations of playing dead ask, 'where else is there to go?', their wager is also that there is a here-and-now to be experienced in this temporal density, without the promise of standard values. This shares something with what Ruth Wilson Gilmore calls 'a dream of justice' among a group of abolition activists on a bus leaving a Methodist church parking lot, whose riders decided 'through struggle, debate, failure, and renewal', that they must 'seek general freedom for all from a system in which punishment has become as industrialised as making cars, clothes, or missiles, or growing cotton' (2007, p. 2). This activism displaces a consortium of citizen-jurors into collectives of poet-judges who are 'acting out, in the details of modest practices, the belief that "we *shall* overcome"' (p. 2), sharing more than just common interests.

The epidemiological plot

What I am calling the epidemiological plot unfolds in the time of progressive historicism, the default position of national timekeeping. In this time, history is made by passing through successive stages of development, each stage overcoming the inadequacies of the last. This model of history corresponds closely to Ernst Haeckel's theory of biological recapitulation: that during the course of development, an organism must pass through its ancestral forms before reaching a more developed stage of being. Building on Charles Darwin's theory of variation by chance (tychism), and Jean-Baptiste Lamarck's theory of progressive evolution (agapasticism), Haeckel looked at odd details of human embryos – gills and tails – to identify evolutionary lineages that extend between human and nonhuman species.

Knowing what we have been also requires knowing what we are. Stephen Jay Gould writes: 'recapitulation also provided an irresistible criterion for any scientist who wanted to rank human groups as higher and lower'; it 'served as a general theory of biological determinism' whereby 'all "inferior" groups – races, sexes, and classes – were compared with the children of white males' (1981/1996, p. 144). Used to insist on the evolutionary supremacy of white people, recapitulation reproduces an adjacent colonial fear: miscegenation, the mixing of racial types. Bulwarking this fear is a biological argument about the contamination of bloodline. Maintaining racial purity requires developing immunity against infectious, deviant and degenerative bodies. The epidemiological plot relies on a standardisation of authentic and normative 'good' (the uncontaminated, the non-diseased, the healthy) through a set of narrative techniques that inveigle a literate bourgeois and empirically minded public into consensus around its terms of entry.

As well as registering *fin-de-siècle* anxieties over imperial degeneration and the evolutionary effects of miscegenation, the emergence of the epidemiological plot can also be understood as part of a broader rivalry between the realist novel and the development of sociology in the eighteenth and nineteenth centuries. Wolf Lepenies historicises this conflict as a 'competition over the claim to be the rule of life appropriate to industrial society' (1988, p. 13). Sociography competed with literary realism 'over claims to offer adequate reproduction of the "prose of everyday circumstances"' (p. 13). On the other side of this were the natural sciences, whose methods the social sciences imitated, eradicating feelings and 'abandon[ing] inspiration in favour of science' (p. 13). A growing suspicion of literary stylisation corresponded to the ambitions of literature and men of letters to compete with the realism of sociological enquiry, and to the ambitions of sociology to match the natural sciences' hostility to stylisation in favour of 'simple facts'. What resulted from this competition were hybrid forms – literary sociography, scientific fiction and quantitative methods in the social sciences – while the more descriptive natural histories of Georges Buffon and Lamarck fell out of favour.

A recent example of this collusion between progressive historicism and the epidemiological plot has been the UK's development of a COVID-19 vaccine. The quest to develop the vaccine required collaboration across a number of different research centres within the UK, and the international sharing of data in open access databases. This has required new and speculative forms of collaboration 'outside existing structures', in microbiologist Sharon Peacock's words (2021), as well as an increased workload for a workforce of scientists and technicians unprepared to serve at the forefront of a global pandemic. The peculiar dissonance of describing Britain's response to the pandemic as a success story has been tempered only by a few references to the importance of gathering diverse data sets in future. This, while the disproportionate black and brown death rates fall from public memory, and the distribution of the vaccine rehearses imperial trade routes. Des Fitzgerald has figured this phenomenon as 'viral nationalism', when 'a moment of biological and political crisis effloresce[s] into a distinctive form of border-fever' (2021, p. 5). The vaccine quest attached itself to wartime metaphors of sacrifice and resilience, and reinscribed a national body politic as the prime beneficiary of any future vaccine. Propping up this national narrative were the closing of public spaces and furloughing of service workers; the mass rollout of the vaccine within the UK was accompanied by the spectacle of pubs reopening and stadiums filled to capacity. The vaccine promised a universal and science-driven consensus around investing in a cure through genomic investigation, and part of this consensus has been guided by the managed desire to repopulate these deserted public spaces.

Imagining the UK's crisis management as a success story means privileging vaccine development as the principal mode of virus management, and national health as the primary site of mitigation, upholding forms of assessment that make vaccine nationalism both possible and common sense (Eaton, 2021). A 'cultural politics of heredity' continues to determine the development and distribution of biomedicine and health globally, and a symptom of 'the intertwinement of . . . biology and law within a new era of ethno-nationalist state projects' (Fitzgerald et al., 2020, p. 1161). In this ethnonational contemporaneity, processes of racialisation are part of the production of progress as synonymous with historical time. The vaccine story has unfolded through various strands of plot gathered together to create a sense of transformation. Science steps in to save the species as well as to save the sense that the species should be saved; the reason the species should be saved is because it is capable of producing a vaccine to protect itself against destruction.

This circuitous psychodrama has a precedent in late nineteenth-century mappings of cancer that imagined modernity as a contaminant, and which posited cancer as a 'disease of civilisation' and 'pathology of progress', as Agnes Arnold-Forster (2020) has argued. While there were attempts 'to explain why "civilised" races might be more prone to cancer than their "barbarous" counterparts', Arnold-Forster argues that cancer was characterised as a problem of lifestyle and 'the civilised *way of living*' (p. 181). This conflation of a declining national body with new epidemiological maps of colonised territories registered the shifting relationship between empire and public health towards the close of the century, as well as modernism's nascent concern with western civilisation as both contagiously degenerative and in need of a cure.

This is by no means out-of-step with a recapitulation model of progress if it is understood that the post-Westphalian right to sovereignty is secured by a nation-state's imagined ability to manage its own degeneracy. Liberal and communitarian futurisms share an interest in positing an analogous, if not ontological, relation between historical and evolutionary forms of transformation. History moves through stages of socio-political organisation, and historicism is the labour of capturing the recapitulation of past forms as part of a process of progressive social evolution. Darwin's theory of natural selection as the survival of biological traits corresponded, for Marx, to class struggle as the selection of socio-economic forms of organisation. For Sean Sayers, this means that neither Marx nor Darwin repudiate teleology, but render it 'in naturalistic terms that are consonant with modern natural science' (2019, p. 59). Sayers makes the case for Marx as a thinker of historical emergence, where unities of commons exist first as possibilities, and then develop into reality as 'different groups come into contact with one another [and] more concrete and developed forms of relation begin to grow and to acquire an increasingly determinate form' (p. 52). Historical development is blind (causal), but it is also moving towards a future of increasing collective autonomy, and has to be in some sense purposeful.

Gregory Moore goes one step further in his reading of Nietzsche's 'ironic distortion' of biologism, suggesting that in the nineteenth century, evolution could not replace Judeo-Christian teleology *tout court*: scientists' 'faith in progress was an essential means of reassuring themselves that whatever the short-term suffering, there was a meaningful goal to be achieved, that evolution was a process leading inexorably towards moral and intellectual improvement' (2002, p. 9). The contingency of variation is a more insecure starting position than combining natural selection with biological purpose. The latter offers a place for progressive history to go, and it means that some form of natural law is assured as embedded in the process of biological progress.

Assuming the embeddedness of natural law in theories of historical and biological progress means that the process of progressive historicism can justify the management or administration of emergency uses of force. Justice, in this limited sense, is a mechanism for the negotiation/selection of legal constraints. But what exactly happens in these spaces of negotiation, or as Arto Laitinen puts it, these 'intermediate phases' between different historical stages (2017, p. 245)? To rehearse the oscillation between Walter Benjamin and Jacques Derrida: can justice be found between law-positing and law-preserving violence (Benjamin, 2004), or resolve the relation between the singular and the universal by 'appealing to force from its first moment' (Derrida, 1992, p. 10)? In organisations of ordinary time that privilege progressive historicism, consensus is prefigured. In the following section, I explore the prefiguration of consensus in a reading of *Dracula*. The text seeks to cultivate its reader as a sociological worker, required to do the work of assessing plot and investing in the narrative momentum to manage the text's syndrome: vampirism.

Dracula's prefiguration of consensus

Dracula was published in the decade when, in Saree Makdisi's words, 'the realist novel enters its modernist crisis', and Stoker effects his own 'modernist breakdown' of nineteenth-century literary realism (1998, p. 9). Expected from the outset to participate in the novel's demanding labour of assessing evidence, the reader of *Dracula* might be too distracted – exhausted, even – by the volume of documentation, the changes in perspective, the jumps in time, and the gaps in the plot to question the allegiance they have been asked to share with the consortium. The novel's awkward resolution lies somewhere between contamination and vaccination, and it is unclear whether or not a cure has been found, or to what end. The vampire moves beyond his metaphorical function as embodiment of national syndrome to deliver his own judgement, loitering menacingly in the bloodlines of his human antagonists, and exceeding their combined expertise. In their efforts to annihilate the vampire, the consortium invents a medical syndrome that keeps the borders between vampire and human porous and indeterminate. *Dracula* is not just an allegory for a late nineteenth-century fixation on national degeneration as a result of colonial misadventure; it also challenges the reproduction of the nation as a public that should (or can) be kept healthy.

What is the epidemiological plot, aside from a plot which foregrounds the management of some mass syndrome? First, the epidemiological plot does not figure progress as transformation, but as cure. It is generated out of the stabilisation of binaries (illness and good health, contaminant and remedy, alienation and integration), and privileges an equilibrium model of social change. Second, the epidemiological plot relies on a consortium to evaluate, measure and ensure this equilibrium. Third, the epidemiological plot cultivates its reader as a sociological worker, training this reader-worker to believe in both the necessity and the possibility of a cure, and to participate in the labour of assessing the threat. Stoker's novel registers a transformation of narrative-making at a particularly fragile juncture of British imperialism at the end of the nineteenth century, where practices of policing, state-funded mapping and medical intervention fortified national borders and cultivated consensus around national security.

Vampirism, like COVID-19, is infection, illness and physical type, crossing social metaphor, physiological symptom and raciology. The novel's plot follows an international consortium deciphering and eventually defeating a life-obliterating force, the eponymous vampire, a premodern Transylvanian monster with an unspecified but nonetheless lethal and enduring grudge against Anglophone modernity (Arata, 1990). The narrative is motivated by its characters' fears of miscegenation, contamination and national decline, adjacent anxieties which the genre permits the narrative to register as one and the same problem: the vampire. Horror's dramatic axis is composed of the shadow worlds that emerge alongside familiar and often domesticated ones, that may or may not be relied upon to protect their inhabitants. In *Dracula*, this protection relies on a model of community that asserts the domestic veto power of the nation and its parochial processes of decision-making with regard to who does and does not count as part of its extensions of temporary or permanent citizenship. The group that works to piece together information about the vampire is composed of a solicitor and his wife – Jonathan and Mina Harker – a psychiatrist, John Seward, an aristocrat, Arthur Holmwood, a rich American businessman, Quincey Morris, and a Dutch polymath, Abraham Van Helsing. This consortium model initially centres England as a vulnerable and breached space in need of protection, where America and Holland, rising and fallen empires respectively, step in to help on the mission. This consortium is reliant on imperial collaboration and foreign expertise, the latter in the form of labour that can be incorporated and made useful to securing national borders. As the plot goes on, the consortium participates in criminal activities to track down the vampire, most notably breaking into his house; these uses of emergency powers outside the law are justified in the quest to eradicate the threat.

Recapitulation influenced theories of criminal pathology. *Dracula*'s epidemiological plot pitches an eighteenth-century Romantic, aristocratic solo genius against a nineteenth-century bourgeois research consortium (the Count is an excellent letter writer, while Van Helsing records himself on his phonograph). Gould notices that the amateur vampire hunters Jonathan and Mina Harker describe Count Dracula, indirectly and directly, as '"of criminal type"', his features corresponding to Cesare Lombroso's description of criminal phrenology, for whom criminals are 'evolutionary throwbacks in our midst' (Gould, 1981/1996, p. 153): aquiline nose, big and bushy eyebrows, and pale and pointed ears, an aberration on the border of a species that has already left him behind. The Harkers' mutual consensus on Count Dracula's atavism – stemming in part from his racialisation as Eastern European – is legible to their colleagues because it is positioned in a broader historical-evolutionary shift from a less advanced stage of human development to a more advanced one.

The consortium rehabilitates national values by distributing a parochial form of justice, managing disparate and muddled observations through a pooling together of medical theories, past and present. As Martin Willis notes, these include a combination of folklore, contagionism, miasmatism, sanitary science and germ theory. In 1890s Britain, Willis argues, the intertwinement of miasmatism and germ theory in particular 'achieved an ongoing connection of disease to immorality that had always between present in sanitary science' (2007, p. 314). This intertwinement of theories for the sake of finding a treatment enables the consortium both to secure the boundaries of national belonging and to define the parameters of moral conduct. This anticipates vampirism becoming a term 'for sexual predation, or the calculating, carefully targeted exploitation of sex appeal', as David Trotter notes (2020, p. 42). The effort to correct this viral exploitation is played out most dramatically through the group killing of the contaminated, promiscuous Lucy Westenra, the consortium's primary test subject.

The novel's form is an extended performance of sociological consensus. The narrative is composed of correspondence between members of the group, their journal entries, phonograph transcriptions, relevant newspaper cuttings and invoices, compiled by an anonymous editor. This editor admits their power of curation over the organisation of the narrative immediately, while resigning any interpretative or descriptive intervention. As Godfrey Frank Singer notes in his study of the epistolary novel, this was also Samuel Richardson's technique in *Pamela* (1740), where the author 'pretends to be but the arranger of existing material that has fallen into his hands' (1933, p. 170). Stoker demonstrates his own act of literary recapitulation, resurrecting the realism of the epistolary novel in an irreal form, as if to say that this denial of editorial investment is not to be trusted, if only by dint of this generic mutation from realism to realist horror.

Before Jonathan Harker's first journal entry, 'leaving the West and entering the East' (Stoker, 1897/2003, p. 7), a short, untitled paratext sits across from the first chapter:

> How these papers have been placed in sequence will be made manifest in the reading of them. All needless matters have been eliminated, so that a history almost at variance with the possibilities of later-day belief may stand forth as simple fact. There is throughout no statement of past things wherein memory may err, for all the records chosen are exactly contemporary, given from the standpoints and within the range of knowledge of those who made them. (D, 6)

This disclaimer creates another character: the reader as sociological worker, recruited as an extension of this research consortium. The note levels an immediate expectation of trust between reader and editor, where the work of the reader is to assess these records, rather than to interpret them. 'Made manifest' implies a latent direction of events, as if this sequence were both self-explanatory and inevitable. The circumlocution of the first sentence is thrown into relief by the admission that there is information external to this narrative that has been disregarded, and which has not made it into the selection that composes what follows. This editing, the 'eliminat[ion]' of 'needless matters', is justified in the name of history. This organisation of documentation into a particular sequence, it is to be assumed, has been necessary to give the text credibility. 'Later-day belief' here reads as a euphemism for scientism, the 'simple fact' that comes after superstition. The note ends by repeating its assumption of readerly trust.

Dracula's opening paratext – the declaration of an editor's disinterested organisation and the curious handing over of the power of assessment to the reader – is a closed circuit: the arrangement of these papers will make sense because the reader will make them make sense. The paratext cannot guarantee that it will be read; left to its own devices, there is the danger that it will become stuck in time, an unanswered call, dependent on an external source for authentication. That said, its trustworthiness is guaranteed by the economy of its style. This constructs the narrative as a bibliographic resource, dividing the labour of progressive historicism between the curation of the editor, the accounts of the characters, and the reader's labour of assessment. The paratext requires the reader only to weigh up the evidence to be presented (to assess), rather than to intervene in its construction as fact (to interpret), positioned as part of the jury, not as judge.

Stoker's use of the epistolary parodies realism's preoccupation with cultivating a reader complicit in establishing fiction as 'simple fact', one who will conform to the text's idiosyncratic rendering of narrative time as historical time. The various contradictions and loose ends of the documents gathered together indicate the fragility of scientific method in the ongoing trialling of hypotheses about the vampire, and in managing the threat he poses. The mutation of realism to horror forces the management of contagion into the realm of improbable and unverified folklore. In lieu of scientific rigour, the subject of the text moves from the vampire to the process of mitigating vampirism. Vampirism, in turn, does not function as a simple metaphor for national borders, but is produced as a scientific object of investigation through the shared desire of the characters for a conclusion based on established fact. What is privileged is not the supposed subject of investigation, but the development of a research group invested in the cause of progress: they are doing what they are doing and working together because it will help history move forward. The consortium configures modes of conduct formed by progressive historicism: the determination of a historical subject, knowledge exchange, gathering a consensus of accounts, and compiling these accounts into a complete text. What Singer describes as *Dracula*'s 'sense of completeness' is an orchestrated ruse that establishes a consensus around conduct by the various negotiations made between its characters as well as the contract that the reader is explicitly required to enter into when beginning the text: to take responsibility for understanding why the sequence of documentation appears as it does, an executive lure held out in lieu of a cure.

The epidemiological plot prefigures progress as the ongoing, ameliorative process of rehabilitating the emergent subject of progressive historicism out of past forms of social organisation: the professional bourgeoisie. *Dracula*'s sense of historical process is organised around the elimination of 'needless matters' and the formation of consensus around this elimination. This consensus emerges through the need to account for why certain actions are taken to mitigate particular forms of harm, for the sake of reaching a new stage in history. The epidemiological plot relies on a selective mechanism as the basis of national progress: history as the eradication of unwanted or dysgenic material. Stoker uses the novel's composition as its own technology of selection, a site for the preservation of traits, the rehabilitation of 'good' cultural forms, and the elimination of bad ones. It becomes a technology of standardisation. Vampirism is produced as an epidemiological deviation from a standard value of good health, and this deviation is what makes its story of national health both possible and imaginable. *Dracula*'s unsettlement of sociological realism shows the orchestration of these interests and their anticipated attachments, tied to a vision of progress organised around rehabilitating the national body politic through the invention of a new modern subject: the sociological worker in a consortium.

The Lonely Letters and ecstatic congregation

In the consensus to act as detectives of everyday life, and to share the labour of emergency governance, *Dracula*'s civil society exists in a state of paranoia. I have argued that the epidemiological plot registers dependency on the cure as the just end to an unjust present while permitting emergency forms of crisis management, and cultivates the reader as a sociological worker in the labour of assessing, rather than interpreting, evidence. I return now to some of the questions that populate this article: what sense of the possible can political community organise around after progress? If to hope for a cure is to fall for the promise of justice not only within existing structures of law, but also national figurations of historical time, then when can a cure take place, and in what form? In Michael Denning's recent and emphatic reading of Antonio Gramsci's interest in the orchestra, a multiplicity is 'united through the friction of individuals' through the 'horrible cacophony' of establishing consensus (2021, p. 43). This means learning the technicality of instrument (how I play) alongside how to negotiate with others (how we play). It imagines conduct as the working-out of social permission through the everyday dissonance of getting it wrong. It moves from a consensus of shared code to a consensus of shared arrangement, and retrieves the social power of adjudication from the agreement that national legislation should constitute the commons.

Ashon Crawley gets to this in *The Lonely Letters*, asking if it is possible to share ecstatic moments without committing to the possessiveness of identity, and whether this might engender forms of cure without an end, 'like intimacies that happen even if they are disclaimed and renounced', as he writes elsewhere (2020b). This, after he has loosed himself from religious commitment, a lapsed member of the Pentecostal church, documenting his ongoing connection with spiritual aesthetics through memory and rehearsal. *The Lonely Letters* falls somewhere between theory, memoir and letter, a quasi-fictional epistolary sequence punctuated by the sound effects of routine breaks and bar ends. These are arranged in a secular generation of ecstatic congregation, a form of solidarity repeated throughout the letters in temporary acts of judgement, where solidarity is a wager on shared relevance, 'an event of the coming to matter of things', situated and, in the broadest sense, local (Savransky, 2016, p. 25).

Like *Dracula*, Crawley's text begins with a note to the reader that declares an informal memorandum of understanding. It starts in the autobiographical mundane – sitting in a corner desk in Emory University's Woodruff Library, taking up a reading suggestion from an unnamed friend. Through the echo of the scene – a scholar, a library, a desk, a table, a friend – a tendril of intimacy reaches out that at once encloses and expands the possibility of relating to the text: the bracketing of the year into academic timekeeping ('the summer of 2006, or maybe the early fall semester') and the unlikeliness of the reader sharing this privileged site of scholarship ('I was in a master's program') are met by an act of drawing in. That is, it does not deny the specificity of composition nor attempt to generalise for the sake of cultivating a reader, but moves through it on the off chance that something might resonate.

The practice of drawing out and being drawn in that follows from this preface starts with a suspended connection: someone seeing 'something familiar in me that he'd not ever named' (LL, 16), and the other's hesitation to act on it. Initially, this missed opportunity is coded through queer desire. The letters begin with this moment of hesitation and go on to explore other forms of unnamed recognition that forge temporary community, and this community emerges through acts of holding off or raising up, a reflex or rejection that facilitates a form of participation drawn out across the space of paragraphs or several letters, and an exchange that creates its own environment of reciprocation. The letters are a one-sided conversation that states 'the desire for friendship as a way of life' as its opening gambit (LL, 11). They are dispatched at irregular intervals ('It's been some time'), and punctuated by self-conscious asides ('but I'm rambling'): the acknowledgement of missing and being missed, while the space of the letter becomes a place to practise thinking across temporalities of diversion and distraction.

The letters move between the apophatic and the hyperbolic: from saying the saying of nothing, to saying something so emphatically that its meaning has to shift and split. Instead of asking the reader to assemble these modulations into coherence, the author's insistent address to the absent, code-named interlocutor draws the reader into the middle of a conversation for which they only have half the information they need to make sense of it. The difference between the lack of information here and *Dracula*'s paratextual admission of elimination is that this absence offers a space in the text where the reader can arrange an imaginary response. They are offered the power to play – to skip past and circle back, to move around and out of the text – rather than forced to make sense of its compilation:

Dear Moth,

I hear you, I do. I understand that you think I'm not necessarily being fair to mystics but that's not the case at all. (LL, 24)

Dear Moth,

What I'm saying is we breathe, and in the fact of our breathing, we experience – not optimism per se but – the plural event of possibility as beyond exhaustion. We keep going. (27)

Dear Moth,

You said it was beautiful, that you believed me, but didn't say much else. (137)

Dear Moth,

Yes, sorry for forgetting to respond to that part of your message but yes, I really dug what Wynter said about Aretha too. (161)

Dear Moth,

What I thought I needed to say was this: (168)

The letters begin with the acknowledgement of what has come before, and they stay with it. This staying with, or keeping on, allows the writer to demonstrate their understanding of the absent letters that sit between the gaps between theirs, clarifying something that was said, questioning why something more has not been said, apologising for forgetting to respond properly. They indicate sometimes writing at speed, prepositions and pronouns left out, or slowing down to make space for not hearing back. These changing speeds generate a sense of a presence on the other side who wants to be heard and read, and to hear and read.

This shared desire is disturbed by the possibility of not being able to demonstrate and reciprocate through the medium of letter writing, because there is always a chance that someone will lose concentration or put off replying because something else comes up, or that details will be lost or misplaced during the process of composition. This mode of address demonstrates the effort of working out a way of relating, generating enough material to elicit a response, acknowledging the strategy, pulling back and holding off, then going towards again. The form of the letter permits the circularity of relation to be registered as a modulation rather than repetition, a tone moving between registers, alteration that does not anticipate transformation on either side. *The Lonely Letters* keeps going without seeking a way into the routes of progressive historicism. To return to Denning and Gramsci, it circumvents the fanaticism of a technical relationship between conductor and orchestra by refusing that this relation should determine its horizon of justice.

This is judgement without the promise of progress, in forms motivated by asynchronous movement. Crawley's account of Blackpentecostalism is that it is 'an aesthetic practice that was sent and is about being sent' (2016, p. 5). There is an analogy here between the body and writing – I was *here* and now I am *there* and still *here*. The congregation emerges through this modulation, out of considering the simultaneous defamiliarisation and coming-towards that emerges out of letter-writing, which means that 'I'm writing to you but also, mostly and most fundamentally, writing to me':

> We begin songs in one key, kinda like how we dance and shout, trying to withhold energy until the vamp, the drive. And then finally, we let them have it, we exert all that we have within us. Modulation occurs in some songs, making audible migration and movement and motion, modulation as that sonorous refusal of stillness and being stilled (though of course, being stilled is merely another 'movement'). And the audience sits until they can't sit anymore, the modulations moving them so much, so the audience stands and is moved and amazed and surprised and enraptured by the heights achieved that were not initially imagined. (LL, 165)

This scene does not go anywhere. It is the 'changing, moving – the transitioning – from one tonal center to another' (LL, 165). This transitioning is facilitated by the practice of judging where best to move, but not requiring this 'being affected' to deliver justice. The movement between these tonal centres creates a particular rhythm with history, where past forms are modulated rather than exceeded, outdone or surpassed. The subject is dispersed into the 'sonic zones' of the practice space, 'every voice a bit of a fugitive, on its run away from regulative function and form' (LL, 166).

Is this cure or cult? Does this reader miss the comparative *knowingness* of sociological labour and the security of a team, faced instead with the uneasiness, even embarrassment, of the space in the text left empty for a preacher to fill? Or, to follow Clive Nwonka, when reduced to a banal kind of relatability, does a possible relation with this empty space risk leaving a space open for 'the neoliberal aestheticisation of black death' (2020, p. 13)? I want to stay with the possibility of modulation as a cure without plot, returning to the figure of judgement with which this article began. Writing on Amiri Baraka, Dhanveer Singh Brar rejects Simone White's appellation of him as a 'poet-legislator' in the latter's *Dear Angel of Death* (2018). He writes, 'I would prefer to think about him as an adjudicator, issuing fiery wild judgements under constant revision' (2021a, p. 6). This distinction is important, because 'judgements can always be contested':

> The congregation can always question the judgement, or actually the congregation isn't necessary for the judgement to function. There's a counter-play, there's a folding back and forth. In a sense, you can think about the preacher not as leading a flock, but the preacher as an emanation of the collective desire of the flock. (Brar, 2021b).

In *The Lonely Letters*, Crawley creates a space for an absent judge-preacher, removing the requirement to be cultivated into the desire of a particular plot. The relation is reversed. These practice spaces are their own kind of cure, allowing the temporary relief of symptoms, and produce an image of a world outside the syndrome. Where *Dracula*'s plot leads the reader through historical tunnel vision to produce a world in which living without the threat of vampirism is no longer thinkable, *The Lonely Letters* does not resolve itself by conceding to this progressive narrowing towards justice. This matters because becoming attached to the plot of justice, to the possibility of curing contagion in some projected future while implementing emergency measures to manage it in the present, means being routed back to the national as a space of recapitulation. This means that any possibility of general justice is already compromised. Crawley's ecstatic congregation is entangled in the time of judgement in spaces of half-empty correspondence, arranging ordinary time so that new forms of social permission can be experienced collectively, after the constraints of progressive historicism.

Conclusion

I started this article with international demonstrations of playing dead, which declare that overlapping contemporary crises exceed the boundaries of national management. Their reverberations have challenged forms of emergency governance that seek to recapitulate state interests. I have argued that the epidemiological plot is a way of narrating the national as a body politic in need of rehabilitation. This plot enables the continued emergence of historical-evolutionary subjects who might best undertake this labour of rehabilitation. In the epidemiological plot of COVID-19 where neoimperial nations emerge triumphant in the race to produce a vaccine, the problem is not the production of the vaccine, but that vaccination manages the crisis. *Dracula*'s exhaustion of its compliant reader through the proliferation of data offers an analogy for a normative and mainstream socio-scientific literacy that serves, increasingly, as a condition for full participation in public life. Against this, I considered Crawley's invitation to arrange cures without plots, where the time of justice is suspended for the time of judgement, in a move from legislation to adjudication. This troubles the horizon of a normative cure for a social reality so deeply entangled in the infrastructure of colonial-capitalism. It displaces a sense of shared life 'after' the syndrome, configuring community in the here-and-now.

Acknowledgements

Presenting drafts of this article at the National Syndromes symposium at the Wellcome Centre for Cultures and Environments of Health, at the UCL Institute of Advanced Study's seminar series, and in conversation with Dhanveer Singh Brar has helped to expand and refine its parameters.

Funding

This work was supported by the Wellcome Trust (Grant number: 203109/Z/16/Z).

References

Arata, S. (1990). The occidental tourist: *Dracula* and the anxiety of reverse colonisation. *Victorian Studies*, *33*(4), 621–645.

Arnold-Forster, A. (2020). 'A rebellion of the cells': Cancer, modernity, and decline in *fin-de-siècle* Britain. In M. Dickson, E. Taylor-Brown, & S. Shuttleworth (Eds.), *Progress and pathology: Medicine and culture in the nineteenth century* (pp. 173–193). Manchester University Press.

Benjamin, W. (2004). Critique of violence (E. Jephcott, Trans.). In M. Bullock & M. W. Jennings (Eds.), *Selected writings volume 1, 1913–1926*. Harvard University Press.

Brar, D. S. (2021a). Knowing manufacture of an RnB feeling. *Darkmatter Hub (Beta)*. https://darkmatter-hub.pubpub.org/pub/3x25j469

Brar, D. S. (2021b). *Knowing manufacture of an RnB feeling: A conversation with Dhanveer Singh Brar*. Seminar as part of the Exeter Decolonising Network's 'Racism and Social Justice' series.

Crawley, A. (2016). *Blackpentecostal breath: The aesthetics of possibility*. Fordham University Press.

Crawley, A. (2020a). *The lonely letters*. Duke University Press.

Crawley, A. (2020b). Lifting voices in the key of Blackqueer YES. *LA Review of Books*. https://lareviewofbooks.org/article/lifting-voices-in-the-key-of-blackqueer-yes/

Denning, M. (2021). Everyone a legislator *New Left Review*, *129*, 29–44.

Derrida, J. (1992). Force of law: The metaphysical foundation of authority. In D. Cornell, M. Rosenfeld, & D. Carlson (Eds.), *Deconstruction and the possibility of Justice* (pp. 3–67). Routledge.

Eaton, L. (2021). Covid-19: WHO warns against 'vaccine nationalism' or face further virus mutations. *BMJ*, *372*, 292.

Fitzgerald, D. (2021). Normal island: COVID-19, border control, and viral nationalism in UK public health discourse. *Sociological Research Online.* https://doi.org/10.1177/13607804211049464

Fitzgerald, D., Hinterberger, A., Narayan, J., & Williams, R. (2020). Brexit as heredity redux: Imperialism, biomedicine, and the NHS in Britain. *The Sociological Review, 68*(6), 1161–1178.

Freeman, E. (2019). *Beside you in time: Sense methods and queer sociability in the American nineteenth century.* Duke University Press.

Gilmore, R. W. (2007). *Golden gulag: Prisons, surplus, crisis, and opposition in globalizing California.* University of California Press.

Gould, S. J. (1996). *The mismeasure of man.* Norton (Original work published 1981).

Laitinen, A. (2017). Dewey's progressive historicism and the problem of determinate oughts. *The Journal of Speculative Philosophy, 31*(2), 245–259.

Lepenies, W. (1988). *Between literature and science: The rise of sociology.* Cambridge University Press.

Makdisi, S. (1998). *Romantic imperialism: Universal empire and the culture of modernity.* Cambridge University Press.

Moore, G. (2002). *Nietzsche, biology and metaphor.* Cambridge University Press.

Nwonka, C. J. (2020). The black neoliberal aesthetic. *European Journal of Cultural Studies.* Advance online publication. https://doi.org/10.1177/1367549420973204

Peacock, S. (2021, June 29). *Genomics and the COVID-19 response: Lessons learned and improving preparedness to respond to future health threats* [Public Talk]. Westminster Health Forum: Next steps for the use of genomics in healthcare.

Polidori, J. (2008). *The vampyre and other tales of the macabre.* Oxford University Press (Original work published 1819).

Richardson, S. (2008). *Pamela; Or virtue rewarded.* Oxford University Press (Original work published 1740).

Savransky, M. (2016). *The adventure of relevance: An ethics of social inquiry.* Palgrave.

Sayers, S. (2019). Marx and teleology. *Science & Society, 83*(1), 37–63.

Singer, G. F. (1933). *The epistolary novel: Its origin, development, decline, and residuary influence.* University of Pennsylvania Press.

Stoker, B. (2003). *Dracula.* Penguin (Original work published 1897).

Trotter, D. (2020). Come-hither looks: The Hollywood vamp and the function of cinema. *Critical Quarterly, 62*(2), 37–53.

White, S. (2018). *Dear Angel of Death.* Ugly Duckling Presse.

Willis, M. (2007). 'The invisible giant,' *Dracula,* and disease. *Studies in the Novel, 39*(3), 301–325.

Author biography

Lara Choksey is lecturer in Colonial and Postcolonial Literatures in the Department of English at University College London, and specialises in meetings of literature, science and technology, and political philosophy. She is the author of *Narrative in the Age of the Genome* (Bloomsbury, 2021), and has had articles and chapters published in *Medical Humanities, Journal of Historical Geography, Journal of Literature and Science, Sanglap: A Journal of Literary and Cultural Inquiry, The Palgrave Handbook of Twentieth and Twenty-First Century Literature and Science,* and *Ethical Futures and Global Science Fiction* (Palgrave, 2020).

Article

MONOGRAPH SERIES

Waiting for Tindaya: Modern ruins and indigenous futures in Fuerteventura

The Sociological Review Monographs
2022, Vol. 70(2) 82–98
© The Author(s) 2022
Article reuse guidelines:
sagepub.com/journals-permissions
DOI: 10.1177/00380261221084431
journals.sagepub.com/home/sor

Isaac Marrero-Guillamón

Department of Anthropology, University of Barcelona, Spain

Abstract

Since the mid-1990s, the mountain of Tindaya (Fuerteventura, Canary Islands, Spain) has been in limbo. Despite being listed as a Natural and Cultural Asset by virtue of its environmental singularity and indigenous engravings, the conservation plans have never been implemented. Instead, the state institutions designated it as the location for artist Eduardo Chillida's *Monument to Tolerance* (a huge, bare cubic cave to be dug in its interior) – a controversial project that remains suspended, neither in construction nor abandoned. To complicate matters, the mountain also features three quarries, and speculation over the mining rights associated with them resulted in a long series of trials and appeals. Tindaya is therefore a site of truncated futures, fragments of which are still to be found in and around the mountain. This article works with these material traces as a way of activating the mountain's role in a plurality of strategies of anticipation, from the economic and cultural superabundance ascribed to Chillida's project by the state to the indigenous rituals and offerings that took place in the mountain. It is argued that Tindaya stands today as an unintended monument to the ruins of a modernity envisaged in the language of economic development and artistic abstraction, but also represents the possibility of enacting other, minoritarian futures, connected to the poorly understood indigenous lifeworlds attached to the mountain and its surroundings. The critique of the former is accompanied by the cultivation of the latter through an exercise in speculative ethnography.

Keywords

Eduardo Chillida, fiction, indigenous heritage, progress, speculative methods

Introduction

The village of Tindaya (Fuerteventura, Canary Islands; population: 510) is home to an extraordinary concatenation of truncated futures. Upon entering the village, one finds the

Corresponding author:
Isaac Marrero-Guillamón, Department of Anthropology, University of Barcelona, C/ Montalegre, 6–8, Barcelona, 08001, Spain.
Email: imarrero@ub.edu

Casa Alta Museum, sited in a restored manor house and dedicated to artist Eduardo Chillida's grand project for the mountain of Tindaya: a huge cubic cave to be hollowed from within, connected to the outside by two vertical shafts and an entry tunnel. Models, drawings and 3-D simulations visualise the *Monument to Tolerance*, described in the texts that punctuate the exhibition as the pinnacle of Chillida's work *and* a turning point for the island's development. Omitted is the fact that the Monument dates back to the mid-1990s and has neither been built nor abandoned – it remains suspended, entangled in a complex controversy surrounding the right to intervene in a mountain that is also a protected natural environment, a listed archaeological site and a mining resource.

A few hundred metres away from the Museum is Bar María, an establishment frequented by older locals and occasional tourists. Among the items decorating the walls there are five posters made by environmental activists in response to Chillida's project. Slightly faded after more than two decades, they introduce Tindaya's natural and cultural 'value' to the general public. A key focus of the posters is the mountain's exceptional archaeological remains – most notably the hundreds of foot-shaped engravings that marked Tindaya as a ritual centre and sacred site for the indigenous population of the island, the Mahos. The posters argue that, while it is officially protected, Tindaya's pre-Spanish heritage remains understudied and under threat, both by Chillida's proposed Monument and by the mountain's several quarries. A case is made that a sustainable future for Fuerteventura hinges on Tindaya's 'proper' conservation, including the recognition of its indigenous significance and the immediate ceasing of all mining activity.

Continuing northbound on the same road, with the mountain itself now dominating the view, one finds a menhir-shaped slab of Tindaya hidden behind outgrown palm trees on an unassuming traffic island. On closer inspection, the object reveals itself as the municipality's homage to Eduardo Chillida. The plaque at the bottom, dated 2003, thanks the artist for his 'grandiose contribution to art and culture, and for the international exposure it has given to the village thanks to his Monument'. This somewhat premature celebration is complemented by Chillida's undaunted statement, chiselled on the stone: 'I do not know about races or colours, I only know that the horizon is the homeland of all men.'

This strange sequence of mediated encounters with Tindaya culminates at the end of the same road. Here, the walls of an abandoned football pitch frame the view of the mountain, its straight lines echoing the scars left by the now empty quarries. Standing on the harsh gravel pitch, I would think of the young men who played football on it, their scabbed knees and footprints now replaced by tyre tracks and traces of 360° spins. I could not help but picture the scene in my head: the quad bikes and their riders enveloped in dust, exhaust fumes and engine noise – an image of nihilist abandon that seemed the perfect counterpoint to the grand futures once imagined for Tindaya (see Image sequence 1).

The traces of Tindaya's various 'former futures' (Koselleck, 2004) – projected in relation to mining, modernist art, or heritage preservation – constitute the point of departure for this article. I activate these material remains in order to empirically engage with the politics of progress; to understand how ideas of linear time, endless growth and inexorable advancement have shaped the relationship between people, indigeneity and land. I argue that Tindaya stands today as an unintended monument to the ruins of a modernity envisaged in the language of monumental art and development, and at the same time represents the possibility of cultivating an alternative futurity that reactivates the

Image sequence 1. Encounters with Tindaya.

lifeworlds once attached to the mountain and its surroundings – an indigenous future *after and against progress*.

The mountain of Tindaya has played an important role in the prosperous futures envisaged by the state in Fuerteventura, first through mining, then tourism and art. These visions of progress relied on unimpeded access to land-as-resource as much as they did on the effacement of indigenous history. The inevitability of future progress was shaped, sustained and legitimised by a range of technologies of anticipation such as forecasting, modelling or predicting. The critique of this orientation towards time and land is by now well-established (Scott, 1998). I will also briefly engage in it below, but my ultimate goal is rather to experiment with the possibility of imagining an alternative scenario, one that excavates the truncated histories of the Mahos in order to put indigenous afterlives at the centre of the island's future. 'If we are to think beyond the self-devouring growth drive', Julie Livingston writes, 'then we must open those repositories of the imagination – the before, the against, and the besides – that have been or are now being crushed by it' (2019, p. 9). Hence, the article moves from a critical analysis of the already existing to the cultivation of the what-if; from the indicative to the subjunctive. I engage in a specu-lative exercise that seeks to nurture more tentative and inventive forms of thinking with indigenous heritage. In so doing, I join several others who have reclaimed speculation as a useful sensibility for the social sciences, as we engage in the urgent task of imagining futures otherwise (Benjamin, 2016; Haraway, 2013; Rao et al., 2014; Wilkie et al., 2017). Following a practice well-established in fine art, design and architecture (Dunne & Raby, 2013), I argue that speculative methods can help shift the discussion around indigenous heritage in the Canary Islands by asking unlikely questions, envisaging improbable futures, and encouraging unforeseen desires.

Drawing from fieldwork conducted in 2016–17,[1] this article mobilises ethnographic insight to creatively engage with a plausible alter-future for Tindaya, one existing after, and in tension with, the dominant progress-oriented imagination. I call the result 'ethno-speculation', a practice whose purpose is the *empirically-grounded cultivation of the otherwise*. If ethnography may be described as the study of social relations through social relations, the kind of speculative ethnography I am interested in fostering here involves the additional gesture of creatively reconfiguring said relations. The point of doing so is to enlist ethnographic insight in the task of fostering new possibles and disturbing the so-called inevitable (see Collins, 2018). As Juan Francisco Salazar has argued, specula-tion and ethnography can be considered complementary practices, capable of enriching one another in a 'future-facing cultural inquiry that enables research to follow forked directions, to both respond and anticipate phenomena that may not simply be held, observed and acted upon' (2017, p. 154). Like Salazar, I am interested in developing inventive modes of ethnographic practice that engage with 'possibility and potentiality, not just actuality'.

As I expand on below, any discussion of indigenous matters in the Canary Islands is confronted with the fact that the arrival of European colonisers in the fifteenth century resulted in the annihilation of the indigenous population. The resulting discontinuity between the past, the present and the future of indigeneity in the archipelago constitutes a formidable challenge – but also the very condition of possibility for envisaging new and alternative scenarios, crafted from a sense of care and responsibility towards these destroyed lifeworlds. In Tindaya, the Mahos constitute an absent presence mediated by archaeologists and activists, tangible only in the form of traces, remains and hauntings.

Accordingly, I have directed my ethno-speculative efforts towards reimagining their place in the island's heritage policy. As a practice that curates and animates an inherited history, that attempts to negotiate its spectres, heritage provided an obvious stage to craft alternative articulations between the past and the future of indigeneity.

A prosperous future, suspended

The Canary Islands is a volcanic archipelago located off the West coast of Africa. It has been a Spanish territory ever since it was colonised by the Crown of Castile during the fifteenth century. At that point in time, all seven islands were inhabited by groups of Amazigh descent, collectively referred to as Guanches, that had settled in the Canaries probably around the beginning of the Common Era. Indigenous lifeworlds did not survive the multiple forms of colonial violence that ensued: their social, economic and religious practices were forbidden in the name of Christianity and civilisation, and those who resisted – as well as many who did not – were killed or enslaved (Adhikari, 2017). In the case of Fuerteventura, the indigenous population, the Mahos, saw their semi-nomadic way of life organised around common land and freely roaming livestock replaced by the imposition of crop agriculture, private property and forced labour.

Soon after the conquest, the archipelago became an ideal periphery for colonial experiments, starting with slavery and the plantation economy (Fernández-Armesto, 1982). Over time, other forms of extractivism such as cash crops, free trades areas or more recently mass tourism were implemented. Fuerteventura – the driest and windiest of the islands – played a singular role in this process. Much less fertile than the rest of the Canaries and subject to the permanent threat of fatal droughts, it was favoured as a military outpost. It was not until the 1960s, still under Franco's dictatorship, that the island started its transformation into a tourist destination with the construction of the first hotels, the airport and the water desalination plant. Fuerteventura's entry into the mass tourism circuit meant the inauguration of a brand-new official future for the island: a new age of progress, prosperity and modernity. It is hard to overestimate the impact this vision was to have: in 1980, the first year for which there are data, approximately 62,000 foreign tourist arrivals were registered, in an island with 30,000 inhabitants. Ten years later, there were approximately 320,000 foreign tourist arrivals and 49,000 inhabitants. By 2000, these figures had increased to 1.3 million and 63,000, respectively. In 2008, the year of the economic crash, tourist arrivals neared 1.5 million and the population passed 100,000.[2] These numbers provide only a glimpse of the speed and intensity of the transformation; they were accompanied by an equally frantic development of the island's real estate and infrastructures. To be sure, Fuerteventura's metamorphosis echoed a process taking place in Spain at large. Tourism and property development became the country's economic pillars once it joined the European Economic Community in 1986 (López & Rodríguez, 2011). An era of developmental paroxysm followed, fuelled by foreign investment and punctuated by global events such as the Barcelona Olympics, Seville's Universal Exhibition or the inauguration of the Guggenheim-Bilbao.

It was in this context that, in 1996, the island and regional governments decided to adopt Eduardo Chillida's *Monument to Tolerance* as a flagship project. An encounter with the sensibility of that era is made possible at the Casa Alta Museum mentioned in the introduction. Within the museum, the arrival of the Monument is imminent and its realisation as inevitable as the benefits it will bring to the island. The text panels, the audio clips, the artist statements are all delivered exactly as they were in the 1990s – their prophecy only betrayed by subtle signs such as the anachronistic texture of the digitalised videotapes. Chillida's cubic void is presented as Fuerteventura's ticket to developing a more 'prestigious' and 'sustainable' form of tourism. Indeed, the exhibition makes the argument that the project 'sets the standard' for how to intervene in a protected site. According to the official narrative, the Monument does not interfere with the indigenous engravings, since the former is located in the interior of the mountain and the latter on its surface. Furthermore, the monumental scale and transcendental aspirations of Chillida's project would add a contemporary spin to Tindaya's ancient sacredness.

In my conversations with those responsible for commissioning Chillida's Monument it quickly became apparent that the aspiration to partake in this new wave of development was a key component of their elation with the project. If everyone else was doing it, why couldn't they? If Lanzarote (the closest of the Canary Islands) had been able to successfully turn artist César Manrique's interventions in the landscape into a tourist package, why wouldn't they succeed with Chillida's Monument? Even if the model of culture-as-resource was somewhat dated, a high official told me, it could still work; in any case, it was a matter of 'sovereignty', of exercising his generation's right to 'mark the territory' just like the Mahos had done back in the day. The construction of this grand Monument by an artist of such reputation was Fuerteventura's chance to shift gears and become a top destination for land art. Why not profit from the land – he added – one of the few resources they did have? I needed to understand that the Monument was an *investment*, not an expenditure; that it would bring with it progress and a cascade of opportunities.

The state officials' persistent optimism regarding Chillida's Monument sits oddly with its actual fate. Soon after it was declared a 'project of general interest for the region' in 1996 – a designation that carried with it access to large amounts of public funds – the Monument got entangled in a series of legal disputes. Faced with two companies that held mining rights in Tindaya, the regional government made a deal: it bought off one of them and made the other a partner in the project, thereby linking their mining rights to the construction of the Monument. This resulted in the incorporation of PMMT, a public-private company owned in equal parts by Cabo Verde Inc. and the Canary Islands Government. Paradoxically, it was precisely this instrument, designed to expedite the Monument's construction, that became largely responsible for its indefinite suspension and the closure of the quarries. The valuation and trading of the mining rights, the partnership agreement and the contract underpinning the construction of the Monument were all taken to court by activists, prompting a series of trials and appeals that have stalled the project to this date (see Marrero-Guillamón, 2021). The evidence released in the trials shows how the grand futures for Fuerteventura attached to Chillida's Monument were entangled with rather pedestrian practices of speculation with and trading of the mining rights. So much so, that the financialisation of future prosperity resulted in the truncation of its very foundation, the construction of the Monument.

Standing on the ruins of progress

While the plans for the Monument crumbled, the relentless pursuit of progress through development continued elsewhere on the island: new hotels and apartment complexes mushroomed along the coastline, new roads inaugurated, large areas rezoned and earmarked for development. The island was booming, but would soon bust. The 2008 financial crash quickly revealed the shaky foundations of the model: the real estate market collapsed, construction work came to a halt, tourism declined, thousands of workers lost their jobs. The scars of two decades' intense development followed by a sudden interruption were present everywhere on the island at the time I conducted fieldwork (2016–17). The crisis may have been officially over by then, but whatever direction I drove in, whichever locality I visited, I would encounter abandoned buildings, unfinished structures, or faded billboards selling homes that never were (see Image sequence 2).

This may be one of the reasons why I was drawn to the abandoned football pitch in Tindaya, why I thought its rusty net-less goals, lightless floodlights and derelict changing rooms offered a privileged standpoint on the mountain. Ruins confront us with the 'lingering remains of the past in the present' (Carse & Kneas, 2019, p. 20), as well as past conceptions of the future, or 'futures past' (Koselleck, 2004). As Walter Benjamin (2002) famously argued, modern ruins are negative forms capable of disrupting the 'dream world' of modernity and revealing its destructive force. Tindaya's football pitch was certainly a reminder of the shortcomings of the state's vision of progress; but more importantly, these humble ruins evoked the many others that punctuated the island's landscape. Standing on it I felt as if the suspension of Chillida's Monument resonated with a larger condition affecting the island, one of interruption and waiting. This was a perception amplified by the way in which politicians I spoke to talked about their expectation of a future improvement in conditions, after which their plans could resume (presumably in very similar, if not identical terms as before). Despite the proliferation of ruins, the lure of progress, understood quantitatively as the development of infrastructures, the creation of jobs and so on, remained as powerful as ever – even in the face of ecological meltdown.

As an abstraction that has become policy, modern progress relies as much on *promise* as it does on *erasure*; progress is 'always more than just a category: it is an operation of exclusion that has always already taken place' (Alonso, 1998, p. 20). Its linear temporality involves not only an endless progression of domination over space, but also necessitates the effacement of other temporalities, of other forms of attachment to time (and space). It constitutes 'a single diachronic line in which non-European peoples, modes of coexistence, forms of knowledge, and even parts of the Earth were regarded, like the myths and stories by which they lived, as inhabiting Europe's past' (Savransky, 2021, p. 273). This is certainly the case when it comes to indigenous heritage and lifeworlds in the Canary Islands, systematically reduced to anecdotal evidence of an era not only past but surpassed; that is, proof of the self-fulfilling prophecy of progress. In my conversations with politicians and civil servants during fieldwork, a sort of fear of regression, of 'becoming savages again', seemed to be a trigger response to any critique of progress.[3] What was I suggesting, going back to living in caves and off the goats? Did I even know the hardness of life on the island before the arrival of modern infrastructures? People had

Image sequence 2. Progress in ruins.

starved, or else had to migrate in dire circumstances. It was all very well for academics such as myself to entertain primitivist fantasies, but they had been elected by the people to deliver more opportunities, not fewer.

But perhaps the question is less one of regression than of derailment. That is, of extricating our political imagination of the future from the narrow confines of progress, development, growth, etc. The analogy of a derailment seems appropriate to me, as it points at both the existence of a seemingly inexorable path and the violence associated with deviating from it. Such is the risk involved in parting ways with progress. Such is the risk associated to formulating another future for Tindaya, imagined from the ruins of futures past and with the traces of indigenous lifeworlds still available to us.

Indigenous futures

As Tindaya's monumental futures were being imagined, inflated and traded, the activist posters that decorate Bar María are a humble inscription of some of the ways in which a much less visible task, that of making sense of the indigenous lifeworlds attached to the mountain, was also underway. The posters were part of a public campaign aimed at disseminating archaeological research and gathering support for the abandonment of Chillida's project and the 'full protection' of the mountain. In effect, the state's unveiling of Chillida's project had acted as a catalyst for a sustained series of events, talks, guided visits, direct actions, publications and legal actions aimed at 'saving' Tindaya. Led by a very small group of committed activists grouped under the umbrella of the Tindaya Mountain Coordinating Committee (*Coordinadora Montaña Tindaya*), this was a task of great difficulty, on account of how little the general public knew or cared about Tindaya. Colonial violence did not only efface the indigenous population of the archipelago; it also translated into centuries of institutional disregard for indigenous heritage which displaced the latter to the margins of public life (Farrujia, 2013). Archaeologists and activists have often remarked that this may be because indigenous heritage raises uncomfortable questions for the image of the islands that has been successfully marketed; it brings to the fore their connection with the Amazigh cultures of Northern Africa, the history of Spanish colonialism, as well as the undisturbed continuity of the elites and the extractive economies they have favoured.

The activists' goal of 'Saving Tindaya', therefore, went beyond protecting a mountain – it meant challenging established notions of modern progress and cultivating the idea that the traces of indigenous lifeworlds may indeed constitute a form of valuable heritage. The regional state's cultural heritage policy has systematically favoured post-conquest practices and forms: generous funding, for instance, has been allocated to the restoration of colonial architecture, including military and religious buildings and the homes of the elite. In other words, large amounts of public funds have been used to preserve, and celebrate, the (often private) patrimony of those directly responsible for colonial power and violence. Moreover, these structures have been projected onto the future as valuable tourist attractions.

The story of Tindaya's engravings is telling in its contrast. They were (re)discovered in 1979; until then, Tindaya was just another mountain where goats roamed, where cereal was grown, where partridges were hunted. Although local folk knew about the 'marks' at the top of the mountain, they did not make much of them. It took a young amateur archaeologist, Pedro Carreño, to notify the authorities about the existence of hundreds of foot-shaped petroglyphs to kickstart institutional and professional interest in Tindaya.

Following preliminary studies that confirmed the importance of the findings, the mountain was listed as a Historic Monument and therefore legally 'protected'. But the Department of Culture did not commission the further studies required for the delimitation and conservation of the site until much later.[4] In fact, it took 40 years since the re-discovery of the engravings for an official excavation to be funded or permitted, and for any signalling to appear on the mountain.

The current interpretation of the engravings, and of the pre-colonial practices associated to Tindaya more generally, highlights the mountain's centrality for indigenous life and cosmovision. Archaeologist María Antonia Perera describes it as the religious epicentre of the Mahos, evidenced by the sheer concentration of foot-shaped carvings, unseen anywhere else on the island, the remains of meeting places around the mountain, as well as the latter's distinct and commanding presence in the surrounding landscape. Indeed, this type of engravings was also used by Amazigh populations in Northern Africa to sacralise certain spaces and is interpreted as a collective expression linked to ritualistic practices. In the case of Tindaya, Perera et al. (1996) have argued that the fact that 80% of the engravings point towards the West, more specifically to the Winter Solstice's sunset, which takes place right before the rain season starts, may be an indication of a shamanic rain ritual. Maho society was largely dependent on these seasonal rains for survival, and their proto-religious practices are well-documented in the historical archive.

What if this patchy, tentative knowledge about the Mahos was redeployed as a line of flight for the imagination of a future for Tindaya after progress? What would taking care of Tindaya's heritage look like, if the latter were understood as the task of looking after untold histories and cultivating (im)possible futures? I believe speculative methods can be a useful tool in this regard. As Carin Kuoni (2014, p. 11) writes, speculation is a methodology that facilitates the 'awareness that things could be different', that fosters the imaginary as a 'realm of the simultaneous presence of multiple temporalities or conditions' – that offers, in short, a framework for harvesting a politics of the otherwise. The purpose of so doing would not be to suggest how things *should* be, but rather how they *could* be, and what this fictional future scenario may reveal about our present horizons – 'to unsettle the present rather than predict the future' (Clark, cited in Dunne & Raby, 2013, p. 99). My aim in the remainder of the article is to mobilise ethnographic and archaeological insight to disrupt what passes as 'normal', 'possible' or 'commonsensical' in Tindaya. To craft an alternative scenario – an ethno-speculation – which may provide a platform for reimagining a politics of heritage after (and against) progress.

During fieldwork, I was often told that Tindaya was 'special'. I met someone who had, on several occasions, spent the night laying on it, looking at the stars and letting his body feel the rock underneath. A young man told me he climbed to the top every January 1st, as a personal cleansing ritual marking the start of a new cycle. A hunter described experiencing the most beautiful sunsets from the mountaintop, sitting on the rocks where his ancestors had once sat. A tour guide nonchalantly confirmed Tindaya's sacredness, as attested by her and her clients' feelings when visiting it. I was also told the story of the camel that once appeared inexplicably at the top of the mountain, surely the work of witches. Or that of the fireballs that used to come down the mountain slope, possibly sparks produced by rockfalls.

My own relationship with Tindaya tangibly shifted once I was able to see the engravings myself. It was a clear full moon night. In the dark, the mountain's hard rock became a sturdy, slightly slippery surface. But when the archaeologist leading us told us to gather around her and turned on her flashlight pointing at the floor, the harsh shadows revealed an astonishing series of foot-shaped engravings. She took us to several spots, each revealing an ever more impressive collection of shapes. Guided by her, we experienced what I can only describe as the aura of these inscriptions – the strong sensation that their rudimentary form carried with it the vibrations of something much more powerful and yet elusive (see Image sequence 3).

Finding ways of hosting and encouraging the bundle of affect linked to Tindaya I encountered during fieldwork, including my own, became an important concern in the process of developing the ethno-speculative experiment below. In this regard, I found inspiration and encouragement in a recent body of work devoted to 'indigenous futures' (Lempert, 2018; Raheja, 2017). The aforementioned challenge of thinking with indigeneity in the Canaries, in the absence of an indigenous people, made this strand of speculative, decolonial work particularly relevant. I shared with it an interest in creatively nurturing indigenous futurity, thereby dismantling the dominant association between indigenous lifeworlds and the past – and its corollary, the fantasy of their disappearance (Dillon, 2012). Cultivating indigenous futures, for these authors, involves the refusal of settler frameworks that fossilise indigeneity (Simpson, 2017) as well as the pursuit of narratives of 'survivance' as opposed to mere survival (Vizenor, 2008). As Turtle Mountain Chippewa scholar Danika Medak-Saltzman puts it:

> Indigenous futurisms, like Afrofuturisms and other similar movements, provide authors, readers, filmmakers, audiences, and our communities with opportunities to explore beyond what is and what has been and moves us toward imagining, creating, and manifesting a variety of possibilities that better represent our understandings of, our place in, and our responsibilities to this world and to those yet to come. (2017, p. 143)

The annihilation of Fuerteventura's Mahos cannot be mitigated, but placing their traces at the centre of the reimagination of the future may help to interrupt their mummification as mere indexes of the past. I see experimenting with ethno-speculative scenarios as one way – among many others needed – to foster indigenous futurities in a context in which the latter are radically absent from public life. What follows in the next section is a short ethnography of the future, of another future – one which reshuffles and rearranges the elements I have analysed so far. To be clear, I do not intend to resuscitate the Mahos, but rather to conjure unprescribed afterlives for their traces; to imagine the possibility of a world in which their ghosts have a place (see Tsing et al., 2017).

Waiting for Tindaya: An ethno-speculation

Few could imagine that the enactment of the Local Sovereignty Act would have such profound impact in Tindaya. It was widely known that the Act was tailored to the interests of big landowners and developers, who relentlessly lobbied for 'unleashing the full potential' of local government after the Big Crash. In addition to complete autonomy in

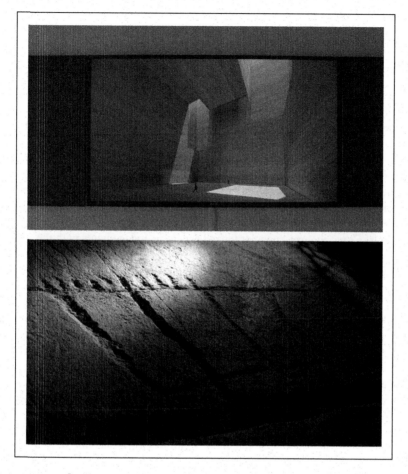

Image sequence 3. Monumental pasts/Indigenous futures.

most realms other than defence, this meant using 'developmental cost-effectiveness' analysis to 'optimise' municipal boundaries. Fuerteventura, for instance, was divided into two local authorities as a result of the Act: the Coast, whose territory was deemed highly profitable, and the Interior, whose area was 100% classified as 'cost-ineffective'. The Coast went on to become a sort of vanguard for the tourist industry: attracted by zero tax policies, developers flocked in, offering every imaginable experience, catering to every market segment. It was a lucrative if highly unequal model – apart from endemically unstable and ecologically damaging.

The Interior, in contrast, was faced with economic collapse at first. Population decreased, investors and creditors stayed away, infrastructures decayed. Only then things started to change. A wave of grassroots 'repossession', 'rewiring' and 'repurposing' actions paved the way for the eventual success of the Slow Party, an eclectic offshoot of the environmental movement. The party's motto, 'living and dying otherwise', translated into ambitious experiments in food and energy harvesting, economic degrowth, school curricula and heritage policy. Somewhat paradoxically, many of these initiatives were ultimately funded by the Coast's huge energy needs, which had created a profitable market for the Interior's surplus.

In Tindaya, the Interior's Department for Sovereign Futures found the ideal site to nurture a growing interest in indigenous heritage, particularly among schoolchildren. The result of decades of collaboration with archaeologists, schools and residents are apparent from the moment one sets foot in the village. 'Welcome to Maho land', says the sign at the entrance. Behind it, surrounded by solar panels, stands the Tibiabín & Tamonante Lab. Sited in what used to be the Casa Alta Museum and named after the Maho priestesses, the Lab was conceived as a public resource and a working space. It makes available a huge archive of material related to indigenous lifeworlds, from colonial records to contemporary archaeo-astronomic and DNA analysis. Rather than favouring a particular interpretation, however, the Lab rather encourages their proliferation. The space is almost always busy with researchers and children working and playing with the materials. Contradictory, speculative and eccentric engagements with the Mahos are pursued without apparent hierarchy, and often replaced by new ones. One installation, for instance, turned the colonial archive inside out, as it were, through a series of decentring interventions: documents were tactically redacted and/or annotated, the narrative of discovery retold from an imagined indigenous witness, and the colonial language of progress and civilisation unmade from the point of view of the crops forced onto inhospitable soil. The Lab's work with schoolchildren has resulted in some of its most compelling speculative excursions, including wild accounts of the lives and aspirations of young Mahos and their goats, affirmatively post-humanist in tone and scope.

The Lab's youthful energy is also tangible in the village's social centre, Bar María. Here, locally harvested food is prepared in the cooking school, meetings of all kinds take place in the Free Association rooms, and children roam free in the Reclaim Play/Ground that occupies the backyard. In the main space, a small exhibition entitled Waiting for Tindaya inconspicuously hangs on the walls. It offers a loose account of the controversy that surrounded the mountain at the turn of the century, when it was almost emptied out in the name of a 'Monument to Tolerance'. Interviews with the protagonists and a selection of documents provide candid insight into how ideas of 'progress' and 'development' were used to efface indigenous heritage and restrict the possibility of alternative futures. To avoid the risk of forgetting this episode, the village council decided that rather than destroying the materials associated to the *Monument to Tolerance* it was best to let them decay naturally. And so the Old Football Pitch – locally known as the Cemetery – was repurposed as a decommissioned art park of sorts. The old municipality's homage to Eduardo Chillida; the models, drawings, films and simulations used to promote the Monument; samples of the 1,650 metres of rock that were extracted during the test drillings; and even an old helicopter that was used during the latter can all be found there, in various stages of ruination.

Although tourism is not encouraged in the Interior, the area does attract a small but steady number of visitors. Tindaya in particular has become relatively well-known and respected in heritage circles. Following a thorough archaeological campaign, several indigenous structures were excavated at the base of the mountain: the remains of meeting and dwelling spaces were restored, and supplemented by a number of interactive materials addressing the Mahos's cultural, social, economic and religious life. Similarly to the Lab, the purpose of these digital materials is not to provide a fossil-like window into the past, but rather to facilitate learning from indigenous lifeworlds. Hence, rain rituals, common-land rules, cheese making or polygamy are explored as 'infrastructures for living', partially connected to contemporary concerns.

As for the mountain itself, the heritage plan established that the best way to care for and protect its dormant sacredness was to designate it a restricted site. It can only be accessed a few days every year (on the Winter Solstice and in relation to other solar and lunar events), at night, in small guided groups and for a minimum of five hours. The visit is entirely analogue, and all forms of image capture are forbidden too. Somewhat contentious at first, deemed excessive by some, these measures turned out to be rather uncontroversial in the end. The astonished eyes of those who return from the mountaintop, their haunted tales, the new forms of veneration that have sprouted since – they all seem to have done the work of silencing critics.

Walking around Tindaya, one is left with the impression that people there have allowed themselves to be affected by the traces of the Mahos, that they have learned to live in the company of spectres.

Coda

Arguably, the suspension of the state's grand plans for Tindaya has resulted in an impasse with unique analytic and political affordances. The inevitability and linearity of 'progress' has cracked. Ruins have flourished. Indigenous heritage has emerged as a matter of public concern. By moving from critique onto speculation, I have aimed to inhabit this interstice and contribute to envisaging an alternative future for Tindaya – to cultivate other possibles using and rearranging insight gained through ethnography.

It was not difficult, during fieldwork, to entertain the idea of the Monument never being built. Less easy was to picture a more affirmative scenario in which the distinction between 'indigenous pasts' and 'modern futures' was reshuffled, or rather upended – in fact, as I crafted the scenario above, I could only imagine it following an undetermined catastrophic event ('the Big Crash') and existing in tension with a reverse utopia (the Interior/Coast antagonism). To a large extent, my ethno-speculation was constructed as a game of inversions between the buried and the excavated, the preserved and the ruined, the valued and the disposable. Quite literally, I attempted to project indigeneity into the future – as a condition of the land, and a collective resource for the cultivation of the otherwise – and conversely to treat today's modern progress as a relic of the past.

There is no doubt that the result is a fraught, perhaps even dangerous exercise. Does it make sense to reclaim indigeneity in a context where an indigenous people no longer exists as such? Doesn't the speculative method risk speaking for (absent) others? What are the politics of composing such heritage utopia in an academic text, as opposed to in the public domain? These are good questions; they point at tensions that were central to the writing of this article – and for which I only have partial answers. I would argue that the absence of the Mahos/Guanches as a living people, together with the indisputable presence of their traces, create the conditions – and constitute the very challenge – for inventive approaches to indigenous heritage. I therefore think of the vignette above as an opening, as an invitation to the task of collectively envisaging and creating new horizons of possibility for Tindaya. As Vyjayanthi Venuturupalli Rao puts it (2014, p. 24): 'The speculative moment – in which a new world is envisioned and striven for – is therefore the moment in which radical change is possible, but only through the enactment of a "space of reception," as yet unborn.' Sharing and discussing drafts of this article – including at the *After Progress* seminar series – provided a tentative beginning for such conversation. My interlocutors' concerns regarding the purpose of imagining a 'heritage utopia' or the politics of situating myself in a God-like position; their doubts about the public reach of such exercise; but also the associations it triggered and the pedagogical potential they saw in it were all hugely enriching and became part of each re-draft. The usefulness of the exercise, as I see it, may reside precisely in discussing its limitations or shortcomings – for identifying these is another way of composing the otherwise.

My hope remains that staging an alternative future after and against 'progress', and offering it up for discussion, may generate what Chris Moffat calls an 'untimely interference', that is, 'a sense of responsibility to that which is not present, whose corporeal existence has been extinguished' (2019, p. 2). Encouraging the proliferation of afterlives for the Guanches/Mahos may be one way to disturb the homogeneous time of modernity and think instead of 'endings that are not over' (Gordon, cited in Moffat, 2019, p. 6). In other words, taking care and responsibility for these ghosts can contribute to interrupting the linearity of progress and pluralising/complicating the relationship between indigenous pasts, present and futures (Rifkin, 2017). I am certainly aware that extricating Tindaya from the futures currently envisaged by the state is a colossal task that cannot be possibly resolved by speculative exercises. And yet, I would argue that the latter constitute a helpful complement to critique when it comes to disrupting the 'problem-space of the normal, the probable and the plausible' and cultivating 'the eruption of what, from the standpoint of the impasse of the present seems, in all likelihood, to be impossible' (Savransky et al., 2017, p. 7).

Ash Watson (2021) has recently reflected on the increasing interest in using fiction and creative writing in sociology. Compared to traditional scholarship, 'sociological fiction' can provide a more engaging interface with the public, a more welcoming platform for collaboration with research participants, and a richer engagement with sensory and embodied forms of knowledge. I certainly agree, and welcome the ways in which using fictional forms contributes to expanding what we understand by empirical qualitative research. My argument for ethno-speculation adds an explicit interest in the disruptive affordances of speculative fiction, i.e. its capacity to challenge narratives of inevitability and experiment with different possibilities. As Ruha Benjamin (2016) argues, it is a matter of studying the world empirically and reflecting on it speculatively, so that we may expand our visions of what is possible and encourage situated alternatives – daring to imagine an otherwise is arguably part of the task of bringing it about.

Funding

The research underpinning this article was funded by a Leverhulme/British Academy Small Research Grant (SG152145). It is associated to the research group TURICOM (PGC2018-093422-B-I00).

Notes

1. As of December 2021, the plans for the protection and dissemination of the mountain's environment and indigenous heritage remain a work in progress and Chillida's Monument – while no longer a priority for the island's current coalition government – still remains 'in the books'.
2. All figures calculated from the Regional Government's publicly available data (Instituto Canario de Estadística [ISTAC], 2019).
3. This paragraph (and the article more generally) draws generously from discussions that took place during the *After Progress: Modernity in Ruins* seminar series organised by Martin Savransky and Craig Lundy in 2019. I thank the conveners, speakers and attendees for creating such a stimulating environment.
4. Their inaction stands in contrast to the proactivity of the Ministry of Industry and Energy, which during that period granted the mining concessions that underpinned the quarries.

References

Adhikari, M. (2017). Europe's first settler colonial incursion into Africa: The genocide of Aboriginal Canary islanders. *African Historical Review*, *49*(1), 1–26. https://doi.org/10.1080/17532523.2017.1336863

Alonso, C. J. (1998). *The burden of modernity: The rhetoric of cultural discourse in Spanish America*. Oxford University Press.

Benjamin, R. (2016). Racial fictions, biological facts: Expanding the sociological imagination through speculative methods. *Catalyst: Feminism, Theory, Technoscience*, *2*(2), 1–28. https://doi.org/10.28968/cftt.v2i2.28798

Benjamin, W. (2002). *The arcades project*. Harvard University Press.

Carse, A., & Kneas, D. (2019). Unbuilt and unfinished: The temporalities of infrastructure. *Environment and Society*, *10*(1), 9–28. https://doi.org/10.3167/ares.2019.100102

Collins, S. G. (2018). Anthropology's latent futures. *Theorizing the Contemporary, Fieldsights*. https://culanth.org/fieldsights/anthropologys-latent-futures

Dillon, G. (Ed.). (2012). *Walking the clouds: An anthology of indigenous science fiction*. University of Arizona Press.

Dunne, A., & Raby, F. (2013). *Speculative everything: Design, fiction, and social dreaming*. The MIT Press.

Farrujia, J. (2013). *An archaeology of the margins: Colonialism, Amazighity and heritage management in the Canary Islands*. Springer.

Fernández-Armesto, F. (1982). *The Canary Islands after the conquest: The making of a colonial society in the early sixteenth century*. Clarendon Press.

Haraway, D. J. (2013, November). SF: Science fiction, speculative fabulation, string figures, so far. *Ada: A Journal of Gender, New Media & Technology*, 3. https://adanewmedia.org/2013/11/issue3-haraway/

Instituto Canario de Estadística. (2018). *Anuario estadístico de Canarias* [Annual statistics for Canary Islands]. www.gobiernodecanarias.org/istac/temas_estadisticos/sintesis/operacion_C00052A.html

Koselleck, R. (2004). *Futures past: On the semantics of historical time*. Columbia University Press.

Kuoni, C. (2014). Foreword. In V. V. Rao, P. Krishnamurthy, & C. Kuoni (Eds.), *Speculation, now* (pp. 10–13.). Duke University Press Books.

Lempert, W. (2018). Indigenous media futures: An introduction. *Cultural Anthropology*, *33*(2), 173–179. https://doi.org/10.14506/ca33.2.01

Livingston, J. (2019). *Self-devouring growth: A planetary parable as told from Southern Africa*. Duke University Press.

López, I., & Rodríguez, E. (2011). The Spanish model. *New Left Review*, *69*, 5–29.

Marrero-Guillamón, I. (2021). More than a mountain: The contentious multiplicity of Tindaya (Fuerteventura, Canary Islands). *Journal of the Royal Anthropological Institute*, *27*(3), 496–517. https://doi.org/10.1111/1467-9655.13547

Medak-Saltzman, D. (2017). Coming to you from the indigenous future: Native women, speculative film shorts, and the art of the possible. *Studies in American Indian Literatures*, *29*(1), 139–171. https://doi.org/10.5250/studamerindilite.29.1.0139

Moffat, C. (2019). *India's revolutionary inheritance: Politics and the promise of Bhagat Singh*. Cambridge University Press.

Perera, M. A., Belmonte, J. A., Esteban, C. E., & Tejera, A. (1996). Tindaya: Un estudio arqueoastronómico de la sociedad prehispánica de Fuerteventura [Tindaya: An archaeo-astronomical study of the prehispanic society of Fuerteventura]. *Tabona: Revista de prehistoria y de arqueología*, *9*, 165–196.

Raheja, M. (2017). Imagining indigenous digital futures: An afterword. *Studies in American Indian Literatures*, *29*(1), 172–175. https://doi.org/10.5250/studamerindilite.29.1.0172

Rao, V. V. (2014). Speculation, now. In V. V. Rao, P. Krishnamurthy, & C. Kuoni (Eds.), *Speculation, now* (pp. 14–25). Duke University Press Books.

Rao, V. V., Krishnamurthy, P., & Kuoni, C. (Eds.). (2014). *Speculation, now*. Duke University Press Books.

Rifkin, M. (2017). *Beyond settler time: Temporal sovereignty and indigenous self-determination*. Duke University Press.

Salazar, J. F. (2017). Speculative fabulation: Researching worlds to come in Antarctica. In J. F. Salazar, S. Pink, A. Irving, & J. Sjoberg (Eds.), *Anthropologies and futures: Researching emerging and uncertain worlds* (pp. 151–170). Bloomsbury Academic.

Savransky, M. (2021). After progress: Notes for an ecology of perhaps. *Epherema: Theory & Politics in Organization*, *21*(1), 267–281.

Savransky, M., Wilkie, A., & Rosengarten, M. (2017). Introduction: Speculative implications. In A. Wilkie, M. Savransky, & M. Rosengarten (Eds.), *Speculative research: The lure of possible futures* (pp. 1–18). Routledge.

Scott, J. C. (1998). *Seeing like a state: How certain schemes to improve the human condition have failed*. Yale University Press.

Simpson, L. B. (2017). *As we have always done: Indigenous freedom through radical resistance* (3rd ed.). University of Minnesota Press.

Tsing, A., Swanson, H.A., Gan, E., & Bubandt, N. (Eds.). (2017). *Arts of living on a damaged planet*. University of Minnesota Press.

Vizenor, G. (Ed.). (2008). *Survivance: Narratives of native presence*. University of Nebraska Press.

Watson, A. (2021). Writing sociological fiction. *Qualitative Research*. Advance online publication. https://doi.org/10.1177/1468794120985677

Wilkie, A., Savransky, M., & Rosengarten, M. (Eds.). (2017). *Speculative research: The lure of possible futures*. Routledge.

Author biography

Isaac Marrero-Guillamón is a Serra Hunter Lecturer in Anthropology at the University of Barcelona. Prior to that, he was Senior Lecturer in Anthropology at Goldsmiths, University of London, where he convened the MA in Visual Anthropology. His work explores the politics and aesthetics of development, grassroots activism and heritage in the context of spatial conflicts. He has conducted ethnographic research in Spain and the United Kingdom.

MONOGRAPH SERIES

Tilting relationalities: Exploring the world through possible futures of agriculture

The Sociological Review Monographs
2022, Vol. 70(2) 99–115
© The Author(s) 2022
Article reuse guidelines:
sagepub.com/journals-permissions
DOI: 10.1177/00380261221084778
journals.sagepub.com/home/sor

Henrietta L. Moore and Juan M. Moreno
Institute for Global Prosperity, UK

Abstract

Demography has driven increases in agricultural productivity and is in the limelight once again with questions about how we intend to feed 9 billion people on the planet. The scale of this challenge and the ecological threat from collapsing resources has generated a sense of impending crisis, but remarkably little action. The frames of reference tend towards climate change and the Anthropocene, but perhaps a more fruitful approach is to reflect on developments in agriculture and agroecology to examine the scale and significance of the ecological challenges we face. In this article, we use agriculture as a nodal point through which to engage with the emerging and dislocating human–planetary relations of the contemporary world, reflecting on past, current and future notions of 'progress', and on how ongoing developments and experiments in making a living with others (human, non-human and more-than-human others) might offer potential pathways for positive social transformation and future flourishing. As we argue throughout the article, reassessing notions of progress does not mean the mere return to traditional forms of knowledge and practice, nor embracing a form of luddite politics absent of advances in modern science and technology. Instead, we propose this is about opening spaces where diversity, pluralism and contending perspectives and agencies are engaged on their own terms, creating and sharing alternative knowledge and ways of doing and being. Here, the role for the social sciences and humanities is not to describe or pretend to represent these emerging relationalities, but instead to enable and actively engage them. Doing this responsibly and effectively will require us to inhabit the disorienting and discomforting ruins of progress, eschewing the turn towards finalised solutions and outcomes.

Keywords

agriculture, agroecology, Anthropocene, more-than-human, other, progress, relationality

Introduction

The world is literally tilting, pulled off its true axis by glacial melt pouring into the oceans (Deng et al., 2021). Day by day, we are bombarded by impending Anthropocene

Corresponding author:
Henrietta L. Moore, Institute for Global Prosperity, Maple House, 149 Tottenham Court Rd, London W1T 7NF, UK.
Email: igpdirector@ucl.ac.uk

crises with their narratives of despair and insurmountable challenges: extractivist industries and intensive agriculture, the climate emergency, mass migration, displacement and conflict arising from inequalities and poverty, all compounded by rising global population, socio-economic transformation, changes in dietary patterns, the depletion of water and land resources, and soil degradation. In this article, we use agriculture as a nodal point through which to engage with the emerging human–planetary relations of the contemporary world, reflecting on past, current and future notions of 'progress', and on how ongoing developments and experiments in making a living with others (human, non-human and more-than-human others) might offer potential pathways for positive social transformation and future flourishing.

We explore these questions through three main parts. In the opening section, we first take pause and account for the breath, intensity and plurality of forms of enabling and constraining interactions, conditions, knowledges and ways of doing and being that plough the planet, its crises and opportunities. We like to refer to these as 'tilting relationalities'; imagined, actualised and remembered, both comforting and troubling, encounters with ourselves and the many others that inhabit and share, willingly or not, Planet Earth. We cannot pretend to understand all these relationalities, and this article is by no means an attempt to overview and synthesise them. Yet, it is only by acknowledging and embracing these welcome and unwelcome relations as we stumble upon them that we will then be able to envisage, acquiesce and action true, honest, transformational change. In the second section, we critically examine some developments in agriculture and agroecology, as a lens through which to reformulate notions of progress. We argue that progress, within the context of agriculture and beyond, must be understood and approached as a relational process based on an ethics of care across human/non-human, local/planetary divides, one that could and should reconfigure the broader context of value chains and investment that structure our food systems. Finally, in the third section, we discuss our insights considering current and future human–planetary challenges and interventions, such as developments in agroecology and other knowledge and technological systems, as well as the role of the social sciences and humanities.

Whose planet and whose crisis?

The planetary crises we face derive from a series of failures across interlocked and intersecting systems with non-linear dynamics. How to intervene in these systems requires a consideration not just of the limits of human agency, but of questions of ethics, power and responsibility across new frontiers of human/non-human interactions and forms of care and solidarity (Myers, 2017; Puig de la Bellacasa, 2017). Arguably, humans have wrought many changes on the worlds they inhabit, but they have never had to organise human societies before to regenerate the planet and the natural systems on which they depend across the breadth of the Earth. Imagining the forms of change, governance, thought, power and resource mobilisation necessary to initiate and sustain such transformations is far from easy, and it sets an unprecedented challenge for all forms of social theory right across the full range of humanities and social science disciplines. However, while understanding social change is the purview of the social sciences, transfiguring and redesigning how societies relate to the biosphere is of a quite different order of magnitude. Specific outcomes such as carbon reduction, biodiversity conservation, the emergence of liveable cities, and reduced plastic in oceans are all fundamental form part of a wider set of transformations designed to remake the relations between humans and the natural world. The crucial point here is that technological innovation will not be enough to bring about the transformations we require, the enabling necessities for which reside in the realms of ethics, governance, imagination and social innovation. In these spheres of human life, we at once encounter issues of diversity and conflict with their multifarious links to social justice and self-determination.

As a planetary challenge, whole system change presses upon the question of what it means to live well with others, and whether and how this is possible. These others are not simply other humans, but non-humans, as well as other materials, objects and potentialities that form the constitutive elements of all our environments. Our 'reciprocal capture' by our many others (Stengers, 2010) – for the charge and agency to understand and intervene in the world is both plural and not exclusive to humans – is not only a form of embedded, co-constitutive embodiment (Haraway, 2015), but also of a necessary politics and an ethics (Moore, 2012, 2014). Indigenous environmental activists have long articulated the Earth as a living being that humanity must respect and nurture, and recent legal and constitutional changes have begun to demand recognition of the rights of non-human others (de la Cadena, 2015a, 2015b; Szerszynski, 2016; Walsh, 2018; Wilson & Lee, 2019). The incorporation of these others into ethical and legal frameworks necessitates an expansion of the ethical imaginations for most of the world's populations, affecting both their scope and character.

Yet, this is not simply a matter of taking account of local cultural views, but rather of the incorporation of distinctive new versions of the non-human into the self–other relation (de la Cadena, 2015a, 2015b). Such a refashioning is simultaneously radical and familiar. It is a feature of social life that our most intimate self–other relationships are energised by visions of the world outside them, just as our connections with international capitalism, global warming and planetary boundaries take form within the specifics of work, sex, food and leisure (Moore, 2020). We understand this intuitively when we think of how many are inspired by the climate emergency to become vegan and simultaneously change their relationship to their own bodies and to the planet. It is evident then that when we speak of the ethical imagination – the many framing devices we have for understanding and experiencing self–other relations – it is never just a matter of the local and the cultural. It is also equally apparent that the ethical imagination develops and changes as a response to certain historical challenges (Moore, 2011), and is therefore fully engaged in how we envision planetary regeneration and socially just futures.

New ethical sensibilities are empowering alter-globalisation movements and climate activism, stretching notions of care and relationality to confront long-established forms of violence and exclusion as evidenced in the Black Lives Matter protests and the powerful demands for restitution and recognition in the face of the exclusion and dispossession of indigenous peoples (Crook et al., 2018). A manifest demand to 'defamiliarize' and 'deterritorialize' our mental habits (Braidotti, 2017, p. 89; 2019, p. 77) draws a clear link between hierarchical, oppositional and domineering classifications of the human and non-human (Neimanis et al., 2015; TallBear, 2015), and the violence of systemic exclusion and dispossession (Wynter, 2003; Yusoff, 2019). The desire for non-violent and less destructive relationships with the planet and all other earthlings (Haraway, 2016) requires a definitive move away from instrumental and productivist modes of domination, and the dehumanising effects of dominant masculinity. Yet, while new forms of radicalism may be seeking more life-enhancing connections to the natural world through the development of alternative social and ecological relationships (Sachs, 2017), there is considerable disquiet and justifiable anger about an Anthropocene politics that fails to register its own erasures and subjugations (Yusoff, 2019, p. 12).

Far from ignoring its salience as a 'contemporary meta-narrative that seeks to make sense of the "earth-system" as a whole' (Chernilo, 2017, p. 44), in this article we abstain from defining the Anthropocene and limit ourselves to acknowledging it as both a historically and socioculturally charged 'boundary object'; that is, an instantly recognisable but highly disputed term that brings different consequences and distributions of power each time it is defined or framed. This is primarily so because for '[a]ll its scientific, philosophical and even political merits . . ., the Anthropocene debate is built on a very narrow understanding of what a human being is and what human life consists of' (Chernilo, 2017, p. 56). One in which, the event or date chosen as its inception affects 'the stories people construct about the ongoing development of human societies' (Lewis & Maslin, 2015, p. 178).

Black, feminist, indigenous and posthumanist scholars have argued against the exclusionary and universalising category of man contained within the Anthropocene vision of a natural world reshaped by humanity. The current ecological emergency is a crisis of inequality, dispossession, subjugation and non-recognition (Montenegro de Wit, 2021, p. 100) not just because the poor of the Global South suffer most under climate change and its precipitating factors, but because its foundations are scaffolded upon systemic structural disadvantage and exclusion. Without examining the history of the framing of non-white as non-being in the extractive onslaught that has produced the material outcomes relabelled the Anthropocene, there are few possibilities to interrogate anew how regimes of production, extraction and consumption were built on the desecration of others' lives and their losses (Francis, 2020).

The Anthropocene as a framing device and a boundary object is producing both subjects and material worlds, fundamentally shaping the ways and means through which we can envisage alternative futures (A. Moore, 2016). Without examining its history of deadly erasure, enslavement and death, the result can only be a failure to rethink the possibilities for genuine transformation and change, a 'rebirth without possibility' (Yusoff, 2019, pp. 8–9), extending whiteness into the future (Erickson, 2020). The powerful point here is that colonialism and racism make possible the boundary marking of the very distinction between the human and the natural that now requires transcendence (Åsberg, 2017; Francis, 2020). There is a long history of environmental protection embedded in colonialism. We need to consider of transformation and future possibilities that do not reinstitute the past: 'If the Anthropocene is viewed as a resurrection of the impulse to re-establish humanism in all its exclusionary terms of universality, then any critical theory that does not work with and alongside black and indigenous studies (rather than in an extractive or supplementary mode) will fail to deliver an epochal shift at all' (Yusoff, 2019, p. 18).

Certainly, the Anthropocene does provide an unparalleled opportunity to guide action, attitudes, choices, policies and resources to develop a more just, ecologically diverse and prosperous world. But how this will be done is a matter of great contention. Those who argue for a new social contract with the planet are often unwilling to adequately address the exclusionary terms of what they imagine to be the plural art of living and flourishing well with others where fossil fuels are the issue rather than politics (Nightingale et al., 2020; Trebeck & Williams, 2019). The result is a ghostly version of neoliberal wishful thinking where improving our relationship with the planet will have benefits for all. A world that is 'socially, ecologically and economically desirable is likely to differ radically from the world in which we presently live' (Bennett et al., 2016, p. 442), and this means that our collective futures are constrained, not only by the limits of our radicalisms, but also by competing conceptions of the good life. These differing conceptions do not just sit across obvious distinctions such as Euro-American versus indigenous, or Brown versus Green solutions, but drive fundamental cleavages between and within histories, politics, communities, regions and intellectual movements, enlivening differences between competing visions of what a sustainable world should look like from agroecologists and ecofeminists to ecomodernists and techno-optimists (Hedlund-de Witt, 2014; Pickerill, 2018).

The science of the Anthropocene moment is powerful, but scientific facts cannot resolve matters of politics and value; they do not signpost appropriate trade-offs, nor do they provide answers to critical questions such as 'who should decide what course of action is taken?' or 'what counts as betterment of the human condition? (Bai et al., 2016). Human agency has brought about a series of changes with unintended consequences, not all of which human actors are aware of, and consequently human actors can change or ameliorate. Beyond this, the Anthropocene as a boundary object – brought into being through a specific set of scientific framings – drives further forms of human agency that are deepening and accelerating the co-evolution of social and environmental systems, driven in part by evolving scientific knowledge, complexity theory and systems thinking (Bai et al., 2016; Moore et al., 2014; Sharpe et al., 2016). These new forms of co-evolution are creating novel circumstances and intersections, giving rise to new forms of nature, framings of time and space and modes of politics (Lövbrand et al., 2015; Mathews & Barnes, 2016). This accounts in part for the fractious debates around the Anthropocene itself and whether it should be renamed as Capitalocene (J. W. E. Moore, 2016), Chthulhucene (Haraway, 2016) or Plantationocene (Haraway, 2015), and the increasing anxiety of whether as a boundary object it hinders or helps the swift action that needs to be taken. The Anthropocene will continue to be an emergent complex and contested phenomenon, and how we navigate it will depend on the kind of world we want to live in and leave for future generations.

The Anthropocene is not the only boundary object in contention. The notion of the planet itself, and revisions of human–planetary relations, imply a singularity in framing enhanced through scientific achievement, that forecloses alternative ways of imagining the entanglements of natural and social worlds, reducing the range and viability of alternative meanings and political trajectories. It is not merely a question of who speaks for the Earth, but which Earth we are speaking about (Lövbrand et al., 2015). Consequently, the future of the Earth must encompass a much wider range of knowledge traditions and communities, enabling larger imaginative engagements for future flourishing. One of the key issues here concerns presumptions of scale. Alternative knowledge traditions are very frequently consigned to the local, their relevance discounted when it comes to whole system change. This becomes evident with notions of sustainability and their recent reformulation in terms of planetary boundaries and their maintenance (Biermann & Kim, 2020; Rockström & Klum, 2015) which appear to be scientifically neutral while very often failing to recognise alternative knowledges, perspectives and experiences (McGregor et al., 2020; Samuel, 2019; Williams, 2018). The role of indigenous and local communities in managing biodiversity and climate change, and the significance of their knowledge systems and intellectual framings are still under-recognised and deployed (Crook et al., 2018; Etchart, 2017; Hill et al., 2020; Sobrevila, 2008; Virtanen et al., 2020); the embedded and localised character of that knowledge both lauded and disregarded. Creating mechanisms to learn effectively and collaborate positively with alternative knowledges, visions and experiences is a crucial part of developing sites of resistance and forms of experimentation for innovative and diverse formulations for future flourishing (Blok & Jensen, 2019).

Any formulation of future flourishing will depend on the nature of ours and others' agency to engage with and be shaped by the plethora of enabling and constraining conditions, knowledges and ways of doing and being of the world. As we anticipated earlier, we cannot pretend to synthesise let alone understand all these relationalities for they are emergent and ever changing. Instead, we must acknowledge and embrace them as the bare bones that will guide our future envisioning, acquiescence and actioning for true, honest, transformational change.

Treating the Earth like dirt

Clearly, future flourishing on a regenerated planet involves the realisation of a world that is better than the present one; it thus encodes notions of progress. For all the critiques of progress in recent years, there are few ways of expressing human betterment – and now indeed planetary wellbeing – that do not bring it back into focus. All the communities of the world have rights to a better quality of life (Waas et al., 2011), but they start from very different places precisely because older notions of progress and modernity structurally required systemic inequalities to function, extracting value from some locations, processes, materials and lives and depositing it elsewhere. Sustainable development as popularised in the 1990s was aimed at meeting the requirements of the present without compromising the needs of future generations. As a framework and as a set of practices, it had the potential to drive economic and environmental reform, but in reality it served to justify the actions of those pursuing sustained economic growth. At its heart it contained a contradiction as to whether development and environmental concerns were compatible, often letting go of any commitment to environmentally sustainable development in favour of development as the capacity for sustaining growth in material production and consumption or modernisation (Escobar, 2019); the sustainable and the successful became intertwined, if not interchangeable formulations, with predictable results (de Sousa Santos, 2018).

The notion of growth as progress is deeply sedimented in Euro-American thought, and recent critiques have been voluminous (Jackson, 2021; Macekura, 2020; Mouzakitis, 2017). Since the Second World War, most countries have committed to economic growth measured by GDP. Despite recent and much welcome steps towards social wellbeing, inclusion, equality, good health, opportunity and quality of life (Fioramonti, 2017; Green et al., 2020; Moore, 2015; Moore & Woodcraft, 2019; Stiglitz, 2019), policy initiatives around the world are still focused on economic growth as the key measure of success, accompanied by improvements in productivity and efficiency. The ongoing pandemic has laid bare the structural frailties and systemic injustices of social systems built on economies of optimisation and extraction; and yet, alternatives to inexorable economic growth are deemed unfeasible; capitalist realism holds sway (Fisher, 2009). Neologisms offer promise – e.g. inclusive growth – but deliver little change. The current construct of the economic system continues to incentivise resource efficiency while governments determinedly speak of productivity gains and the curse of low productivity, trying to find ways to extract more from each unit of labour (Sandbu, 2020; Stiglitz, 2019). GDP as the measure of growth and market activity propels these forms of extraction, but this adherence to productivism has not brought wellbeing or quality of life for many. Instead, it has propelled detrimental consequences for the environment, undermined employment through deskilling and job flexibilisation, and driven declines in incomes, health and security for ordinary communities (Foster, 2018).

We see this most dramatically in the context of our food systems, and therefore reflecting on how we might institute change in our agricultural systems provides us with a potentially productive lens through which to view the scale and significance of the challenges we face. Agriculture is one of humankind's oldest pursuits, one of its most innovative and one of its most destructive. Contemporary food systems – at least since the Second World War and the following crisis of hunger and nutrition – have been built on the super scale realisation of productivity and efficiency employing technological means, including mechanisation, non-organic fertilisers and chemicals. In the case of modern agricultural systems, the goal is to extract the maximum yield per hectare and to drive down costs, producing more with less. This has sometimes been termed competitive productivism, and with monocropping, specialisation, intensification, non-organic fertiliser and pest control measures, this is leading to increasing pressures on the environment, rising levels of toxicity, declining biodiversity and augmented threats to future food production and food security (Khoury et al., 2014; Lawrence et al., 2013). In the global south, development programmes and policy are still focused on agricultural productivity and market integration measured by growth, cost efficiency and high yields at the expense of quality of life and ecological wellbeing (Lunn-Rockliffe et al., 2020). Small scale farmers around the world are being driven off the land as increasing concentration of land and other productive resources is driven by processes of accumulation and expansion. Key to the justification of such dispossession is the culturally prevalent connection – across a wide spectrum of cultures – that modernisation and efficiency are the hallmarks of progress, and low-yielding farms need to function like high-yielding ones (Motta & Martín, 2021).

Contemporary food systems are extractive economies on a grand scale, with their true costs externalised, living on borrowed time. Today agriculture is the largest consumer of the world's freshwater resources, and more than one-quarter of the energy used globally is expended on food production and supply (Dunkelman et al., 2018). It is now widely recognised that the pursuit of constantly augmented growth is not sustainable in the context of limited planetary resources (Biermann & Kim, 2020; Raworth, 2017; Rockström & Klum, 2015). The health and environmental costs of global agriculture now exceed the market value of all that is produced (Benton & Bailey, 2019). There is an urgent need to reprioritise and rethink our agricultural futures, and this will involve sundering the connections between productivity, efficiency, optimisation and progress (Benton & Bailey, 2019). There are considerable grounds for hope in that various arguments about the necessity for increasing productivity, efficiency and optimisation in agriculture and the economy more broadly are being routinely challenged across a wide spectrum of policy, civil society and community spaces (Food and Agriculture Organization [FAO], 2018; Lunn-Rockliffe et al., 2020). This is accompanied by a questioning of the subordination of ecosystems and human social and cultural life to economic reasoning, extractivism and efficiency, precisely because markets cannot be relied on to deliver justice, sustainability and value pluralism (Bliss & Egler, 2020), nor to safeguard natural resources and shared public goods.

While it is evident that our food systems are driving climate change and biodiversity loss, and degrading soils and ecosystems, biodiversity loss also applies within agriculture and many historical food stuffs are no longer consumed. This is of concern not just because genetic diversity makes food systems more resilient to climate change, pests and pathogens (Benton et al., 2021), but because in addition to the reductions in biodiversity, optimisation of single food crops has reduced the forms of human knowledge that allow us to work with mechanisms for enriching diversity. For example, in the upper reaches of the Huangpu River, 60 km south of Shanghai, a long history of traditional Jiangnan-style farming involving resource saving and locally adapted agricultural practices was based on deep local understandings of soils and water resources. Farmers dredged mud from the Huangpu River and used animal manure and human waste to fertilise the soil, achieving very high yields without damaging the health of the land or exceeding its production capacity. Resilience in the system involved adopting external innovations as well as passing knowledge from generation to generation (Liu et al., 2016, pp. 1–2). Starting in the 1980s, many of these practices were abandoned due to China's state-led economic and land reforms, the intensification of agricultural production, new irrigation systems, and increased usage of chemical fertilisers and pesticides, declining farm labour in an ageing population, and the hollowing-out of rural areas (Sanders, 2006; Van der Ploeg et al., 2014). Despite growing contemporary demand for more organic and healthy produce from urban centres, reintroducing traditional practices such as the application of river mud, combined with innovative techniques for future sustainable farming scenarios in the region, would require not only cross-sectoral collaboration between different stakeholders in China, but also 'a shift in perceptions of farming, [and] the willingness to engage in cross-generational learning' which has been lost (Liu et al., 2016, pp. 20–21).

Food is about a metabolic exchange with nature, and the links between environmental degradation, monocropping, declining soil fertility, non-organic fertilisers, agrobiodiversity reduction and the impoverishment of famers' livelihoods have been framed in terms of a metabolic rift (Schneider & McMichael, 2010; Wittman, 2009). This is best conceived as a breakdown not just in terms of nutrient cycles, soil fertility, biodiversity, etc., but also in knowledge sharing and transfer and in social and political relations. Agroecological approaches to repairing this rift have gained traction in recent years and have been proposed to transform food systems, ecosystem health, household nutrition and food sovereignty (Bezner Kerr et al., 2019a; FAO, 2018; Gliessman, 2018; Wezel et al., 2020). The guiding principle of agroecology is to mimic natural ecosystems, but it involves more than the implementation of practices such as recycling, reduction of inputs, diversification of resources and species, and soil enhancement. It also encompasses the application of new principles for the redesign of farming systems (Nicholls et al., 2016; Rosset & Altieri, 2017). Endowing landscapes and communities with greater resilience, wellbeing and health has become especially important in the light of the COVID pandemic and the links between the origin and spread of the pathogen and deforestation, monocropping and systemic inequalities (Altieri & Nicholls, 2020; Montenegro de Wit, 2021).

Animal, human and ecological health are closely linked; while future agricultural systems need to minimise risks to humans, non-humans and the planet, they also need to engage with and amplify emergent and future modes of productive entanglement between human and more-than-human flourishing. Evidence shows that agroecology can increase crop yields, improve production resilience through diversification, augment diets and income, reduce farmer dependency on inputs, conserve biodiversity and mitigate climate change. In Tigray in Ethiopia, crop yields of cereals and pulses have almost doubled using agroecological practices such as composting, water and soil conservation, agroforestry and crop diversification (Lappé, 2016). Diverse landscapes also support a larger range of economic activities such as tourism, craft production and beekeeping (Garibaldi & Pérez-Méndez, 2019). Intervening in agricultural systems through agroecology cascades benefits through multiple intersecting environmental, social and economic dimensions. But designing diversified farming systems is not a matter of one size fits all, of a single set of processes and interventions. Agroecology must be closely adapted to local material, environmental and social conditions, with detailed attention to microsites across soils and landscapes.

Thriving in and through conditions of diversity entails close attention to how interventions can most productively function in the enmeshed space of human and more-than-human relations. Agroecology is now a global social movement involving indigenous communities, farmers, activists and scientists, as well as international agencies like the FAO, local governments, civil society organisations and business (de Molina et al., 2019; FAO, 2018). It is not a matter of just returning to traditional knowledge, but of reanimating its productive potential in concert with emerging multiple forms of knowledge and social relations at the local level. Recent work has shown that it is not enough to apply agroecological principles and practices in the hope of regenerating landscapes and community wellbeing because in situations, for example, where women do not control land, harvests and income, they do not necessarily benefit in terms of improved livelihoods. In addition, tasks such as mulching and composting which are essential for agroecological techniques can fall disproportionately on women, increasing their workload and exacerbating gender-based violence. Labour and decision-making are key microsites for building food sovereignty and individual and community wellbeing (Bezner Kerr et al., 2019b), and agroecology requires attention to social innovation as well as ecological.

Similarly, in many colonial contexts in Africa, the British strongly discouraged local practices that served to maintain soil fertility and dietary resilience, including shifting cultivation, fallowing, use of ash and manure, weeds and crop residues, disrupting the productive potential of landscapes further by actively promoting male labour migration. Post-colonial regimes maintained their commitment to maize monocropping and subsidised non-organic fertilisers, while allocation of land to parastatals and political allies resulted in land dispossession for many small farmers (Davies et al., 2014; Moore, 2018). Current attempts to repair the metabolic rift through agroecology must acknowledge the complex consequences of colonialism and slavery and their permutations in the present. As suggested earlier, pathways to sustainable and just food systems have to envision racial relations and systemic injustice as fundamental in repairing the social, political and epistemic dimensions of the metabolic rift (Montenegro de Wit, 2021).

Effective transition and transformation in food systems thus involves questions of social justice and self-determination, but it fundamentally requires a new approach to how social-ecological worlds are made, expanding notions of belonging, care and sociality beyond human worlds. Agricultural productivity understood as an ethic of care across the human/non-human, local/planetary divides could and should reconfigure the broader context of value chains and investment that structure food systems. Imagine if you will a set of concerted actions based on disinvestment in food systems that do not adhere to planetary regeneration, biodiversity and climate resilience, as has been done with fossil fuels. Any envisioning of alternative, decolonial futures for agriculture must start with rethinking multi-species entanglements and relationships, involutions as Myers has described them (Myers, 2017), conversations in the sense given by de la Cadena (2017), or relations of care in Puig de la Bellacasa's formulation (Puig de la Bellacasa, 2017): where ongoing, improvised, experimental encounters can take shape as human and non-humans involve themselves in others' lives in deeper and more productive ways.

Growing the future

There is no doubt that we are inhabiting the ruins of progress in terms of the dominant frame in which it has been understood since the eighteenth century. Focusing on agriculture is salutary here because modern food systems are failing to sustain both people and the natural resources on which they rely, representing an existential threat to us all. Consequently, agriculture and food offer a strategic location for ethical, social and political action in the Anthropocene. But, how to make better nature and human–nature relations is a fraught empirical and political question.

As suggested throughout this article, it involves recognising that humans and non-humans are enmeshed in complex social, ecological and technological systems. Insofar as agroecology is one possible mode of intervention in charting a course towards future flourishing, it must be envisaged as a specific assemblage of plants, people, soil, fertiliser, technologies, animals, fences and infrastructures both material and social. As such it is not a single set of practices or outcomes, but rather a set of relational achievements specific to each context for which diversity is the watchword. It is not a return to a past, to indigenous knowledge or to pre-existent nature. It is a novel amalgam of diverse knowledges, including science, of political and social practices, of forms of governance, and of relations of care and attention linked to future flourishing (Šūmane et al., 2018). Its aim is the shaping of emergence, the drive towards richer permutations in relationships between humans and the many others who share the planet together. As a story of unfolding, tilting relationalities, its fecundity is allied to forms of sharing that enhance complexity.

Constructing liveable futures requires unearthing violently erased practices, wisdoms and knowledge (Myers, 2017), the historical lifeworlds of what de la Cadena calls the 'Anthropos-not-seen' (de la Cadena, 2015b). This process is fundamental for the envisioning of future flourishing in a manner that allows for and requires the simultaneous disruption of the present. Modern science and technology are part of this process too. Moving away from productivism and extraction as forms of progress overweeningly committed to efficient optimisation and the asinine goal of outsmarting nature does not mean embracing a form of luddite politics which cuts the world off from advances in health care, technology, learning, systems thinking, ecology and more. It means generating spaces 'where diversity, pluralism, and contending perspectives are present on their own terms but also deeply invested in engaging others in creating and sharing information and knowledge' (Sardar & Sweeney, 2016, p. 3). The process of sharing must be set within broader goals and value systems, and as noted earlier there is currently little consensus as to what these should be, and divisions are further exacerbated by power, elitism, corporatism, greed and systemic injustice. A focus on agriculture and food affords a shared space for debate over these issues, and more than that a set of potential shared practices that can translate into a shared understanding of nature, of the new forms of human and more-than-human interaction required, and of visions for future flourishing. Shared understandings arising from practice create new imaginaries, new ways of relating to self and other, new forms of the ethical imagination.

In this context, productivity must be rethought as relationality rather than as extraction or optimisation. If there is to be progress it is in terms of deepening complexities that enhance future flourishing, where prosperity is an emergent property of complex systems (Moore & Mintchev, 2021). These tilting relationalities should include and draw sustenance from the many elements of life already created through sharing and diverse forms of sociality, including social and cultural resources like open-source software, scientific knowledge, libraries, dance, and platforms for indigenous knowledge and languages. A renewed relation of humans to the planet needs to include all these elements; they must be harnessed as opportunities for realising desirable and plausible futures. Productivity is not an output but a process, a form of productive entanglement that creates new forms of relationality and must necessarily include the material and the non-material, the biotic and the abiotic, expanding the remit of what we understand by the terms sociality, knowledge, nature, ecology; breaking down old binaries.

If there is to be a good Anthropocene or even a post-Anthropocene, it will have to be a diverse one, since there are only multiple futures for future flourishing; these enhanced forms of relationality will arise in complex locales and spaces, and will not necessarily share similar theoretical or ideological foundations (Bai et al., 2016; Bennett et al.,

2016). The hope is that new practices of care for non-human others and the planet will generate new forms of agency and politics (Sharpe et al., 2016), as well as new forms of the ethical imagination that will drive further entanglements and transformations. Key to such processes will be to keep the uncertainty of the outcomes visible, to invest in experimentation with the potentialities of diversity, to ensure that we do not reduce the future down to formulations of progress or sets of development objectives, to render power explicit, and to continually interrogate terrains like gender and race that hold concrete material, social and ecological implications (Preiser et al., 2017).

The role for the social sciences and humanities here is not to describe or pretend to represent these emerging forms of relationality; they escape tightly bound prescriptions because they are dynamic, non-linear, and often intangible. Instead, they must enable and actively engage these relationalities. Doing this responsibly and effectively will require us to inhabit the disorienting and discomforting ruins of progress, eschewing the turn towards finalised solutions and outcomes. In short, 'after' progress we will need to learn to live with the worlds' many others, and that can only be done by honestly and humbly accepting and committing to the sustainable emergence of alternative ways of knowing, doing and being.

Funding

The authors received no financial support for the research, authorship, and/or publication of this article.

References

Altieri, M. A., & Nicholls, C. (2020). Agroecology: Challenges and opportunities for farming in the Anthropocene. *International Journal of Agricultural and Natural Resources*, *47*(3), 204–215. doi:10.7764/ijanr.v47i3.2281

Åsberg, C. (2017). Feminist posthumanities in the Anthropocene: Forays into the postnatural. *Journal of Posthuman Studies*, *1*(2), 185–204. doi:10.5325/jpoststud.1.2.0185

Bai, X., van der Leeuw, S., O'Brien, K., Berkhout, F., Biermann, F., Brondizio, E. S., Cudennec, C., Dearing, J., Duraiappah, A., Glaser, M., Revkin, A., Steffen, W., & Syvitski, J. (2016). Plausible and desirable futures in the Anthropocene: A new research agenda. *Global Environmental Change*, *39*, 351–362. doi:https://doi.org/10.1016/j.gloenvcha.2015.09.017

Bennett, E. M., Solan, M., Biggs, R., McPhearson, T., Norström, A. V., Olsson, P., Pereira, L., Peterson, G. D., Raudsepp-Hearne, C., Biermann, F., Carpenter, S. R., Ellis, E. C., Hichert, T., Galaz, V., Lahsen, M., Milkoreit, M., López, B. M., Nicholas, K. A., Preiser, R., . . . Xu, J. (2016). Bright spots: Seeds of a good Anthropocene. *Frontiers in Ecology and the Environment*, *14*(8), 441–448. doi:https://doi.org/10.1002/fee.1309

Benton, T. G., & Bailey, R. (2019). The paradox of productivity: Agricultural productivity promotes food system inefficiency. *Global Sustainability*, *2*, e6. doi:10.1017/sus.2019.3

Benton, T. G., Bieg, C., Harwatt, H., Pudasaini, R., & Wellesley, L. (2021). *Food system impacts on biodiversity loss. Three levers for food system transformation in support of nature.* UN Environmental Programme. www.unenvironment.org/resources/publication/food-system-impacts-biodiversity-loss

Bezner Kerr, R., Hickey, C., Lupafya, E., & Dakishoni, L. (2019a). Repairing rifts or reproducing inequalities? Agroecology, food sovereignty, and gender justice in Malawi. *The Journal of Peasant Studies*, *46*(7), 1499–1518. doi:10.1080/03066150.2018.1547897

Bezner Kerr, R., Kangmennaang, J., Dakishoni, L., Nyantakyi-Frimpong, H., Lupafya, E., Shumba, L., Msachi, R., Boateng, G. O., Snapp, S., Chitaya, A., Maona, E., Gondwe, T., Nkhonjera, P., & Luginaah, I. (2019b). Participatory agroecological research on climate change adaptation improves smallholder farmer household food security and dietary diversity in Malawi. *Agriculture, Ecosystems & Environment, 279,* 109–121. doi:https://doi.org/10.1016/j.agee.2019.04.004

Biermann, F., & Kim, R. E. (2020). The boundaries of the planetary boundary framework: A critical appraisal of approaches to define a 'safe operating space' for humanity. *Annual Review of Environment and Resources, 45,* 497–521.

Bliss, S., & Egler, M. (2020). Ecological economics beyond markets. *Ecological Economics, 178,* Article 106806.

Blok, A., & Jensen, C. B. (2019). The Anthropocene event in social theory: On ways of problematizing nonhuman materiality differently. *The Sociological Review, 67*(6), 1195–1211.

Braidotti, R. (2017). Critical posthuman knowledges. *South Atlantic Quarterly, 116*(1), 83–96. doi:10.1215/00382876-3749337

Braidotti, R. (2019). *Posthuman knowledge:* Polity Press.

Chernilo, D. (2017). The question of the human in the Anthropocene debate. *European Journal of Social Theory, 20*(1), 44–60.

Crook, M., Short, D., & South, N. (2018). Ecocide, genocide, capitalism and colonialism: Consequences for indigenous peoples and glocal ecosystems environments. *Theoretical Criminology, 22*(3), 298–317.

Davies, M. I., Kipruto, T. K., & Moore, H. L. (2014). Revisiting the irrigated agricultural landscape of the Marakwet, Kenya: Tracing local technology and knowledge over the recent past. *Azania: Archaeological Research in Africa, 49*(4), 486–523.

de la Cadena, M. (2015a). *Earth beings: Ecologies of practice across Andean worlds.* Duke University Press.

de la Cadena, M. (2015b). Uncommoning nature. *E-flux Journal, 65,* 1–8.

de la Cadena, M. (2017). Matters of method; Or, why method matters toward a not only colonial anthropology. *HAU: Journal of Ethnographic Theory, 7*(2), 1–10. doi:10.14318/hau7.2.002

de Molina, M. G., Petersen, P. F., Peña, F. G., & Caporal, F. R. (2019). *Political agroecology: Advancing the transition to sustainable food systems.* CRC Press.

de Sousa Santos, B. (2018). *The end of the cognitive empire: The coming of age of epistemologies of the South.* Duke University Press.

Deng, S., Liu, S., Mo, X., Jiang, L., & Bauer-Gottwein, P. (2021). Polar drift in the 1990s explained by terrestrial water storage changes. *Geophysical Research Letters, 48*(7), e2020GL092114. https://doi.org/10.1029/2020GL092114

Dunkelman, A., Kerr, M., & Swatuk, L. A. (2018). The new green revolution: Enhancing rainfed agriculture for food and nutrition security in eastern Africa. In L. A. Swatuk & C. Cash (Eds.), *Water, energy, food and people across the global south* (pp. 305–324). Springer.

Erickson, B. (2020). Anthropocene futures: Linking colonialism and environmentalism in an age of crisis. *Environment and Planning D: Society and Space, 38*(1), 111–128.

Escobar, A. (2019). Thinking-feeling with the Earth: Territorial struggles and the ontological dimension of the epistemologies of the south. In B. de Sousa Santos & M. P. Meneses (Eds.), *Knowledges born in the struggle* (pp. 41–57). Routledge.

Etchart, L. (2017). The role of indigenous peoples in combating climate change. *Palgrave Communications, 3*(1), 1–4.

Fioramonti, L. (2017). *The world after GDP: Politics, business and society in the post growth era.* John Wiley & Sons.

Fisher, M. (2009). *Capitalist realism: Is there no alternative?* John Hunt Publishing.

Food and Agriculture Organization. (2018). *Scaling up agroecology to achieve the sustainable development goals*. Paper presented at the Second International Symposium on Agroecology. Food and Agriculture Organisation, Rome. www.fao.org/about/meetings/second-international-agroecology-symposium/en/

Foster, K. R. (2018). *Productivity and prosperity*. University of Toronto Press.

Francis, R. (2020). The tyranny of the coloniality of nature and the elusive question of justice. In E. Benyera (Ed.), *Reimagining justice, human rights and leadership in Africa: Challenging discourse and searching for alternative paths* (pp. 39–57). Springer.

Garibaldi, L. A., & Pérez-Méndez, N. (2019). Positive outcomes between crop diversity and agricultural employment worldwide. *Ecological Economics, 164*, Article 106358. https://doi.org/10.1016/j.ecolecon.2019.106358

Gliessman, S. (2018). Defining agroecology. *Agroecology and Sustainable Food Systems, 42*(6), 599–600. doi:10.1080/21683565.2018.1432329

Green, M., Harmacek, J., & Krylova, P. (2020). *Social progress index*. www.socialprogress.org/static/37348b3ecb088518a945fa4c83d9b9f4/2020-social-progress-index-executive-summary.pdf

Haraway, D. (2015). Anthropocene, capitalocene, plantationocene, chthulucene: Making kin. *Environmental Humanities, 6*(1), 159–165.

Haraway, D. J. (2016). *Staying with the trouble: Making kin in the Chthulucene*. Duke University Press.

Hedlund-de Witt, A. (2014). Rethinking sustainable development: Considering how different worldviews envision 'development' and 'quality of life'. *Sustainability, 6*(11), 8310–8328.

Hill, R., Adem, Ç., Alangui, W. V., Molnár, Z., Aumeeruddy-Thomas, Y., Bridgewater, P., Tengö, M., Thaman, R., Yao, C. Y. A., Berkes, F., Carino, J., da Cunha, M. C., Diaw, M. C., Díaz, S., Figueroa, V. E., Fisher, J., Hardison, P., Ichikawa, K., Kariuki, P., . . .Xue, D. (2020). Working with Indigenous, local and scientific knowledge in assessments of nature and nature's linkages with people. *Current Opinion in Environmental Sustainability, 43*, 8–20. https://doi.org/10.1016/j.cosust.2019.12.006

Jackson, T. (2021). *Post growth: Life after capitalism*. Polity Press.

Khoury, C. K., Bjorkman, A. D., Dempewolf, H., Ramirez-Villegas, J., Guarino, L., Jarvis, A., Rieseberg, L. H., & Struik, P. C. (2014). Increasing homogeneity in global food supplies and the implications for food security. *Proceedings of the National Academy of Sciences, 111*(11), 4001–4006.

Lappé, F. M. (2016). Farming for a small planet: Agroecology now. *Development, 59*(3), 299–307. doi:10.1057/s41301-017-0114-9

Lawrence, G., Richards, C., & Lyons, K. (2013). Food security in Australia in an era of neoliberalism, productivism and climate change. *Journal of Rural Studies, 29*, 30–39.

Lewis, S. L., & Maslin, M. A. (2015). Defining the Anthropocene. *Nature, 519*(7542), 171–180.

Liu, P., Moreno, J. M., Song, P., Hoover, E., & Harder, M. K. (2016). The use of oral histories to identify criteria for future scenarios of sustainable farming in the South Yangtze River, China. *Sustainability, 8*(9), Article 859.

Lövbrand, E., Beck, S., Chilvers, J., Forsyth, T., Hedrén, J., Hulme, M., Lidskog, R., & Vasileiadou, E. (2015). Who speaks for the future of Earth? How critical social science can extend the conversation on the Anthropocene. *Global Environmental Change, 32*, 211–218.

Lunn-Rockliffe, S., Davies, M. I., Willman, A., Moore, H. L., McGlade, J. M., & Bent, D. (2020). *Farmer led regenerative agriculture for Africa*. Institute for Global Prosperity at UCL Report. https://seriouslydifferent.org/igp-data/farmer-led-regenerative-agriculture-for-africa

Macekura, S. J. (2020). *The mismeasure of progress: Economic growth and its critics*. University of Chicago Press.

Mathews, A. S., & Barnes, J. (2016). Prognosis: Visions of environmental futures. *Journal of the Royal Anthropological Institute, 22*(S1), 9–26.

McGregor, D., Whitaker, S., & Sritharan, M. (2020). Indigenous environmental justice and sustainability. *Current Opinion in Environmental Sustainability, 43*, 35–40.

Montenegro de Wit, M. (2021). What grows from a pandemic? Toward an abolitionist agroecology. *The Journal of Peasant Studies, 48*(1), 99–136. doi:10.1080/03066150.2020.1854741

Moore, A. (2016). Anthropocene anthropology: Reconceptualizing contemporary global change. *Journal of the Royal Anthropological Institute, 22*(1), 27–46.

Moore, H. L. (2011). *Still life: Hopes, desires and satisfactions*. Polity.

Moore, H. L. (2012). The fantasies of cosmopolitanism. In R. Braidotti, P. Hanafin & B. Blaagaard (Eds.), *After cosmopolitanism* (pp. 107–120). Routledge.

Moore, H. L. (2014). Living in molecular times. In B. Blaagaard (Ed.), *The subject of Rosi Braidotti: Politics and concepts* (pp. 47–55). Bloomsbury Academic.

Moore, H. L. (2015). Global prosperity and sustainable development goals. *Journal of International Development, 27*(6), 801–815.

Moore, H. L. (2018). Prosperity in crisis and the longue durée in Africa. *The Journal of Peasant Studies, 45*(7), 1501–1517. doi:10.1080/03066150.2018.1446001

Moore, H. L. (2020). The habitat of the subject: Exploring new forms of the ethical imagination. In M. Ege & J. Moser (Eds.), *Urban ethics: Conflicts over the good and proper life in cities* (pp. 28–46). Routledge.

Moore, H. L., & Mintchev, N. (2021). *What is prosperity?* UCL Institute for Global Prosperity Working Paper. https://discovery.ucl.ac.uk/id/eprint/10126424

Moore, H. L., & Woodcraft, S. (2019). Understanding prosperity in East London: Local meanings and 'sticky' measures of the good life. *City & Society, 31*(2), 275–298.

Moore, J. W. E. (2016). *Anthropocene or capitalocene? Nature, history, and the crisis of capitalism*. PM Press.

Moore, M. L., Tjornbo, O., Enfors, E., Knapp, C., Hodbod, J., Baggio, J. A., Norström, A., Olsson, P., & Biggs, D. (2014). Studying the complexity of change toward an analytical framework for understanding deliberate social-ecological transformations. *Ecology and Society, 19*(4), Article 54.

Motta, R., & Martín, E. (2021). Food and social change: Culinary elites, contested technologies, food movements and embodied social change in food practices. *The Sociological Review, 69*(3), 503–519. https://doi.org/10.1177/00380261211009468

Mouzakitis, A. (2017). Modernity and the idea of progress. *Frontiers in Sociology, 2*. https://doi.org/10.3389/fsoc.2017.00003

Myers, N. (2017). From the Anthropocene to the Planthroposcene: Designing gardens for plant/people involution. *History and Anthropology, 28*(3), 297–301. doi:10.1080/02757206.2017.1289934

Neimanis, A., Åsberg, C., & Hedrén, J. (2015). Four problems, four directions for environmental humanities: Toward critical posthumanities for the Anthropocene. *Ethics & the Environment, 20*(1), 67–97.

Nicholls, C. I., Altieri, M. A., & Vazquez, L. (2016). Agroecology: Principles for the conversion and redesign of farming systems. *Journal of Ecosystems and Ecography, S5*(1).

Nightingale, A. J., Eriksen, S., Taylor, M., Forsyth, T., Pelling, M., Newsham, A., Boyd, E., Brown, K., Harvey, B., Jones, L., Kerr, R. B., Mehta, L., Naess, L. O., Ockwell, D., Scoones, I., Tanner, T., & Whitfield, S. (2020). Beyond technical fixes: Climate solutions and the great derangement. *Climate and Development, 12*(4), 343–352, doi:10.1080/17565529.2019.1624495

Pickerill, J. (2018). Black and green: The future of Indigenous–environmentalist relations in Australia. *Environmental Politics*, *27*(6), 1122–1145.

Preiser, R., Pereira, L. M., & Biggs, R. (2017). Navigating alternative framings of human–environment interactions: Variations on the theme of 'Finding Nemo'. *Anthropocene*, *20*, 83–87. doi:10.1016/j.ancene.2017.10.003

Puig de la Bellacasa, M. (2017). *Matters of care: Speculative ethics in more than human worlds.* University of Minnesota Press.

Raworth, K. (2017). *Doughnut economics: Seven ways to think like a 21st-century economist.* Chelsea Green Publishing.

Rockström, J., & Klum, M. (2015). *Big world, small planet.* Yale University Press.

Rosset, P. M., & Altieri, M. A. (2017). *Agroecology: Science and politics.* Practical Action Publishing.

Sachs, W. (2017). The sustainable development goals and *Laudato si'*: Varieties of post-development? *Third World Quarterly*, *38*(12), 2573–2587. doi:10.1080/01436597.2017.1350822

Samuel, S. (2019). Witsaja iki, or the good life in Ecuadorian Amazonia: Knowledge co-production for climate resilience. In A. Ahearn, M. Oelz & R. K. Dhir (Eds.), *Indigenous peoples and climate change* (pp. 51–63). International Labour Organization.

Sandbu, M. (2020). *The economics of belonging: A radical plan to win back the left behind and achieve prosperity for all.* Princeton University Press.

Sanders, R. (2006). A market road to sustainable agriculture? Ecological agriculture, green food and organic agriculture in China. *Development and Change*, *37*(1), 201–226. doi:10.1111/j.0012-155X.2006.00475.x

Sardar, Z., & Sweeney, J. A. (2016). The three tomorrows of postnormal times. *Futures*, *75*, 1–13. doi:10.1016/j.futures.2015.10.004

Schneider, M., & McMichael, P. (2010). Deepening, and repairing, the metabolic rift. The *Journal of Peasant Studies*, *37*(3), 461–484.

Sharpe, B., Hodgson, A., Leicester, G., Lyon, A., & Fazey, I. (2016). Three horizons: A pathways practice for transformation. *Ecology and Society*, *21*(2), Article 47. doi:10.5751/es-08388-210247

Sobrevila, C. (2008). *The role of indigenous peoples in biodiversity conservation: The natural but often forgotten partners.* The World Bank Report. www.iccaconsortium.org/wp-content/uploads/2017/06/RoleofIndigenousPeoplesinBiodiversityConservation-2008.pdf

Stengers, I. (2010). *Cosmopolitics (Vol. 1).* University of Minnesota Press.

Stiglitz, J. (2019). *People, power, and profits: Progressive capitalism for an age of discontent.* Penguin.

Šūmane, S., Kunda, I., Knickel, K., Strauss, A., Tisenkopfs, T., Rios, I. d. I., Rivera, M., Chebach, T., & Ashkenazy, A. (2018). Local and farmers' knowledge matters! How integrating informal and formal knowledge enhances sustainable and resilient agriculture. *Journal of Rural Studies*, *59*, 232–241. doi:10.1016/j.jrurstud.2017.01.020

Szerszynski, B. (2016). Praise be to you, earth-beings. *Environmental Humanities*, *8*(2), 291–297.

TallBear, K. (2015). An indigenous reflection on working beyond the human/not human. *GLQ: A Journal of Lesbian and Gay Studies*, *21*(2–3), 230–235.

Trebeck, K., & Williams, J. (2019). *The economics of arrival: Ideas for a grown-up economy.* Policy Press.

Van der Ploeg, J. D., Ye, J., & Pan, L. (2014). Peasants, time and the land: The social organization of farming in China. *Journal of Rural Studies*, *36*, 172–181.

Virtanen, P. K., Siragusa, L., & Guttorm, H. (2020). Introduction: Toward more inclusive definitions of sustainability. *Current Opinion in Environmental Sustainability*, *43*, 77–82.

Waas, T., Hugé, J., Verbruggen, A., & Wright, T. (2011). Sustainable development: A bird's eye view. *Sustainability*, *3*(10), 1637–1661.

Walsh, C. (2018). Constructing the pluriverse. In R. Bernd (Ed.), *Development as buen vivir: Institutional arrangements and (de)colonial entanglements* (pp. 184–194). Duke University Press.

Wezel, A., Herren, B. G., Kerr, R. B., Barrios, E., Gonçalves, A. L. R., & Sinclair, F. (2020). Agroecological principles and elements and their implications for transitioning to sustainable food systems. A review. *Agronomy for Sustainable Development*, *40*(6), Article 40. doi:10.1007/s13593-020-00646-z

Williams, L. (2018). Climate change, colonialism, and women's well-being in Canada: What is to be done? *Canadian Journal of Public Health*, *109*(2), 268–271.

Wilson, G., & Lee, D. M. (2019). Rights of rivers enter the mainstream. *The Ecological Citizen*, *2*(2), 183–187.

Wittman, H. (2009). Reworking the metabolic rift: La Vía Campesina, agrarian citizenship, and food sovereignty. *The Journal of Peasant Studies*, *36*(4), 805–826.

Wynter, S. (2003). Unsettling the coloniality of being/power/truth/freedom: Towards the human, after man, its overrepresentation – An argument. *CR: The New Centennial Review*, *3*(3), 257–337.

Yusoff, K. (2019). *A billion black anthropocenes or none*. University of Minnesota Press.

Author Biographies

Henrietta L. Moore is the Founder and Director of the Institute for Global Prosperity and the Chair in Culture, Philosophy and Design at University College London. Ongoing research interests in globalisation, mass migration, gender, social transformation and livelihood strategies, new technologies and agroecology have shaped her career and her engagement with policy making: igpdirector@ucl.ac.uk

Juan M. Moreno is a Research Fellow at the Institute for Global Prosperity at University College London, and at the Values and Sustainability Research Group at University of Brighton. Juan Manuel has an interdisciplinary and cross-sectoral background in history, political science, international migration, community development and humanitarian work. His research experience and interests bring together memory, oral history, socio-political analysis, shared values, social justice and community resilience: juan_m_moreno@outlook.com

MONOGRAPH SERIES

The Sociological Review Monographs
2022, Vol. 70(2) 116–137
© The Author(s) 2022
Article reuse guidelines:
sagepub.com/journals-permissions
DOI: 10.1177/00380261221084780
journals.sagepub.com/home/sor

Implicated by scale: Anthropochemicals and the experience of ecology

Dimitris Papadopoulos
Institute for Science and Society, School of Sociology and Social Policy, University of Nottingham, UK

Abstract
If our worlds are unimaginable, or, ironically, perhaps even unsustainable without anthropogenic chemicals, what does it mean to live and navigate the toxic regime, this historical moment where human-made substances are so entangled with ecologies and societies that a clean up and an 'after' to our polluted worlds is almost unthinkable? Anthropogenic chemicals are produced and used at such scale that humans need a tremendous scale of alternative chemicals to replace them. Scale, the organising principle of growth, is the source of ecological degradation and, simultaneously, is a necessary component of many remediation attempts. As life is becoming more and more chemical, chemical practice is gradually becoming conscious of its flagrant disregard of its own ecological boundaries. The attempt to restore a holistic experience of ecology shapes many current attempts to develop alternative chemical practices. When chemical practice becomes obliged by ecology to respond to the environmental crisis, the search for a different approach to scale emerges. With obligation comes the quest for reparation, both as repair and as compensation for the social and ecological damage done.

Keywords
chemical pollution, ecological experience, limits of growth, material milieu, production scale, reparation ecology, science and technology

Being implicated: Anthropochemicals

In the print *Peace Through Chemistry* (1970), Roy Lichtenstein depicts a tree branch along test tubes and microscopes to mix cubism, art moderne, pop art and the scale of muralism into a promise and a vision for science's contribution to peace. Peace is something that very few would associate with chemistry, even in the 1970s where the

Corresponding author:
Dimitris Papadopoulos, Institute for Science and Society, School of Sociology and Social Policy, University of Nottingham, University Park, Nottingham, NG7 2RD, UK.
Email: dimitris.papadopoulos@nottingham.ac.uk

creation of new synthetic compounds and materials corroborated the rise of consumerism and the plastic culture. Lichtenstein's *Peace Through Chemistry* feels more in line with the extensive and carefully planned public relations, press and international diplomacy campaign of the US government to ease people's and allies' Cold War anxieties (Orr, 2006) and simultaneously to prepare the build-up of the US nuclear weapons arsenal – a campaign that was marked by President Eisenhower's UN General Assembly speech *Atoms for Peace* in 1953. One wonders if Lichtenstein was ironical in his apotheosis of science and in elevating chemistry to a guarantor of peace just eight years after the publication of Rachel Carson's *Silent Spring* (1962) and in a historical moment where the US military was deploying extensive chemical warfare in Vietnam and was spraying Agent Orange across Southeast Asia to destroy forests, crops, livelihoods and people. As much as the promise of chemistry might be detached from the reality of chemical substances, in today's environmental conditions this statement appears more pertinent than ever; it becomes in fact an imperative for action and an imperative for transformation.

We can turn the title of this series of lithographs and say that if there is no peace through chemistry then there will not be any. From plastics to endocrine and hormone disrupting compounds, from the depletion of rare earth metals to persistent environmental pollutants, from the multiplication of public health hazards to the decline of food pollinating insects, anthropogenic chemicals pose a vital challenge to social and ecological worlds. The embeddedness of human-made chemicals in modern societies and in industry is so deep that we can talk of the anthropogenic chemicalisation of the social and natural world (Barry, 2005; Bensaude-Vincent & Stengers, 1996; Fortun, 2014). Anthropochemicals, all these human-made synthetic substances that reign over our everyday lives and environments, have become the most visible and ubiquitous marker of industrial humanity as a geological agent (Masco, 2021) investigated by the Working Group on the Anthropocene (Zalasiewicz et al., 2011, 2016). Fewer than 10% of all human-made chemicals are environmentally, socially or clinically benign, leading to detrimental problems on a planetary scale (Boudia et al., 2018; Sanderson & Anastas, 2011). Anthropochemicals protract life for some and administer death to others; they secure life and they let die. In contemporary Global North societies, the production of life truly relies on chemicals. More than 95% of all manufactured products contain some form of synthetic chemicals. Life and death is governed through anthropochemicals.

Anthropochemicals reveal the differential effect that the sourcing, production, use or afterlife of manufactured chemicals has on certain social groups and on certain places and its human and nonhuman inhabitants rather than other. It is to say that securing life today for some populations cannot happen without letting other populations die. There is a planetary system of production, circulation, application and disposal of chemicals that imposes the effects of toxicity and pollution more on certain places and social segments than others (Bullard, 1994; Davies, 2018; Nixon, 2011). Race, class and geographical location are vectors that navigate how environmental damage is attached only to certain places and people. 'People are struggling to breathe, and more so in some places than others', as Kim Fortun says (Fortun, 2014, p. 326; Nunn, 2018; Roberts et al., 2008).

But things are perhaps even more complicated as the interrelatedness of life and death does not only affect differentially and disproportionately certain groups of humans and nonhumans but increasingly most human and nonhuman bodies as many substances have planetary reach and simultaneously sustain and cause bodily harm. Security and risk, invigoration and destruction coincide in human bodies, our neighbourhoods, our ecologies, our worlds. The pervasiveness of anthropochemicals implicates social groups and places which otherwise seem less vulnerable than those which are disproportionately affected by toxicity and pollution.

Despite this inextricable link between chemicals, ecologies and societies, there is a broad underlying assumption that anthropochemicals can be eventually detached and the social and political body can be "purified". There is a widespread belief that our societies can be separated from the toxic chemicals that they produce. There is often an implicit assumption to this belief: that the proliferation of anthropochemicals is primarily the outcome of economic interests. Chemicals have been simultaneously the source and the product that drives multiple operations in human production systems. The consequence of this approach is that the current capitalist mode of production is elevated to a singular historical subject of agency that has the capacity to adopt (or ideally reject) the production and use of harmful substances. Chemicals are implicitly conceived here as both constraints of human action and simultaneously as action enabling tools that can be discarded if the system would decide to do so. These two poles represent two widespread popular understandings of science and technology that have been extensively discussed within Science and Technology Studies: technoscientific determinism on the one hand and the political determination of technology on the other (for a discussion of both see Winner, 1980; Wyatt, 2008). Common to both is that knowledges, materials and technologies – including anthropogenic chemicals that I discuss in this paper – are made to be the mere object of human will. Within this unreflectively humanist and anthropocentric view of our worlds, materials and technologies represent the ontologisation of will.

Anthropochemicals are so deeply and inextricably linked to human societies that the idea that they can be simply disengaged from human bodies, human technologies and ecologies by some form of global political will is evidently impossible. But even if in a thought experiment human societies would be able to arrive at a global decision to eradicate harmful chemicals, they would be faced with the insurmountable problem of the mundane spread of chemicals: technoscientific objects, the bio- and geosphere, and human everyday life are linked to each other in ways that are ungraspable and, indeed, ungovernable by human politics whether there is political will or not. Anthropogenic molecules are produced in so many different multifaceted processes and contexts that rather than being explainable through an economistic approach to the current mode of production, they can perhaps help us explain the function and system of production itself. When it comes to chemicals, the capitalist mode of production is not the explanans but the explanandum.

Anthropochemicals implicate us because they cut across and reconfigure power divides, social asymmetries, political injustices, ecological imbalances, and material conflicts in multiple ways (Papadopoulos et al., 2021). As much as chemicals are a core component of the supply chains and production networks of contemporary Global North societies, they are also intrinsic to many material, cultural, psychosocial and biosocial ways of being that cannot be disentangled from one another. Anthropochemicals implicate humans because they enable them in so many ways that they are impossible to be dissociated from their damaging effects. Almost every anthropochemical is simultaneously enabling and damaging. This entanglement is relentless and there is no possibility of erasing the presence of chemicals in our societies. So, what is the escape route from this unavoidable grip of human societies by chemicals? Anthropochemicals implicate us and we need to remake them differently in order to escape them. We escape with them rather than from them. In a sense the antidote to chemicals are chemicals. A utopian scenario would be a radical programme for replacing all current chemicals with fully benign substances and this can be a programme that starts from the individual level through the community level all the way to societal governance. It has become impossible to maintain life without anthropochemicals. In these conditions the transition to anthropogenic benign chemicals has become an imperative (Anastas & Zimmerman, 2018).

In what follows I want to discuss the condition of being implicated by anthropochemicals and the imperative to replace harmful substances with sustainable and benign chemicals through the problem of growth and scale. The scale of production and use of harmful chemicals is intimately linked to the continuous growth of human societies. A no growth alternative appears to be the only reasonable solution. However, the size of any programme that would materialise the transition to sustainable and benign chemicals requires a transformation of such a scale that complicates the polarity between growth and no growth. What is an appropriate scale of change that can enable the social transformation towards sustainable chemicals? How can we imagine our present otherwise and our worlds composed differently (Savransky, 2021b) when a clean up of our damaged ecologies and an 'after' to our polluted environments is impossible? In the following section I will discuss how the problematic of scale complicates our understanding of growth and questions the binary growth/no growth. In the third section I will move to explore how scale is embedded in an ecological milieu and how the experience of ecology can drive the reparation of damaged environments. Finally, in the concluding section I will introduce some alterative conceptualisations of scale that may contribute to a discussion of the transition to sustainable and benign chemicals.

The problematic of scale and the double limits of growth

In practices that involve chemicals everything is about scale. Scale embodies the powers and the pitfalls of chemistry and although it is probably true that there is chemistry without scale, it also true that there cannot be modern chemistry without scale (Bensaude-Vincent, 2013; Bensaude-Vincent & Simon, 2008; Klein, 2005; Lefèvre & Klein, 2007). The difference is minimal and yet has considerable implications. Modern chemistry is predicated on the *imperative of transcendence*: Transcending the obstacles in the manufacturing of a molecule in order to make it widely accessible. The drive for transcendence makes modern chemistry a typical technoscience. In the technosciences the main concern is to overcome the concrete barriers that emerge in the making of novel substances, materials or technologies and then step by step, challenge by challenge, obstacle by obstacle to scale them up through the manufacturing process so that they circulate through economy, society, and everyday life. In the technosciences, and of course in modern chemistry as one of them, the loops between research and potential applications, between knowing and making, between the multiple human and nonhuman actors that participate in the creation of science, and between research experimentation, technological design, the production process and everyday life are short and polyvalent (Bensaude-Vincent, 2013; Bensaude-Vincent & Loeve, 2018; Haraway, 1997; Ihde & Selinger, 2003; Ravetz, 2006).

As much as modern chemistry is driven by the imperative of transcendence it is also an empirical-practical science. Transcendence is resolved and achieved on each singular specific step along the way from making a novel substance to its application; and if it is not achieved within each step then transcendence collapses: the molecule is no longer produced and vanishes into the scientific archive, research papers or engineering logbooks. The empiricism of modern chemistry lies with the fact that it solves the challenges and obstacles it encounters always internally. It does not follow an external plan or grand theory but a myriad of mundane attempts to negotiate and settle uncertainties, complications, and difficulties that emerge at every specific step in the making and production of a molecule. Paradoxically the imperative of transcendence is always dealt with immanently. Modern chemistry is a radically empiricist science that constantly strives to transcend the scale of what it makes.

Between 2019 and 2022 I conducted as a Leverhulme Fellow an ethnographic fieldwork study on the emergence on green and sustainable chemistry. When I mentioned the empirical nature of modern chemistry to a leading chemist on 'catalyst discovery', he said: 'if you read an academic paper in chemistry it makes it sound as though it's all worked out that we had some hypothesis, we had some target molecule we were doing and we went in there and did it and of course it virtually never happens like that, . . . we may have a process in mind and we design a catalyst we think is going to work and you know, part of that is calculation and part of it of what people have done before but you know, more than half of it is just our intuition for it kind of this feels like it might be the right thing to do and most of the time they don't work and so what do we then? Well certainly what we do in my group is say "Okay, well it's not worked for this process but why don't we try it for this or why don't we try it for that?"' (Field interview B331). And as much as this mundane empiricism is what constitutes research in chemistry, the drive and challenge is to scale up the production of molecules. The same scientist told me: 'as scientists we can keep discovering new, interesting things and, you know, new specific transformations, new solvents. Of course, there are scientific challenges in this, you know, I've mentioned one, to develop catalysts that are tolerant of the sort of feed stocks we'd want from biomass. But I think those scientific challenges are less important than the challenge of scaling some of this up, of getting genuine investment in this and having real commercial technology that we can use as an exemplar for the success of this area, the sort of thing that you can show the Minister around to show that this is really delivering for the UK economy and delivering for sustainability and is based on fundamental science that was developed in the UK. I think if we can do that to champion the area then that's more important than the scientific challenges that remain' (Field interview B331).

'Was the reaction atom economic?' (Field interview C328); 'Do you need to get a pure chemical from this process?' (Field interview Y313); 'How many kilograms of waste per kilogram of product does the reaction generate?' (Field interview A334-5); 'How much do we reduce energy consumption by using supercritical CO^2?' (Field interview N330); 'What are these products in the material that we discovered through chromatography and that were not there before?' (Field interview C328); 'How can we minimise the variability of the feedstock?' (Field interview Y371); 'How can I reduce the steps of the reaction?' (Field interview C350); 'How are you going to control the heat of the reaction?' (Field interview B332); 'Do I know enough about the calorimetry and the kinetics of my new polymer forming reaction so that it can scaled up later?' (Field interview N367); 'How can we reduce the size of the reactor to increase safety and efficiency?' (Field interview N402); 'Is there a way that you can redesign a reaction to use an alternative greener solvent?' (Field interview L319) – these are just a few questions extracted from conversations during the lab fieldwork that I conducted as part of the research study I mentioned earlier that exemplify the inherent issues that emerge in each specific step of the invention process of a molecule all the way to its wider manufacturing and point towards the empiricism of modern chemistry. With Deleuze and Guattari (1994, p. 47) we could say that this is a radical empiricism: 'When immanence is no longer immanent to something other than itself it is possible to speak of a plane of immanence. Such a plane is, perhaps, a radical empiricism.' But this radical empiricism of modern chemistry is always paired with the drive to scale up. Scalability is transcendence and transcendence means moving beyond the inherent limits of a specific reaction on a specific scale by staying within the given constraints of this specific scale and overcoming the obstacles that emerge within it. In modern chemistry the immanence of research materialises transcendence and manifests scale.

It is this riddling and improbable coexistence of transcendence and immanence that necessitates to reconsider what is scale in modern chemistry. Scale here does not only mean measure (of volume, mass, intensity, quality or value) but also refers to a specific plane on which research is undertaken and issues are resolved. This plane of immanence of every specific scale in the life of a molecule constitutes the *ecological milieu* that sustains a molecule of a certain quantity and the actual process of its making. On each and every level of scale in the life of a molecule a different ecological and material milieu either secures its further existence or is unable to create the right order and terminates the potential of a molecule to become widely accessible across society leaving only a traceable existence in chemistry research papers and perhaps the process design briefs of engineers.

Consider the case of the urgently needed transition to safe alternatives of hazardous solvents – the non-active substances in countless commercial and industrial solutions – which introduces a series of complex social and material issues at each one of the different phases of their development (Jessop, 2016; Poliakoff & Licence, 2015). For example, the alternative solvent dihydrolevoglucosenone which was invented at the Green Chemistry Centre of Excellence, University of York (Clarke et al., 2018) is a novel compound derived from biomass and food waste that could be used as replacement for NMP, a widely used organic compound which is a known substance of very high concern because of its environmental and health safety effects. The conditions that the novel alternative solvent assembles around itself when created at labscale are very different from the conditions of the compound at demonstrator or production scale. As the compound changes scale a very different set of issues and actors sustain its existence. As dihydrolevoglucosenone moves to production scale issues of standardisation, toxicity metrics, public regulation, innovations in process engineering, industrial entrepreneurship, economic and financial viability and, perhaps most importantly, the sustainable access to biomass become crucial dimensions of its existence. As waste and biomass become a valuable resource in their own right (Dugmore et al., 2017; Poliakoff et al., 2002; Sheldon, 2007; Tuck et al., 2012) a series of questions about a holistic approach to value emerge (Gupta et al., 2018) that encompass the sourcing of feedstocks, energy efficiency, and the afterlife of the solvents (Caillol, 2013; Clark et al., 2016; Kümmerer, 2007).

Every step in changing the scalability of a chemical, every step in extending its scale does not only involve the modification of measure but also the immanent alteration of its ecological milieu. Thus, even if scale appears to be an extension of a linear progressive system of classification it necessitates something much more diverse and complex in order to exist: it necessitates a whole ecology of practices (Stengers, 2021), processes and objects that allow a molecule to exist within the ecological milieu of a specific scale. Such ecologies are complex arrangements that involve a multiplicity of human actors, engineers, chemists, local communities, governing bodies and regulatory authorities, industry and, of course, a multiplicity of nonhuman actors, objects, landscapes, and other species.

Scale is crucial for chemical practice because for the 'same' compound in different measures there is a very different ecology that is involved. Depending on how much this ecological question of scale becomes considered or is erased, the transition to sustainable and benign compounds that incorporate such ecological concerns becomes a more or less urgent question. Scale is, as I mentioned earlier, crucial for the making of modern and contemporary chemistry, but the problematisation of scale is even more crucial for creating alternative green and sustainable compounds. Throughout my fieldwork in green chemistry labs and within the extensive series of interviews with preeminent green and sustainable chemists[1] scale appears as one of the most salient and equally controversial dimensions for green and sustainable chemical practice. What kind of scale do we need? How much of it and how? But probably one thing that seemed to represent most if not all the positions is that there cannot be change in chemistry without scale. So, scale appears to be both the problem and the solution.

So, how much scale do we need to change things? What is the scale of chemicals that is needed if chemicals always implicate us? The problem with scale is that it is an ambivalent concept, we need scale to encounter the depth and width of ecological destruction and simultaneously we know that scale is the engine of productionism and productionism drives growth which is a major cause of ecological destruction. In a shortcut, scale is linked to destruction. And yet, there is something plausible about scale: without scale there is very limited scope for meaningful ecological change. Scale is an ordinary concept as it speaks to a sense of planetary belonging that corresponds to the need of a significant politics of scale to reduce carbon emissions, reverse geo- and biodiversity loss, eliminate pollution and toxicity, and instigate transformative societal programmes.

The urgency of a transition to green and sustainable chemicals exemplifies this Janus-faced meaning of scale: scale is tightly connected to environmental destruction but it is also an indispensable component of environmental action for avoiding catastrophic futures. Within social thought approaches to scale tend to conceive it as a theoretical problem, in fact as something that might not even exist as such. Strathern (2000), Bruun Jensen (2015) and others, for example, make the case that rather than nesting scales we have fractal environments whose complexity is scale invariant as they incorporate many different qualities that traditionally belong to different scales. Tsing (2012, 2015) goes a step further and elevates scalability to a device that performs domination and ultimately social and ecological destruction. Thinking scale with chemicals complicates these approaches: toxic, hazardous and primarily petrobased anthropochemicals are produced and used at such scale that we need a tremendous economy of scale of alternative chemicals in order to replace them. Scale = ecological degradation. Simultaneously: no scale, no ecological transition. As much as scale is historically and geopolitically embedded in a certain form of social organisation, it now exceeds this determination to manifest itself ontologically in the degradation of our ecologies and, simultaneously, in any vision of ecological transition.

Rather than a single issue to be decided for or against, this ontological pervasiveness and inherent ambivalence of scale makes it a problematic (Leistert & Schrickel, 2020; Savransky, 2020): Scale is the organising principle of ecological degradation and simultaneously it is a necessary component of many reparation and remediation attempts. Without some form of scale there is no possibility to confront the extent to which anthropogenic chemicals pervade everything. The fact that human societies are so deeply implicated by chemicals renders this ambivalence of scale all the more present and, indeed, vital. It is this link to the vital threats but also vital possibilities that scale incorporates that makes it so valuable for political strategists of every kind and taste who try to harness current widespread environmental unease and respond to today's ecological urgency: First, those who use scale as a proxy to revolutionary system-wide change in order to overcome capitalist productionism and only alleviate ecological damage afterwards; second, those ultra-neoliberals who use scale to instigate new modes of value creation that largely ignore or are opportunistic towards ecological damage and environmental change; third, those statists who need scale to preserve the elitist make-up of liberal Global North societies through the implementation of a technofix-driven green deal; and fourth, those autocrats and regressive nationalists who use scale to consolidate and expand their power by negating the environmental effects of scale altogether. The ambivalence of scale makes it easily compatible with so many divergent approaches: the revolutionaries, the neoliberals, the liberals, the autocrats (Ghelfi & Papadopoulos, 2022b). And, of course, this ambivalence pertains also to a fifth group: those who refuse to engage with scale altogether because of the danger of co-option. In this view current societies cannot but appropriate scale to reinforce existing power asymmetries and thus any thinking of scale is impossible even if, paradoxically, we think with the notion of scale to describe the grave social and environmental problems that we encounter. In all these five very different positions, the problematic of scale is that you need it but when you have it, it undermines transformational socio-ecological change.

We are implicated by scale both in its destructive pervasiveness and its promissory capacities. This duplicitous character of scale emanates from its deep attachment to economic growth as the single most powerful driver of environmental destruction. But the problematic of scale complicates our relation to growth when it comes to ecological questions today and, in particular, to the pervasiveness of harmful chemicals which is the focus of this article. The scale of toxic chemicals and the scale of alternative benign chemicals that are needed to reduce further ecological degradation sit uneasily with both, the celebration of growth and its outright dismissal. Being implicated by scale means that chemicals and materials production cannot be just stopped, they need to be replaced with other chemicals even if slow growth or degrowth were possible. Growth together with scale are at the heart of the problem of the proliferation of harmful anthropochemicals and simultaneously they need to play a key role in their replacement.

From a materialist perspective on anthropochemicals, limitless growth and no growth, fast and slow, large scale and small scale become impossible to be decided in practical terms, they are 'infernal alternatives' (Pignarre & Stengers, 2011). The category of growth is too universal to be encountered. Its absence mirrors the universality of its presence. If its presence is associated with ecological degradation and loss of nonhuman life, its absence is imposed on those who already feel its destructive consequences: disadvantaged and marginalised social groups, the Global South and large ecosystems and other species. While growth is unevenly and unequally distributed across different regions and spaces of the planet, imposed economic no growth has similar devastating social and ecological consequences to the places that experience it. Steady growth has been always a historical exception reserved for small parts of the Global North and an often vacant promise for so many other places, while the absence of growth or imposed no growth has been the norm for large parts of the Global South and occasionally also in certain parts of the Global North.

The limits of growth extend in two directions: there is always too much growth and there is not enough to prevent conflict and decay. We are in a moment in which growth brings environmental and social destruction and when it slows down it brings pain, deep social conflicts (that on many occasions release fascist-oriented political movements) and ecological destruction (Ghelfi & Papadopoulos, 2022b). From the perspective of chemicals, the absence of growth does not lead to the absence of harmful substances but to the continuation of their proliferation: two literally 'infernal' alternatives. When it comes to chemicals the absence of growth does not mean no growth and reduction of ecological impact, it means a regress to a form of chemical practice and production that continues to neglect its ecological obligations. Scale as well as no scale, growth as well as no growth constitute a negation of the ecological embeddedness of anthropochemicals and their production, use and disposal.

The bifurcation of ecological experience and ecological reparation

I mentioned earlier in the article that scale is not just about measure but about the incorporation of the ecological context into the life of a molecule. When scale/no scale become the only two existing options mirroring the infernal alternatives of growth/no growth, what suffers is the ecological milieu that houses scale. What does the loss of ecology specifically mean in the binary opposition between scale/no scale and growth/no growth? The loss of ecology involves the loss of the continuity between the many distinct registers that constitute what the ecological is: (1) the epistemic register of ecology as a scientific discipline;[2] (2) the ontic register, referring to the relations and becomings among beings doing life together; (3) the lived register of the everyday experience of rootedness and belonging in our surroundings and the embodied understanding of our worldly connections with different beings and spaces; (4) the economic register, which approaches ecology through the lens of value and conceives ecosystems as distinct worldly productive entities; (5) the political register, which involves a multiplicity of social movements and a long tradition of environmental activism and ecological mobilisations; (6) and, finally, the cultural register, from ecological urbanism to the alternative cultures of rural resurgence, from environmental fine art photography to ecopoetry, from ecology as a mode of thought to ecology as a method of enquiry.

All these registers together constitute ecology as experience, a 'general ecology' (Hoerl & Burton, 2017), that is generative (Figueroa Sarriera & Gray, 2016) of experiences and social relations that put the ecological at the heart of worldly existence. The general experience of ecology is not to harmonise the relations between all these different registers that are often in conflict with each other. Rather, in line with an ecosophical approach in Guattari's (1995, p. 91) terms, this is an attempt for a 'generalised ecology' that tries to articulate and re-articulate 'scientific, political, environmental and mental ecologies' (1995, p. 134; see also Hoerl, 2013). Guattari's ecosophical project of a generalised ecology echoes Bateson's (1972) holistic and relational approach to how human mind, technology and the environment are inseparably entwined. There is no dominant subjectivity here, there is no primacy of the human, the socio-technical or the environmental. They all exist on the same plane and constitute the continuous experience of ecology. Such an a-subjective approach breaks away from humanist understandings of the ecological that see humans realising themselves if only they abandon technology, enlarge their identification with broader ecologies, and reinstall a harmony with the natural world – such as in deep ecology accounts in Fox (1990), Mathews (1991) and Naess (1973) (for a discussion see Bogue, 2009; Braidotti, 2006).

Guattari's ecosophical approach is about how the uneasy and conflictual dynamics of the relations between humans, societies, technologies and ecologies create an everyday 'continuous experience' (Stephenson & Papadopoulos, 2006) of ecology (see also Brown & Stenner, 2009; Brown et al., 2011; Schraube & Højholt, 2016). When the continuous experience of ecology is split, ecology is dominated by one singular register. A holistic and continuous experience of ecology is a quest rather than a given. It almost feels an impossibility in today's social and environmental conditions in which ecology bifurcates to different registers. Similar to Whitehead's (1964) 'bifurcation of nature', which laments how modern thought splits the experience of the world into primary qualities – objective and scientific – and secondary qualities – psychological and cultural – (Debaise, 2017; Goffey, 2008; Haas, 2018; Halewood, 2012), the bifurcation of ecology splits the experience, practice and process of ecology into a series of dualisms between distinct registers, each one of them operating independently and often against each other.

The chasm between these different ecological registers shapes the perception of the world excluding or even actively erasing other ecological registers and making certain registers appear as facts. As Whitehead argued: 'The world is not merely physical, nor is it merely mental. Nor is it merely one with many subordinate phases. Nor is it merely a complete fact, in its essence static with the illusion of change. Wherever a vicious dualism appears, it is by reason of mistaking an abstraction for a final concrete fact' (A. N. Whitehead, 1967, p. 190). The lived ecological register during a countryside hike might be experienced as opposite to the political domain for environmental justice, the ontic register of cohabitation of a certain terrain might be experienced as irrelevant to the economic productivity of its ecosystems, and so on. Accepting the current scale of environmental destruction is only possible because of the bifurcation of ecology as different ecologies diverge from each other. The restoration of a general and generative experience of ecology remains a quest that is gradually becoming the drive of many contemporary social movements (Ghelfi & Papadopoulos, 2022a, 2022b).

Anthropochemicals have been a matter of concern for many decades now but it is only recently that they have also become the site of a promise, even if only a minor one. What if the chemicals humans create and use can be made differently? What if we look for substances that are less harmful outside of chemical science? What if chemistry itself can transform to become aware and incorporate its ecological milieu in its own making? Against the imperative of transcendence and the loss of the continuous experience of ecology there is a multitude of attempts to bypass the double impasse of the scale/no scale binary and to explore how chemistry can gravitate around a general ecology: from green and sustainable chemistry to the amateur science of alternative chemical practices, from traditional knowledge systems to community technoscience, chemicals increasingly become a site for experimentation with their ecological implications.

Chemicals become obliged by ecology. Puig de la Bellacasa (2015; 2017, pp. 150ff.) highlights that obligation is not only about a sense of moral responsibility but it primarily involves a practical-material dimension and the urgency for action: being obliged by ecology means that one has no choice but to care for and repair the ecologies one is part of. A wide range of community projects, social movements and environmental justice campaigns move beyond their single focus on protest politics to engage with transforming the materialities in which they find themselves. This multitude of 'more-than-social movements' (Ghelfi & Papadopoulos, 2022a; Papadopoulos, 2018) practise ecological reparation both as repair of damaged ecologies and claiming reparations for the ecological wrongdoings that these human communities and the nonhuman worlds in which they exist have suffered (Papadopoulos et al., 2022). They move beyond more visible institutionalised forms of reconciliation and state reparation – such as large scale compensation policies, formal exchanges between representatives of conflict groups, widespread provision of psychosocial assistance, ceremonial commemorations – to instigate forms of reparation that attempt to restore the cohabitation of the human and the nonhuman world (Cadieux et al., 2019; Cairns, 2003; Caney, 2006; Hale et al., 2014). Inspired by reparative justice (Macleod, 2019; Mora-Gámez, 2016; Perez Murcia, 2013; Walker, 2010; White, 2016), ecological reparation redirects reparations to the repair of interspecies and human–nonhuman relations damaged by racism, extractivism and environmental injustice. Repair is a vital process within ecological reparation (Darwish, 2013; Denis, 2019; Jackson, 2014; Tacchetti et al., 2022): repair as the unfolding of relations, movements and interconnections among diverse humans and nonhumans in the patching up and reclaiming of damaged socio-environmental ecological niches.

Conclusion: Scaling out

So, this is my question: growth aside, what do we do with the planetary and social boundaries to scale that we are currently facing? There are many different conceptualisations of planetary boundaries (e.g. Diamond et al., 2015; Rockström et al., 2009) that point towards the necessity for a different practice of scale. Neither as an answer to growth nor as an alternative to it but because the presence of growth has made any meaningful engagement with social and planetary boundaries impossible. Rather than embracing any of these impossible alternatives that I mentioned earlier, many social movements attempt to create conditions for establishing their own boundaries and installing their own scales (Kallis, 2019), and to become attentive to practices and stories beyond the dominance of growth (Calvário et al., 2022; Savransky, 2021a). The process of constructing these adequate scales is a process of *commoning* the boundaries of socio-ecological life: instead of adopting some external imposed boundaries, many communities negotiate and, most importantly, practise other scales that ascertain ecological boundaries to communal life. This is eco-commoning – groups of humans and nonhumans make and uphold communally maintained spaces and ecologies in order to reclaim and repair damaged ecologies (Bresnihan, 2013; Castellano, 2017; Ghelfi, 2015; Linebaugh, 2008, 2010; Papadopoulos & Puig de la Bellacasa, 2022; Papadopoulos et al., 2022; Reid & Taylor, 2010; Wall, 2014).

There are many examples of such initiatives that often involve experimenting with alternative materials, substances and anthropochemicals. Consider for example urban experimental eco-living (Pickerill, 2020), the creation of community managed localised infrastructural provision (Hodson et al., 2018), alternative energy supply (Angel, 2017), applied degrowth campaigns (D'Alisa, 2015; Demaria et al., 2013; M. Whitehead, 2013), indigenous forms of eco-social life (Mander & Tauli-Corpuz, 2006; Whyte, 2018), post-developmental politics (Escobar, 2015), urban farms (Salvatore Engel-Di Mauro, 2022), environmental justice campaigns (Agyeman et al., 2016; Bullard & Wright, 2009; Dillon, 2014), ecological activism (Gatt, 2017), maker movements (Ottinger & Cohen, 2011), decolonial ecologies (Ferdinand, 2019), post-capitalist economies (Gibson-Graham, 2006), transition towns (Hopkins, 2011), food sovereignty movements (Shattuck et al., 2017), permaculture gardens (Mars et al., 2016), commons transition (P2P Foundation, 2015), climate urbanism (Bulkeley, 2015), environmental citizenship (Dobson & Bell, 2006), social and solidarity economies (Utting, 2015), bioregeneration (Darwish, 2013), the peasant confederation La Via Campesina and agroecology (Rosset, 2017). What is common to all these very diverse examples is that they establish their own planetary and ecological boundaries as they engage in the ecological reparation of the spaces that they inhabit and maintain.

Ecological reparation is inspired by the practices of these and many other social movements that operate with, within and often against instituted technoscience by engaging with the double bind of scale: for many of these movements scale is not about replicating and multiplying the same type of action in order to create change. Rather it is about engaging with the challenge of ecological reparation and developing alternative ontological conditions of existence, *alterontologies* (Papadopoulos, 2018), on the terrain on which each one of these movements and communities live. Rather than copying and repeating the same practice to scale it up, alterontologies proliferate in intensive ways on the everyday life of communities. Experimentalism is not about replication – something already discussed extensively in Science and Technology Studies (Collins, 1985; Hacking, 1983; Knorr-Cetina & Mulkay, 1983). For replication to happen and to create scale a process of delocalisation and the erasure of the ecological milieu is necessary – something that I have discussed earlier in this article in the case of modern chemistry as the imperative of transcendence. Operationalise, purify and transcend many of the actual conditions that made the experiment possible. Scale becomes a model that dominates many locales.

Scaling *out* promotes an alternative approach to scale as replication and domination: different alterontological experiments emerge in different communities and many of these despite their significant differences align with each other to practise ecological reparation and create alternatives on the ground. Consider for example the repair and remediation of chemically polluted ecosystems, in particular through bioremediation technologies. Bioremediation is typically conceived as 'a *natural process*, which relies on bacteria, fungi (mycoremediation), and plants (phytoremediation) to degrade, break down, transform, and/or essentially remove contaminants, ensuring the conservation of the ecosystem biophysical properties' (Masciandaro et al., 2013, p. 399). Other similar definitions emphasise '*harnessing* the degradative potential of biological systems' (Cummings, 2010, p. v). Bioremediation relies on the processes of a nonhuman world: 'Without the activity of microorganisms, the earth would literally be buried in wastes, and the nutrients necessary for life would be locked up in detritus' (Bonete et al., 2015, p. 24). Therefore the use of bioremediation techniques is often seen as 'working with nature' – a trope shared by grassroots, scientific and industrial bioremediation projects (Bharagava, 2017).

Yet bioremediation technologies are not 'natural' or merely 'biological' but naturecultural and socio-technical. They integrate sophisticated lab-based research and applied environmental biotechnology to accelerate the degradation of polluting contaminants. While industrial bioremediation is often based on a clean up and leave approach neglecting follow up and community maintenance as well as the wider effects on local environments and other species, community supported bioremediation projects are not only about cleaning up contaminants but a way of reintegrating anthropogenic chemical practice – including labouring, affective and ethical aspects – in natural cycles by collaborating across different actors and species (Puig de la Bellacasa, 2021). Reparative alterontological bioremediation projects are always situated and context specific and involve interspecies relations of care while simultaneously relying on the circulation of translocal bioremediation knowledge and practice (Darwish, 2013; Hartigan, 2015; Paxson & Helmreich, 2013; Puig de la Bellacasa, 2010, 2012, 2017).

The ecological reparation of such experiments is not to return back to a state free of anthropochemicals. There is no restoration of a prior state of being; neither is it possible to compensate for the damage that anthropochemicals cause on humans, nonhuman others and the environment. Ecological reparation here means creating alterontologies driven by the continuous experience of general ecology. Ecological reparation is experimenting with chemical substances that install a different lived experience of ecological cohabitation. Are these alterontological practices enough to create sweeping societal change? Perhaps at some point, but possibly not. They are enough though to defend and maintain the life of communities facing social-ecological conflict and destruction. Alterontologies are not the same as prefigurative politics that aim to realise some parts of the desired future in the present (Chatterton & Pickerill, 2010; Graziano, 2016; Pickerill & Chatterton, 2006; van de Sande, 2013). Alterontologies do not primarily point towards some sort of other global politics of transformation to come. There is no 'post' in alterontological politics. Their intensive and experimental material engagements in the present is all there is.

Scaling out involves considering the ecological in many different locales, starting from the green and sustainable research in chemistry science labs and in chemical engineering workshops and moving to a multitude of transformative engagements with anthropogenic chemicals in a plethora of spaces outside of the instituted science of chemistry itself. Chemical practice becomes dispersed in society: the creation of 'translocal infrastructures' (Ghelfi & Papadopoulos, 2022a) and the 'distributed invention power' (Papadopoulos, 2018, p. 182) of amateur scientists, indigenous knowledge practitioners, clandestine chemists, DIY biochemists, researchers in green and sustainable chemistry, remediation ecologists, biodegradable designs, underground labs, interspecies collaborations; entheogens and healing compounds, ethnobotanical knowledges and kitchen chemistries, baking bread, making beer, mattering compost; making amateur-led pollution sensing devices, monitoring chemical toxicity, creating vocabularies, images and stories to capture life in contaminated worlds, doing independent chemical experimental lab work, incorporating green chemistry within citizen science – generative chemical practice as an integral part of technoscience that travels and connects the lab, the engineering bench and community projects. Amateur and professional chemical practitioners create alternative ontologies, alterontologies, on the molecular level. There is a dense traffic between the scaling-up practices of instituted technoscience such as green and sustainable chemistry on the one hand and the scaling-out practices of community-based generative chemical practice on the other hand. Rather than opposition and exclusion, instituted green and sustainable chemistry is one of the currents that are necessary for scaling out chemical practice horizontally as they challenge established research norms and customs within chemistry itself. The proliferation of distributed transformative practices through community specificity, material singularity and practical concreteness is what creates change: many alterontological practices. Change, even if minor, emerges from creating alternative ways of existence obliged by the experience of ecology that give birth to novel ecologies, and possibly also to worlds that do not yet exist (Lundy, 2019). The political significance of alterontological chemical practices emerges from the fact that they engage technoscience and other traditional forms of knowledge to secure communal life in midst of socio-ecological conflict.

Funding

I would like to gratefully acknowledge the support of the Leverhulme Trust, UK (grant number RF-2018-338\4) as well as the Biotechnology and Biological Sciences Research Council (BBSRC), UK (grant number BB/W01453X/1 and grant number BB/L013940/1) and the Engineering and Physical Sciences Research Council (EPSRC), UK (grant number BB/L013940/1).

Notes

1. Within the discipline of chemistry itself we have for example green and sustainable chemistry that emerged in the 1990s and aimed to create waste-free, non-toxic, low impact chemical compounds (Anastas & Warner, 1998; Clark et al., 2014; Sheldon, 2016). Rather than the common attempt to limit and regulate the handling and effects of end-of-pipe chemicals of which only very few are already environmentally friendly, green and sustainable research focuses on a 'benign by design' approach that seeks to limit or even eliminate negative environmental consequences already in the process of synthesising molecules (Sanderson & Anastas, 2011). By the end of the 1990s a series of prominent initiatives had helped establish this line of research, such as the US Environmental Protection Agency's Green Chemistry Program, the Green Chemistry Network and the associated journal of the Royal Society of Chemistry in the UK (Anastas et al., 2016; Iles, 2013; Linthorst, 2010; Woodhouse & Breyman, 2005). It is only in the end of the 2000s that the field started to have a wider impact.
2. Although it is important to highlight here that ecological science is in itself very diverse and is intimately embedded in wider ambivalent social, environmental and historical settings, with its historical beginnings linked to colonial expansion, travel writing, and assuming the world from the explorer's perspective (Ferdinand, 2019; Gómez-Barris, 2017; Pratt, 1992). The ecological sciences were invented, at least in North America, as part of a larger socio-epistemic movement that facilitated colonisation and extraction of native lands (see for example Kingsland, 2005).

References

Agyeman, J., Schlosberg, D., Craven, L., & Matthews, C. (2016). Trends and directions in environmental justice: From inequity to everyday life, community, and just sustainabilities. *Annual Review of Environment and Resources*, *41*(1), 321–340. doi:10.1146/annurev-environ-110615-090052

Anastas, P. T., Han, B., Leitner, W., & Poliakoff, M. (2016). 'Happy silver anniversary': Green Chemistry at 25. *Green Chemistry*, *18*(1), 12–13. doi:10.1039/c5gc90067k

Anastas, P. T., & Warner, J. C. (1998). *Green chemistry: Theory and practice*. Oxford University Press.

Anastas, P. T., & Zimmerman, J. B. (2018). The United Nations sustainability goals: How can sustainable chemistry contribute? *Current Opinion in Green and Sustainable Chemistry*, *13*, 150–153. doi:10.1016/j.cogsc.2018.04.017

Angel, J. (2017). Towards an energy politics in-against-and-beyond the state: Berlin's struggle for energy democracy. *Antipode*, *49*(3), 557–576. doi:10.1111/anti.12289

Barry, A. (2005). Pharmaceutical matters: The invention of informed materials. *Theory, Culture & Society*, *22*(1), 51–69. doi:10.1177/0263276405048433

Bateson, G. (1972). *Steps to an ecology of mind*. Ballantine.

Bensaude-Vincent, B. (2013). Chemistry as a technoscience? In J. Llored (Ed.), *The philosophy of chemistry: Practices, methodologies, and concepts* (pp. 330–341). Cambridge Scholars Publishing.

Bensaude-Vincent, B., & Loeve, S. (2018). Toward a philosophy of technosciences. In S. Loeve, X. Guchet, & B. Bensaude-Vincent (Eds.), *French philosophy of technology: Classical readings and contemporary approaches* (pp. 169–186). Springer.

Bensaude-Vincent, B., & Simon, J. (2008). *Chemistry: The impure science*. Imperial College Press.

Bensaude-Vincent, B., & Stengers, I. (1996). *A history of chemistry*. Harvard University Press.

Bharagava, R. N. (Ed.). (2017). *Environmental pollutants and their bioremediation approaches*. CRC Press.

Bogue, R. (2009). A thousand ecologies. In B. Herzogenrath (Ed.), *Deleuze/Guattari & ecology* (pp. 42–56). Palgrave Macmillan.

Bonete, M. J., Bautista, V., Esclapez, J., García-Bonete, M. J., Pire, C., Camacho, M., Torregrosa-Crespo, J., & Martínez-Espinosa, R. M. (2015). New uses of haloarchaeal species in bioremediation processes. In N. Shiomi (Ed.), *Advances in bioremediation of wastewater and polluted soil* (pp. 23–49). Intechopen.

Boudia, S., Creager, A. N. H., Frickel, S., Henry, E., Jas, N., Reinhardt, C., & Roberts, J. A. (2018). Residues: Rethinking chemical environments. *Engaging Science, Technology, and Society, 4*, 165–178. doi:10.17351/ests2018.245

Braidotti, R. (2006). *Transpositions: On nomadic ethics*. Polity Press.

Bresnihan, P. (2013). John Clare and the manifold commons. *Environmental Humanities, 3*, 71–91.

Brown, S. D., Cromby, J., Harper, D. J., Johnson, K., & Reavey, P. (2011). Researching 'experience': Embodiment, methodology, process. *Theory & Psychology, 21*(4), 493–515. doi:10.1177/0959354310377543

Brown, S. D., & Stenner, P. (2009). *Psychology without foundations: History, philosophy and psychosocial theory*. Sage.

Bruun Jensen, C. (2015, May 28–30). *Mekong scales: Domains, test-sites, and the micro-uncommons*. Paper presented at the Sawyer seminar workshop 'Uncommons', University of California, Davis.

Bulkeley, H. (2015). *An urban politics of climate change. Experimentation and the governing of socio-technical transitions*. Routledge.

Bullard, R. D. (1994). *Dumping in Dixie: Race, class, and environmental quality*. Westview Press.

Bullard, R. D., & Wright, B. P. D. (2009). *Race, place, and environmental justice after Hurricane Katrina: Struggles to reclaim, rebuild, and revitalize New Orleans and the Gulf Coast*. Westview Press.

Cadieux, K. V., Carpenter, S., Liebman, A., Blumberg, R., & Upadhyay, B. (2019). Reparation ecologies: Regimes of repair in populist agroecology. *Annals of the American Association of Geographers, 109*(2), 644–660. doi:10.1080/24694452.2018.1527680

Caillol, S. (2013). Life cycle assessment and ecodesign: Innovation tools for a sustainable and industrial chemistry. In J. Llored (Ed.), *The philosophy of chemistry: Practices, methodologies, and concepts* (pp. 35–64). Cambridge Scholars Publishing.

Cairns, J. (2003). Reparations for environmental degradation and species extinction: A moral and ethical imperative for human society. *Ethics in Science and Environmental Politics, 3*, 25–32.

Calvário, R., Kaika, M., & Velegrakis, G. (Eds.). (2022). *The political ecology of austerity: Crisis, social movements, and the environment*. Routledge.

Caney, S. (2006). Environmental degradation, reparations, and the moral significance of history. *Journal of Social Philosophy, 37*(7), 464–482.

Carson, R. (1962). *Silent spring*. Fawcett Crest.

Castellano, K. (2017). Moles, molehills, and common right in John Clare's poetry. *Studies in Romanticism, 56*(2), 157–176.

Chatterton, P., & Pickerill, J. (2010). Everyday activism and transitions towards post-capitalist worlds. *Transactions of the Institute of British Geographers, 35*(4), 475–490. doi:10.1111/j.1475-5661.2010.00396.x

Clark, J. H., Farmer, T. J., Herrero-Davila, L., & Sherwood, J. (2016). Circular economy design considerations for research and process development in the chemical sciences. *Green Chemistry, 18*, 3914–3934.

Clark, J. H., Sheldon, R., Raston, C., Poliakoff, M., & Leitner, W. (2014). 15 years of Green Chemistry. *Green Chemistry, 16*, 18–23.

Clarke, C. J., Tu, W. C., Levers, O., Brohl, A., & Hallett, J. P. (2018). Green and sustainable solvents in chemical processes. *Chemical Reviews, 118*(2), 747–800. doi:10.1021/acs.chemrev.7b00571

Collins, H. M. (1985). *Changing order: Replication and induction in scientific practice*. Sage.

Cummings, S. P. (Ed.). (2010). *Bioremediation: Methods and protocols*. Humana Press Springer.

D'Alisa, G., De Maria, F., & Kallis, G. (2015). *Degrowth: A vocabulary for a new era*. Routledge.

Darwish, L. (2013). *Earth repair: A grassroots guide to healing toxic and damaged landscapes*. New Society Publishers.

Davies, T. (2018). Toxic space and time: Slow violence, necropolitics, and petrochemical pollution. *Annals of the American Association of Geographers, 108*(6), 1537–1553. doi:10.1080/24694452.2018.1470924

Debaise, D. (2017). The modern invention of nature. In E. Hoerl & J. Burton (Eds.), *General ecology: The new ecological paradigm* (pp. 151–168). Bloomsbury.

Deleuze, G., & Guattari, F. (1994). *What is philosophy?* Verso.

Demaria, F., Schneider, F., Sekulova, F., & Martinez-Alier, J. (2013). What is degrowth? From an activist slogan to a social movement. *Environmental Values, 22*, 191–215.

Denis, J. (2019). Why do maintenance and repair matter? In A. Blok, I. Farias, & C. Roberts (Eds.), *The Routledge companion to actor-network theory* (pp. 283–294). Routledge.

Diamond, M. L., de Wit, C. A., Molander, S., Scheringer, M., Backhaus, T., Lohmann, R., Arvidsson, R., Bergman, Å., Hauschild, M., Holoubek, I., Persson, L., Suzuki, N., & Zetzsch, C. (2015). Exploring the planetary boundary for chemical pollution. *Environment International, 78*, 8–15. doi:10.1016/j.envint.2015.02.001

Dillon, L. (2014). Race, waste, and space: Brownfield redevelopment and environmental justice at the Hunters Point shipyard. *Antipode, 46*(5), 1205–1221. doi:10.1111/anti.12009

Dobson, A., & Bell, D. (2006). *Environmental citizenship*. MIT Press.

Dugmore, T. I. J., Clark, J. H., Bustamante, J., Houghton, J. A., & Matharu, A. S. (2017). Valorisation of biowastes for the production of green materials using chemical methods. *Topics in Current Chemistry, 375*(2), 46–95. doi:10.1007/s41061-017-0133-8

Escobar, A. (2015). Degrowth, postdevelopment, and transitions: A preliminary conversation. *Sustainability Science, 10*(3), 451–462. doi:10.1007/s11625-015-0297-5

Ferdinand, M. (2019). *Une écologie décoloniale. Penser l'écologie depuis le monde caribéen* [Decolonial ecology. Thinking about ecology from the Caribbean world]. Édition du Seuil.

Figueroa Sarriera, H., & Gray, C. H. (2016). Generative justice [Special Issue]. *Teknokultura: Journal of Digital Culture and Social Movements, 13*(2), 361–637. doi:10.5209/rev_TK.2016.v13.n1.52388

Fortun, K. (2014). From Latour to late industrialism. *HAU: Journal of Ethnographic Theory, 4*(1), 309–329. doi:10.14318/hau4.1.017

Fox, W. (1990). *Toward a transpersonal ecology: Developing new foundations for environmentalism*. State University of New York Press.

Gatt, C. (2017). *An ethnography of global environmentalism: Becoming friends of the earth*. Routledge.

Ghelfi, A. (2015). *Worlding politics: Justice, commons and technoscience* [PhD dissertation, University of Leicester].

Ghelfi, A., & Papadopoulos, D. (2022a). Ungovernable earth: Resurgence, translocal infrastructures, and more-than-social movements. *Environmental Values*. Advance online publication. doi:10.3197/096327121X16387842836968

Ghelfi, A., & Papadopoulos, D. (2022b). Ecological transition: What it is and how to do it. Community technoscience and green democracy. *Tecnoscienza: Italian Journal of Science & Technology Studies, 13*(1), 5–31.

Gibson-Graham, J. K. (2006). *A postcapitalist politics*. University of Minnesota Press.

Goffey, A. (2008). Abstract experience. *Theory, Culture & Society, 25*(4), 15–30. doi:10.1177/0263276408091980

Gómez-Barris, M. (2017). *The extractive zone social ecologies and decolonial perspectives.* Duke University Press.

Graziano, V. (2016). Prefigurative practices: Raw materials for a political positioning of art, leaving the avant-garde. In F. Malzacher, E. V. Kampenhout, & L. Mestre (Eds.), *Turn turtle! Reenacting the institute: Performing urgency #2.* Alexander Verlag.

Guattari, F. (1995). *Chaosmosis: An ethicoaesthetic paradigm.* Indiana University Press.

Gupta, R. K., Thakur, V. K., & Matharu, A. S. (2018). Editorial overview: From linear to circular economies: The importance and application of recycling and reuse. *Current Opinion in Green and Sustainable Chemistry, 13,* A1–A3. doi:10.1016/j.cogsc.2018.09.002

Haas, M. (2018). *Tiere auf der Bühne. Eine ästhetische Ökologie der Performance* [Animals on stage. An aesthetic ecology of performance]. Kulturverlag Kadmos.

Hacking, I. (1983). *Representing and intervening: Introductory topics in the philosophy of natural science.* Cambridge University Press.

Hale, B., Lee, A., & Hermans, A. (2014). Clowning around with conservation: Adaptation, reparation and the new substitution problem. *Environmental Values, 23*(2), 181–198. doi:10.3197/096327114x13894344179202

Halewood, M. (2012). *A. N. Whitehead and social theory: Tracing a culture of thought.* Anthem Press.

Haraway, D. J. (1997). *Modest_Witness@Second_Millennium. FemaleMan©_meets_OncoMouse™: feminism and technoscience.* Routledge.

Hartigan, J. (2015). Plant publics: Multispecies relating in Spanish botanical gardens. *Anthropological Quarterly, 88*(2), 481–507. doi:10.1353/anq.2015.0024

Hodson, M., Evans, J., & Schliwa, G. (2018). Conditioning experimentation: The struggle for place-based discretion in shaping urban infrastructures. *Environment and Planning C: Politics and Space, 36*(8), 1480–1498. doi:10.1177/2399654418765480

Hoerl, E. (2013). A thousand ecologies: The process of cyberneticization and general ecology. In D. Diederichsen & A. Franke (Eds.), *The whole earth: California and the disappearance of the outside* (pp. 121–130). Sternberg Press.

Hoerl, E., & Burton, J. (Eds.). (2017). *General ecology: The new ecological paradigm.* Bloomsbury.

Hopkins, R. (2011). *The transition companion: Making your community more resilient in uncertain times.* Green Books.

Ihde, D., & Selinger, E. (Eds.). (2003). *Chasing technoscience: Matrix for materiality.* Indiana University Press.

Iles, A. (2013). Greening chemistry: Emerging epistemic political tensions in California and the United States. *Public Understanding of Science, 22*(4), 460–478.

Jackson, S. J. (2014). Rethinking repair. In T. Gillespie, P. J. Boczkowski, & K. A. Foot (Eds.), *Media technologies: Essays on communication, materiality, and society* (pp. 221–240). MIT Press.

Jessop, P. G. (2016). The use of auxiliary substances (e.g. solvents, separation agents) should be made unnecessary wherever possible and innocuous when used. *Green Chemistry, 18*(9), 2577–2578. doi:10.1039/c6gc90039a

Kallis, G. (2019). *Limits: Why Malthus was wrong and why environmentalists should care.* Stanford University Press.

Kingsland, S. E. (2005). *The evolution of American ecology, 1890–2000.* Johns Hopkins University Press.

Klein, U. (2005). Technoscience avant la lettre. *Perspectives on Science, 13*(2), 226–266. doi:10.1162/106361405774270557

Knorr-Cetina, K., & Mulkay, M. J. (1983). *Science observed: Perspectives on the social study of science.* Sage.

Kümmerer, K. (2007). Sustainable from the very beginning: Rational design of molecules by life cycle engineering as an important approach for green pharmacy and green chemistry. *Green Chemistry*, *9*(8), 899–907. doi:10.1039/b618298b

Lefèvre, W., & Klein, U. (2007). *Materials in eighteenth-century science: A historical ontology.* MIT Press.

Leistert, O., & Schrickel, I. (Eds.). (2020). *Thinking the problematic: Genealogies and explorations between philosophy and the sciences.* Transcript.

Linebaugh, P. (2008). *The Magna Carta manifesto: Liberties and commons for all.* University of California Press.

Linebaugh, P. (2010, January 8). Some principles of the commons. *Counterpunch.* www.counterpunch.org/2010/01/08/some-principles-of-the-commons/

Linthorst, J. A. (2010). An overview: Origins and development of green chemistry. *Foundations of Chemistry*, *12*(1), 55–68.

Lundy, C. (2019). The call for a new earth, a new people: An untimely problem. *Theory, Culture & Society*, *38*(2), 119–139. doi:10.1177/0263276419878246

Macleod, C. I. (2019). Expanding reproductive justice through a supportability reparative justice framework: The case of abortion in South Africa. *Culture, Health & Sexuality*, *21*(1), 46–62. doi:10.1080/13691058.2018.1447687

Mander, J., & Tauli-Corpuz, V. (Eds.). (2006). *Paradigm wars: Indigenous peoples' resistance to globalization.* Sierra Club.

Mars, R., Willis, S., & Hopkins, R. (2016). *The permaculture transition manual: A comprehensive guide to resilient living.* New Society Publishers.

Masciandaro, G., Macci, C., Peruzzi, E., Ceccanti, B., & Doni, S. (2013). Organic matter–microorganism–plant in soil bioremediation: A synergic approach. *Reviews in Environmental Science and Bio/Technology*, *12*(4), 399–419. doi:10.1007/s11157-013-9313-3

Masco, J. (2021). The artificial world. In D. Papadopoulos, M. Puig de la Bellacasa, & N. Myers (Eds.), *Reactivating elements: Chemistry, ecology, practice* (pp. 131–150). Duke University Press.

Mathews, F. (1991). *The ecological self.* Routledge.

Mora-Gámez, F. (2016). *Reparation beyond statehood: Assembling rights restitution in post-conflict Colombia* [PhD dissertation, University of Leicester].

Naess, A. (1973). The shallow and the deep, long-range ecology movement: A summary. *Inquiry*, *16*, 95–100.

Nixon, R. (2011). *Slow violence and the environmentalism of the poor.* Harvard University Press.

Nunn, N. (2018). Toxic encounters, settler logics of elimination, and the future of a continent. *Antipode*, *50*(5), 1330–1348. doi:10.1111/anti.12403

Orr, J. (2006). *Panic diaries: A genealogy of panic disorder.* Duke University Press.

Ottinger, G., & Cohen, B. R. (Eds.). (2011). *Technoscience and environmental justice: Expert cultures in a grassroots movement.* The MIT Press.

P2P Foundation. (2015). *Commons transition: Policy proposals for an open knowledge commons society.*

Papadopoulos, D. (2018). *Experimental practice: Technoscience, alterontologies, and more-than-social movements.* Duke University Press.

Papadopoulos, D., & Puig de la Bellacasa, M. (2022). Eco-commoning in the aftermath: Sundews, mangroves and swamp insurgencies. In N. Urbonas, G. Urbonas, & K. Sabolius (Eds.), *Swamps and the new imagination: On the future of cohabitation in art, architecture, and philosophy.* MIT Press.

Papadopoulos, D., Puig de la Bellacasa, M., & Myers, N. (Eds.). (2021). *Reactivating elements: Chemistry, ecology, practice.* Duke University Press.

Papadopoulos, D., Puig de la Bellacasa, M., & Tacchetti, M. (Eds.). (2022). *Ecological repa-ration: Repair, remediation and resurgence in social and environmental conflict*. Bristol University Press.

Paxson, H., & Helmreich, S. (2013). The perils and promises of microbial abundance: Novel natures and model ecosystems, from artisanal cheese to alien seas. *Social Studies of Science, 44*(2), 165–193. doi:10.1177/0306312713505003

Perez Murcia, L. E. (2013). Social policy or reparative justice? Challenges for reparations in con-texts of massive displacement and related serious human rights violations. *Journal of Refugee Studies, 27*(2), 191–206. doi:10.1093/jrs/fet028

Pickerill, J. (2020). Making climate urbanism from the grassroots: Eco-communities, experiments and divergent temporalities. In V. C. Broto, E. Robin, & A. While (Eds.), *Climate urbanism: Towards a critical research agenda* (pp. 227–242). Palgrave Macmillan.

Pickerill, J., & Chatterton, P. (2006). Notes towards autonomous geographies: Creation, resistance and self-management as survival tactics. *Progress in Human Geography, 30*(6), 730–746.

Pignarre, P., & Stengers, I. (2011). *Capitalist sorcery: Breaking the spell*. Palgrave Macmillan.

Poliakoff, M., Fitzpatrick, J. M., Farren, T. R., & Anastas, P. T. (2002). Green chemistry: Science and politics of change. *Science, 297*(5582), 807–810.

Poliakoff, M., & Licence, P. (2015). Supercritical fluids: Green solvents for green chemis-try? *Philosophical Transactions of the Royal Society A, 373*, 20150018. doi:10.1098/rsta.2015.0018

Pratt, M. L. (1992). *Imperial eyes: Travel writing and transculturation*. Routledge.

Puig de la Bellacasa, M. (2010). Ethical doings in naturecultures. *Ethics, Place & Environment. A Journal of Philosophy & Geography, 13*(2), 151–169.

Puig de la Bellacasa, M. (2012). 'Nothing comes without its world': Thinking with care. *The Sociological Review, 60*(2), 197–216.

Puig de la Bellacasa, M. (2015). Making time for soil: Technoscientific futurity and the pace of care. *Social Studies of Science, 45*(5), 691–716. doi:10.1177/0306312715599851

Puig de la Bellacasa, M. (2017). *Matters of care: Speculative ethics in more than human worlds*. University of Minnesota Press.

Puig de la Bellacasa, M. (2021). Embracing breakdown: Soil ecopoethics and the ambivalences of remediation. In D. Papadopoulos, M. Puig de la Bellacasa, & N. Myers (Eds.), *Reactivating Elements. Chemistry, Ecology, Practice* (pp. 196–230). Durham, NC: Duke University Press.

Ravetz, J. R. (2006). *The no-nonsense guide to science*. New Internationalist.

Reid, H. G., & Taylor, B. (2010). *Recovering the commons: Democracy, place, and global justice*. University of Illinois Press.

Roberts, J. A., Langston, N., Egan, M., Frickel, S., Nash, L., Allen, B., Vogel, S. A., Rowe, D. F., Daemmrich, A., & Murphy, M. (2008). Toxic bodies/toxic environments: An interdiscipli-nary forum. *Environmental History, 13*(4), 629–703. doi:10.1093/envhis/13.4.629

Rockström, J., Steffen, W., Noone, K., Persson, Å., Chapin, F. S., Lambin, E., Lenton, T. M., Scheffer, M., Folke, C., Schellnhuber, H. J., Nykvist, B., de Wit, C. A., Hughes, T., van der Leeuw, S., Rodhe, H., Sörlin, S., Snyder, P. K., Costanza, R., Svedin, U., . . . Foley, J. (2009). Planetary boundaries: Exploring the safe operating space for humanity. *Ecology and Society, 14*(2), 32–65.

Rosset, P. a. A. M. (2017). *Agroecology: Science and politics*. Fernwood Publishing.

Salvatore Engel-Di Mauro, G. M. (2022). *Urban food production for ecosocialism: Cultivating the CITY*. Routledge.

Sanderson, K., & Anastas, P. T. (2011). Chemistry: It's not easy being green. Q&A: Paul Anastas. *Nature, 469*(7328), 18–20. doi:10.1038/469018a

Savransky, M. (2020). Problematizing the problematic [Special Issue]. *Theory, Culture & Society*, *38*(2), 3–159. doi:10.1177/0263276420966389

Savransky, M. (2021a). After progress: Notes for an ecology of perhaps. *Ephemera: Theory & Politics in Organization*, *21*(1), 267–281.

Savransky, M. (2021b). *Around the day in eighty worlds: Politics of the pluriverse*. Duke University Press.

Schraube, E., & Højholt, C. (2016). *Psychology and the conduct of everyday life*. Routledge.

Shattuck, A., Schiavoni, C., & VanGelder, Z. (2017). *The politics of food sovereignty: Concept, practice and social movements*. Routledge.

Sheldon, R. A. (2007). The E factor: Fifteen years on. *Green Chemistry*, *9*(12), 1273–1283. doi:10.1039/b713736m

Sheldon, R. A. (2016). Green chemistry and resource efficiency: Towards a green economy. *Green Chemistry*, *18*(11), 3180–3183. doi:10.1039/c6gc90040b

Stengers, I. (2021). Receiving the gift: Earthly events, chemical invariants, and elemental powers. In D. Papadopoulos, M. Puig de la Bellacasa, & N. Myers (Eds.), *Reactivating elements: Chemistry, ecology, practice* (pp. 18–33). Duke University Press.

Stephenson, N., & Papadopoulos, D. (2006). *Analysing everyday experience: Social research and political change*. Palgrave Macmillan.

Strathern, M. (2000). Environments within: An ethnographic commentary on scale. In K. Flint & H. Morphy (Eds.), *Culture, landscape, and the environment: The Linacre lectures 1997* (pp. 44–71). Oxford University Press.

Tacchetti, M., Quiceno Toro, N., Puig de la Bellacasa, M., & Papadopoulos, D. (2022). Crafting ecologies of existence: More than human community making in Colombian textile craftivism. *Environment and Planning E: Nature and Space*. Advance online publication. doi:10.1177/25148486211030154

Tsing, A. (2012). On nonscalability: The living world is not amenable to precision-nested scales. *Common Knowledge*, *18*(3), 505–524. doi:10.1215/0961754x-1630424

Tsing, A. (2015). *The mushroom at the end of the world: On the possibility of life in capitalist ruins*. Princeton University Press.

Tuck, C. O., Pérez, E., Horváth, I. T., Sheldon, R. A., & Poliakoff, M. (2012). Valorization of biomass: Deriving more value from waste. *Science*, *337*, 695–699.

Utting, P. (2015). *Social and solidarity economy: Beyond the fringe*. Zed Books.

van de Sande, M. (2013). The prefigurative politics of Tahrir Square: An alternative perspective on the 2011 revolutions. *Res Publica*, *19*(3), 223–239. doi:10.1007/s11158-013-9215-9

Walker, M. U. (2010). *What is reparative justice?* Marquette University Press.

Wall, D. (2014). *The commons in history: Culture, conflict, and ecology*. MIT Press.

White, R. (2016). Reparative justice, environmental crime and penalties for the powerful. *Crime, Law and Social Change*, *67*(2), 117–132. doi:10.1007/s10611-016-9635-5

Whitehead, A. N. (1964). *The concept of nature: The Tarner lectures delivered in Trinity College November 1919*. Cambridge University Press.

Whitehead, A. N. (1967). *Adventures of ideas*. Free Press.

Whitehead, M. (2013). Editorial: Degrowth or regrowth? *Environmental Values*, *22*(2), 141–145.

Whyte, K. (2018). Critical investigations of resilience: A brief introduction to indigenous environmental studies & sciences. *Daedalus*, *147*(2), 136–147. doi:10.1162/DAED_a_00497

Winner, L. (1980). Do artifacts have politics? *Daedalus*, *109*(1), 121–136.

Woodhouse, E. J., & Breyman, S. (2005). Green chemistry as social movement? *Science, Technology & Human Values*, *30*(2), 199–222.

Wyatt, S. (2008). Technological determinism is dead: Long live technological determinism. In E. Hackett, O. Amsterdamska, M. Lynch, & J. Wajcman (Eds.), *Handbook of science and technology studies* (pp. 165–180): MIT Press.

Zalasiewicz, J., Waters, C. N., Ivar do Sul, J. A., Corcoran, P. L., Barnosky, A. D., Cearreta, A., Edgeworth, M., Galuszka, A., Jeandel, C., Leinfelder, R., McNeill, J. R., Steffen, W., Summerhayes, C., Wagreich, M., Williams, M., Wolfe, A. P., & Yonan, Y. (2016). The geological cycle of plastics and their use as a stratigraphic indicator of the Anthropocene. *Anthropocene, 13*, 4–17. doi:10.1016/j.ancene.2016.01.002

Zalasiewicz, J., Williams, M., Haywood, I., & Ellis, M. (2011). The Anthropocene: A new epoch of geological time? [Special Issue]. *Philosophical Transactions of the Royal Society, 369*(1938), 833–1112.

Author biography

Dimitris Papadopoulos is Professor of Science, Technology and Society, director of the Institute for Science and Society, and founding director of the Interdisciplinary Research Cluster EcoSocieties at the University of Nottingham. He is a Leverhulme Fellow and has been an Alexander-von-Humboldt Fellow at the University of California Berkeley and Santa Cruz. Papadopoulos is currently completing a photography book on *Divergent Ecologies* and a research monograph on *Chemicals, EcoPolitics and Reparative Justice*. His most recent books are: *Ecological Reparation. Repair, Remediation and Resurgence in Social and Environmental Conflict* (Bristol University Press, 2022), *Reactivating Elements: Chemistry, Ecology, Practice* (Duke University Press, 2021) and *Experimental Practice: Technoscience, Alterontologies and More-Than-Social Movements* (Duke University Press, 2018).

MONOGRAPH SERIES

The Sociological Review Monographs
2022, Vol. 70(2) 138–152
© The Author(s) 2022

Article reuse guidelines:
sagepub.com/journals-permissions
DOI: 10.1177/00380261221084781
journals.sagepub.com/home/sor

Re-animalising wellbeing: Multispecies justice after development

Krithika Srinivasan
Institute of Geography, University of Edinburgh, UK

Abstract

This article addresses contemporary socio-ecological crises by proposing a shift from the logics of protection–sacrifice that characterise developmentality, and by developing the idea of 're-animalisation' as a pathway to multispecies justice. The pursuit of 'development' has been a key hallmark of the modern idea of progress. Long-standing critiques of the socio-ecological and other adverse impacts of development have not made much headway in effecting meaningful change. Engaging with this impasse, I argue that specific zoöpolitical notions of human wellbeing that are co-constitutive with developmentality are at the foundation of today's socio-ecological troubles and multispecies justice concerns. Bringing together post-development and animal studies scholarship, I discuss the twinned logics of protection–sacrifice that underlie the pursuit of human wellbeing at societal scales, and that have come to characterise more-than-human responses as well. I build on this, in conversation with environmental philosopher Val Plumwood and degrowth scholar Giorgos Kallis, to suggest that achieving multispecies justice requires a renewed focus on the human in the form of a fundamental re-placement of the social in the rest of the nature. To this end, I offer thought experiments on re-visioning wellbeing via an approach of 're-animalisation' to provoke reflection on crafting new foundations for equitable multispecies presents and futures.

Keywords

degrowth, development, multispecies justice, postdevelopment, re-animalisation

Introduction

The times that we live in are characterised by abundance; they are equally characterised by fear: abundance in relation to how we inhabit the planet and partake of what it offers, and fear that the ways in which we inhabit this world, that this abundance, is destroying the very conditions of possibility that make human life possible. It is this combination of

Corresponding author:
Krithika Srinivasan, Institute of Geography, University of Edinburgh, Drummond Street, South Bridge, Edinburgh, EH8 9XP, UK.
Email: K.srinivasan@ed.ac.uk

abundance and fear that has now found articulation in the epithet 'the Anthropocene' (Mansfield & Doyle, 2017).

The term Anthropocene foregrounds the negative impacts that modern human life-styles have had on the planet and the other creatures that we share it with. But alongside these negative impacts sits a 'more-than-human' turn in the form of widespread public concern and action about the adverse consequences of humankind's interactions with nonhuman nature (encompassing ecological collectivities and individual organisms). This can be seen most obviously in environmental and animal protection initiatives that have emerged worldwide, and also in everyday actions and debate (Peggs, 2020; Schlosberg & Craven, 2019).

While the 'more-than-human' turn has been valuable, in this article I argue for a renewed focus on the *human* as a necessary response to the Anthropocene. Bringing together environmental philosophy, human–animal studies and post-development litera-tures, I suggest that the abundance and the fear that characterise this era are closely tied to a zoöpolitically exceptionalist vision of human wellbeing, and the near-universal pur-suit of the same via the mechanism of development (Srinivasan & Kasturirangan, 2016). Human wellbeing is seen as something that is achieved by overcoming and controlling the risks that are inherent in being a part of nonhuman nature, and by becoming '*more-than-animal*'. The societal pursuit of this vision of human wellbeing has taken the form of 'development', which, as I explain, is reliant on the ethical privileging of humankind over the rest of life and characterised by twinned logics of protection–sacrifice. This ethical privileging and logics of protection–sacrifice produce outcomes that undermine the wellbeing of nonhuman life, and of people in manners that vary across spatial and temporal scales, and across axes of social (including species) difference. These adverse impacts are hard to contest and overcome because they are tied to what is seen as an indisputable 'good', i.e. human wellbeing.

There is thus a need to reconfigure dominant, zoöpolitically exceptionalist notions of human wellbeing in order to effect meaningful change in the processes that have pro-duced the Anthropocene, and that have led to profound multispecies (social, ecological and animal) injustices (Celermajer et al., 2020). To this end, this article contributes prov-ocations on what might be entailed in rethinking human wellbeing in ways that are ori-ented towards multispecies justice. This, I argue, necessitates the imaginative and practical task of re-animalisation, i.e. resituating humanity as one among other animals, and relearning how to inhabit this world accordingly. I further add that this requires a fundamental shift in approaches to wellbeing and justice – a shift away from logics and practices of protection–sacrifice, and towards the redistribution of the risks of earthly living in more equitable directions.

Development, human wellbeing and zoöpolitical exceptionalism

The 'big' socio-ecological problems of the Anthropocene have their roots in the pursuit of particular visions of human wellbeing. Climate change, biodiversity loss, air pollution and water scarcity are all outcomes of societal efforts to foster human progress – what is now commonly referred to as 'development' (McMichael, 2012). Developmental activities, whether agriculture, concrete buildings, trains and cars, flush toilets, or air-conditioning, seek to improve human life, but also undermine it through negative consequences such as pollution, habitat degradation, and the exploitation and displacement of nonhuman life-forms. It is not just more-than-human problems that are the counterparts of development. The pernicious impacts of development on vulnerable people have been widely discussed (Escobar, 1995; Shrivastava & Kothari, 2012).

In effect, the pursuit of development has been a key hallmark of modernity and progress as well as a driver of the socio-ecological and more-than-human crises of the Anthropocene. The vast literature on developmentality's excesses has critically discussed the reasons for this. Capitalist logics of economic growth, commodification and extractivism have received much attention in this regard (Harvey, 2014; Moore, 2017). These problems are not restricted to capitalist regimes, with even community-oriented, left-leaning governments and civil society groups, subscribing to 'utterly conventional development strategies . . . organised around the extraction of natural sources' (Escobar, 2020, p. xviii). Post-development scholarship thus argues for alternatives *to* development that rethink development as a pathway to 'universal betterment' (Kallis, 2019, p. 6; Kothari et al., 2019).

To rethink development, it is useful to ask *why* development is done. At the most basic level, the assumed and stated end-goal of development is human wellbeing – to better human lives. Even if many of the negative impacts of development can be attributed to the profit-motives of privileged individuals or institutions, these profit-motives themselves can be understood as manifestations of the pursuit of wellbeing (of some people) – profits are valued because people and societies perceive them as contributing to their wellbeing (and perhaps that of others, as per the 'trickle-down' narrative). Even colonialism, the precursor of 'development', was justified in relation to the progress of the 'home' country and its peoples, and sometimes in relation to the 'improvement' of the colonised peoples – who were perceived as lacking the capacities and knowledges required to achieve human flourishing (Li, 2007).

This raises the question of how it is that something that is meant to promote human wellbeing ends up harming people, both directly through development-induced displacement, and indirectly, by harming nature.

To understand this, I would like to direct attention to the vision of human wellbeing that lies at the heart of developmentality. As Srinivasan and Kasturirangan (2016) explain, development is driven by a vision of a 'good' human life as something that (1) is achieved through insulation from the threats posed by nature and the vulnerabilities that are inherent to living as part of nature, including death itself; and (2) involves the maximisation of a range of capacities (e.g. intelligence, creativity) that are considered to be uniquely human, thereby finding fulfilment in going beyond the capacities of 'mere' biological organisms.

In order to make their point, they use as an example one of the most basic indicators of development – longevity. The higher the life expectancy at birth in a country, the higher it scores on the Human Development Index. Longevity as a seemingly unquestionable 'good' is taken for granted in mainstream society. (By 'mainstream', I mean all those societies that subscribe to ideas and practices of development. The exceptions would be societies that remain isolated from the rest of the world, and therefore from developmental norms, such as the Sentinelese in the Andaman Islands.)

Death is an integral part of life on Earth. A good human life, however, is seen as achieved only by preventing or delaying the many things that could put an end to life – ill health, storms, other animals. Many of these are things that kill other animals and life-forms, which is usually seen as 'natural'. But when it comes to human society (including those nonhumans that are specially valued, e.g. pets, farmed plants and animals, gardens), death that occurs outside of human intention and purpose is seen as something that must be overcome through socio-technological advances.

Consider other things that are viewed as essential to a good human life: housing that protects us from the elements, assured access to food, healthcare. And also education, heating/cooling of built environments, internet, energy-powered transport, artificial lighting, the occasional holiday, clothes, phones, computers – mainstream societies across the world are characterised by an ever-growing list of 'basic' needs. As Esteva puts it in conversation with Escobar (2020, p. 108), 'development changed the human condition through a grotesque transformation of necessities and desires into prescribed needs'.

All these are things that insulate humans from the 'risks (and inconveniences) that are inherent to living as part of the "more-than-human world"', and that enable us to exceed our animality (Srinivasan & Kasturirangan, 2016, p. 126). This vision of a good human life is built on *zoöpolitical exceptionalisms*: human wellbeing is achieved through separation from nonhuman nature, in particular, from the hazards and vulnerabilities that are part and parcel of being planetary life; at the same time, it is enhanced by activities and processes – such as a certain type of education, holidays, the internet – that are tied to those qualities and desires that are uniquely human in that they are not shared by other animals. This vision entails being and becoming *more-than-animal*.

These ontological nature–society exceptionalisms go alongside ethical exceptionalisms wherein the processes involved in securing development and/or human wellbeing involve 'the use, exploitation and redesign of nonhuman nature' or its destruction (Srinivasan & Kasturirangan, 2016, p. 126). These processes also harm vulnerable human communities who are displaced in service of the greater good, and whose ways of life are often seen as 'inferior', and in need of 'development' (Li, 2007; Shrivastava & Kothari, 2012). Developmental processes and norms therefore have ecological, animal and social justice implications.

Modern medicine, for example, is built on the exploitation of nonhuman organisms for the manufacture and safety testing of healthcare products, and in some instances, including recent COVID vaccination trials, the exploitation of marginalised people (Bhuyan, 2021). Modern healthcare involves the delay of human mortality and the reduction of human vulnerability to disease by deliberately creating ill health in, and hastening the deaths of, other animals. As Kallis (2019, p. 92) writes, 'we attempt to overcome [death] by subduing nature or by shifting death onto others'. While 'animal welfare' might be a concern in medicine and related fields, the normative assumption that other life-forms can and ought to be sacrificed for the sake of human wellbeing (whether in relation to cancer, hypothyroidism, allergies, or COVID-19) remains unchallenged (barring within marginal animal rights discourse).

Other animals manage their health through means that humans do not fully comprehend. For example, they heal serious wounds just through regular licking. There are occasions when such healthcare fails, and ill health and death ensue. The human health-care apparatus, however, is a fundamentally distinct endeavour. The underlying goal is 'more-than-animal' health and protection from the varied threats that all other life-forms have to deal with, and to achieve that at the level of entire societies.

The production of food in today's world is equally implicated in multispecies injus-tices. Petro-chemical agriculture is accepted to have significant socio-ecological impacts, while others argue that these impacts can be traced to much earlier in the history of set-tled agriculture (Scott, 2017; Weis, 2007). Nevertheless, intensive agriculture continues to be the preferred mode of food production because its yields, however unsustainable, tend to be higher than other forms of food production and procurement – and high yields are understood as necessary to achieve ready access to food for people. This narrative, while debunked, dominates societal approaches to food (Emel & Neo, 2015).

All animals procure food for their survival and that of their families or communities. The procurement of such food is usually restricted to their immediate/daily needs, or in some cases, seasonal needs. Contemporary agriculture, by contrast, is a mammoth inter-vention that seeks to maximise and assure a steady flow of large quantities across global spatial and temporal scales – we want to be assured of food not only for the day, but for the foreseeable future, for not only our immediate communities, but geopolitical entities. At these scales, food becomes more than nutrition – it becomes a means of pursuing other wellbeing goals, such as through commerce and leisure.

The above examples of healthcare and food pertain to basic aspects of human wellbe-ing. In both cases, the effort is to achieve a state that is somehow more-than-animal – through insulation from the risks and uncertainties that are core to living as part of nature (e.g. hunger, mortality from disease), and through *more-than-animal* expansion of what wellbeing means, and to pursue it at societal and generational spatial and temporal scales. This maximisation has no theoretical limits – for instance, the idea of what constitutes premature death (in humans) has shifted towards higher and higher ages over time.

Developmental visions of human wellbeing are therefore about cultivating abundance in relation to how humankind inhabits Earth and continually differentiating humankind from the rest of life. Of course, there is enormous variation within humanity with respect to the extent to which different norms of development and human wellbeing are achieved, and even more variation with respect to the responsibility for the linked adverse conse-quences (Bauer & Bhan, 2016). Yet, these differentials are seen as having to be overcome by bringing such norms and associated materialities to those people and societies that do not have access to them – development is the process through which this is undertaken, a process justified by the differentials that it seeks to eliminate, even as it continually creates such differentials through its progressively expanding goalposts of 'needs' and wellbeing. It is in the pursuit of this zoöpolitical vision of humanity that developmental-ity 'colonises and assimilates the lifeworlds of others, human and nonhuman' (Kallis, 2019, p. 58).

More-than-human responses

The multispecies justice impacts of the developmental quest are hard to challenge because they can be justified with reference to human wellbeing. Hydroelectric projects destroy forests, wildlife and communities, but they control flooding, and bring electricity and water to households, industries and farms. Intensive farming severely compromises the lives and deaths of the animals that it uses as well as local and global ecologies, but it provides livelihoods and food. Scientific and medical research similarly exploit other animals in ways that would need trigger warnings to describe, but they promise cures for cancer, dementia and malaria.

For as long as human societies have used animals, ecologies and peoples for such purposes, they have also worried about the ethics of the same – if Descartes came up with his infamous argument that animals are like machines, it is because, as he justifies later on in the same text, it would otherwise be 'criminal' to use them as we do (Descartes, 1991). Environmental and animal protection activism and research have been raising questions about development for decades. Yet, not only have those early concerns *not been* adequately addressed, but rather, they have grown in scale and severity (Bennett et al., 2018). The BBC's *Green Originals* programme captures this when it points out that Greta Thunberg's chastisement of 'grown-ups' for their ecological irresponsibility was eerily similar to the concerns raised by 12-year-old Severn Cullis-Suzuki at the Rio Summit in 1992. In the 30 or so years that have passed, nothing has really changed ('Severn Cullis-Suzuki', 2020).

This, I suggest, is because of the trump card of human wellbeing that is deployed as developmentality's justification. Social, ecological and animal impacts become unfortunate consequences to be managed. Moreover, the response to these impacts tends to replicate and reinforce the logics underlying developmental processes, thereby reproducing their inherent problems. For instance, 'green' technologies are offered as solutions to pollution and resource depletion, wherein 'side-effects' are tackled even while continuing to engage in those activities that cause the problem in the first place. Even approaches to environmentalism that call for social and behavioural change rarely challenge developmental norms:

> . . . the wants fueling a system that destroy the environment remain unquestioned. . . . The problem is that we can't have it, for reasons that go beyond us, so what we should do is to protect and sustain as much of it as we can possibly have. (Kallis, 2019, p. 59)

Animal welfare similarly is directed at tackling some of the worst 'side-effects' of developmental institutions on animals even while continuing to use them (Haynes, 2011). Indeed, the idea of unnecessary suffering that informs animal welfare law and practice in many parts of the world is tied to whether such suffering (of animals) is necessary for the intended human use or not – as opposed to whether such suffering is necessary from the animal's perspective.

Occasionally, special protections are offered to particular animals (e.g. Great Apes in Spain) or plants (e.g. endangered cacti) or habitats (via protected areas) that act as deterrents to their exploitation. These special protections, however, replicate developmental logics: (a) they work by shoring up the ethico-political status of particular organisms or landscapes, much like developmental logics are focused on shoring up the human; (b) while developmentality rests on ethical exceptionalisms between humankind and the rest of nature, a lot of ecological and animal protection action rests on ethical exceptionalisms – between human and nonhuman life as well as between different nonhuman life-forms.

The domain of biodiversity conservation is replete with ethical exceptionalisms – organisms classified as 'invasive alien' are subject to extermination justified by the protection of other more valued organisms, echoing developmental justifications of harm done to vulnerable people and nature in pursuit of a superior human life (Srinivasan & Kasturirangan, 2017). Biodiversity conservation also displays ethical exceptionalisms at different ontological scales – for instance, when individual members of valued species are subject to harms such as captivity, artificial insemination, ranching and hunting in the name of the protection of the species as a whole. Here, the ontological level of species is granted an ethically exceptionalist status, with individuals sacrificed for the sake of the collective (Biermann & Mansfield, 2014).

The domain of animal welfare is equally characterised by ethical exceptionalisms (e.g. rats are attributed less ethical value than primates in laboratory animal welfare protocols) and even between members of the same species in different social locations (e.g. a dog that's a pet is offered more protections from human-induced harm than a dog in a laboratory). Pet food, whether for adult animals or formula for newborns, is almost always made from other animals, and is a co-product of intensive farming. Vaccinating or treating a dog with antibiotics involves privileging that dog over all the other dogs that have been used to develop and safety test the vaccines and medicine.

In essence, societal responses to the more-than-human crises of our times have implicitly retained the zoöpolitical exceptionalism of developmentality by conceptualising nonhuman wellbeing within and in relation to norms about human wellbeing – through approaches that stay anthropocentric, or by shoring up select nonhuman entities via 'an enlargement of the elite and a retention of intensification of conceptual strategies of erasure and denial for excluded groups' (Plumwood, 2002, p. 152). As such, they do not escape the conceptual and material 'side-effects' of developmentality: better more-than-human relations are sought via protection that inevitably goes alongside sacrifice (of 'lesser' Others).

Protection–sacrifice

On the whole, the twinned logics of protection–sacrifice of the developmental apparatus are co-constitutive with the pursuit of human wellbeing, and also suffuse more-than-human responses. The entrenchment of these logics can be seen in the response to COVID-19.

COVID lockdowns are exemplary developmental measures. They are aimed at protecting humankind from getting infected by a nonhuman threat, and in doing so, have serious negative impacts on vulnerable people by suddenly depriving them of their livelihoods in market economies, rendering them destitute. The social, cultural and livelihood displacement generated by lockdowns has been dealt with similarly to how development-induced displacement is dealt with – through social security measures that barely scratch the surface of the human destitution that has been created (Kalu, 2020; Samaddar, 2021).

While COVID lockdowns are meant to protect everyone, in reality, the health benefits they offer are predominantly restricted to the non-poor – those who have the resources to be 'distanced' from others. COVID lockdowns mirror development projects in their inequitable distribution of costs and benefits and have transformed a 'non-discriminatory' virus into a 'disease of the poor'. These impacts have been evident from the beginning, and yet these lockdowns are repeatedly deployed and justified by narratives about safeguarding humanity – just as development justifies itself.

More crucially, the response to COVID has replicated the very same logics and processes that created the conditions of possibility for the infection in the first place. If it is true that the virus has its origins in some animals that are considered wildlife (World Health Organization & China, 2021), and if it is true that people have always cohabited with wildlife, then how is it that we face what is seen as a dangerous (to human society) pandemic? It cannot just be proximal interactions between human society and wildlife, including the consumption of wild animal meat – that is not new.

What has changed are the social conditions under which those interactions take place. These include the farming of domestic animals; the globalised character of human settlements and lifestyles; the transformation of landscapes and their multispecies inhabitants everywhere which has enabled zoonotic transmission and rapid contagion. All of these changed social conditions fall under the umbrella of development.

It is these very same logics of development that the response to COVID reproduces: in the use of sanitisers and disposable personal protective equipment, the exploitation of animals for vaccine production (European Animal Research Association [EARA], 2020), and measures such as lockdowns which have caused immense social displacement. The logics of development have for long justified harm done to marginalised Others, whether human or nonhuman, as necessary in the interests of 'collective' progress. This can be seen in the COVID response too.

These years of COVID have been emblematic of the developmental status quo and of the 'ruins' of progress. The pandemic has been created by developmental logics and zoöpolitical visions of human wellbeing, but it is more of the same that characterises the response to it. The 'new normal' might be the most-used term of recent times, but things have been different only on a very superficial level wherein much of living, for some humans, has been taking place behind computer screens and closed doors – inside mini-fortresses that are serviced by less-privileged human and nonhuman Others. The underlying narrative of human sanctity and ingenuity has not shifted in the slightest, neither has the tacit decision that this can be achieved through the sacrifice of 'lesser' Others; on the contrary, they have been reinforced and strengthened, as seen in the hopes, calls and promises of defeating COVID, whether through lockdowns or vaccines. All of these 'reproduce continually the same elements of failure – including the arrogance and ecological blindness of the dominant culture – even while we seek desperately for solutions within it' (Plumwood, 2002, p. 6).

Reconfiguring wellbeing and justice

In this article, I have argued the most troubling social and more-than-human concerns of our times are tied to a positive vision of what humans are and how their wellbeing can be achieved at societal scales. The back and forth between doing harm through processes of 'improvement' and progress, and trying to undo or mitigate such harm, lies at the root of extreme but highly uneven prosperity, on the one hand, and extreme current and future vulnerability, on the other. Those activities that have 'caused' the Anthropocene are geared towards pursuing a particular vision of human wellbeing – as something that is achieved through separation from and exceeding nature, by becoming more-than-animal. As such, it becomes futile to challenge these activities without changing the vision of humanity they are directed by.

Critical scholarship and action on and in the Anthropocene has devoted much attention to reconfiguring systems of ethics and politics to make space for the more-than-human. But the continued prevalence, and indeed, exacerbation of social, ecological and animal injustices suggest that it not enough to address the negative impacts of developmentality or challenge the ways (e.g. capitalism) in which development is done. Nor is it adequate to shore up the more-than-human or indeed, 'lesser' humans, or to make existing ethico-political frameworks more inclusive of nonhuman life. Such reconfiguration remains incomplete without revisiting the human.

Plumwood (2002, pp. 142, 8) makes this point in her call for a 'reconception of the human self' '[and] a deep and comprehensive restructuring of culture that rethinks and reworks human locations and relations to nature all the way down'. An exciting body of scholarship has taken up this task (e.g. Country et al., 2019; de la Cadena, 2015; Kimmerer, 2013; Kothari et al., 2019). Encompassing scholars, ideas and practices from diverse communities, the overarching tenor has been to explore 'the ontological politics of radical interdependence', in particular, examining relational ontologies for better ways of being on Earth (Escobar, 2020, p. xvi). This work has generated rich discussion, including analyses of how some of these ideas (e.g. rights of nature and buen vivir) have been co-opted by developmental regimes (Laastad, 2020; Merino, 2016).

A key difficulty in rethinking more-than-human relationships lies in identifying when/ at what point human use of the rest of nature becomes problematic. As Plumwood (2002) argues, more-than-human ethics has been dominated by the (flawed) use/respect dualism where respect and use are seen as mutually incompatible. Earthly living is impossible without using human and nonhuman Others. The challenge is in ensuring that relations of use are also respectful of nonhuman Others (e.g. I may use the services of a plumber, but I am concomitantly respectful of her as a fellow being). Not having a sense for when use becomes exploitation and instrumentalism at individual, societal and planetary scales allows for the co-option of even radical ontologies.

It is here that Plumwood's (2002, p. 11) emphasis on tackling the 'human' end of the human–nature relationship becomes vital: 'what requires critical philosophical engagement in the context of anthropocentric culture is self rather than others, the limits imposed by the human rather than the nature side of the ethical relationship'. Nearly 20 years later, Kallis (2019) makes a similar point in showing how what environmentalism sees as the 'limits' of nature, or 'planetary boundaries', is actually tied to the human Self – ecological 'limits' make sense only in relation to human intentions and desires. For instance, freshwater scarcity arises in relation to how human societies use and want to use water. To Kallis (2019, p. 60), the focus on external, ecological limits hides that 'they are ultimately about us and our own wants'.

Both Kallis and Plumwood, in different ways, are advocating for the redirection of more-than-human responses – away from the nonhuman Other, and towards the human Self. Instead of focusing on how to protect nonhuman nature or to what extent nonhuman nature can be used/exploited 'sustainably', the emphasis would be on humans and how they inhabit the planet. Plumwood (2002, p. 2) articulates this in terms of the need to 'situate dominant forms of human society ecologically'. Building on these insights and the article's earlier analyses of dominant concepts of human wellbeing, I suggest that what is needed is the re-placement of humankind in the rest of Earth through the *re-animalisation* of human wellbeing.

From a vision of a good human life premised upon insulation from the vulnerabilities inherent in living on this planet, we need to examine what it means to live as part of nature, as one among other animals. Equally crucial is a fundamental shift in approach to inequities. Instead of addressing social, ecological and animal injustices by 'shoring up' and seeking protections for vulnerable human or nonhuman Others, the focus would be on more equitably distributing the risks of living on this earth so that they are not borne primarily by marginal people and nature.

Re-animalising the human

How might we approach this task? We might start by asking what it means to live as part of nature, as animals. Given that other animals inhabit Earth without causing the kind of devastation (some) humankind does, this could offer a way of understanding the difference between respectful use and exploitation. As I explain below, re-animalising the human entails upturning some of our most basic ideas of what (human) wellbeing is.

In these times, the idea that humankind is ontologically a part of nature is widely accepted (Mansfield & Doyle, 2017). And yet, most scholarly and public discourse retains zoöpolitically exceptionalist visions of human wellbeing. It remains unimaginable that humans should live like other animals: with shorter life-spans perhaps, and unsupported by the infrastructures of agriculture, medicine and engineering that currently insulate many people from the vulnerabilities that are inherent to being a part of nature, including being killed by other animals. So while on the one hand there is awareness and acceptance of the idea that humankind is part of nature, this coexists with the assumption that human life and wellbeing are and ought to be more important than, and therefore different to, the rest of nature.

On a practical, everyday level, what would it look like to reject exceptionalist visions of the human and re-place people *as* animals? It might mean that I stop using flea medication on my cat. It might mean that I stop benefiting from all those animal lives that have been sacrificed at the altar of biomedicine. It might mean that I learn to cohabit with rats, tigers, elephants, cockroaches, gulls, wolves and pigeons instead of expecting far-off rural communities in India or Zimbabwe to protect wildlife. It might mean that a person being killed by an elephant or a virus is seen as no worse than a person being killed by a car or a hen being killed by a person. It might mean that I live with risks, inconveniences and mortal threats that I am accustomed to seeing only in the lives of more vulnerable human and nonhuman Others. Crucially, it might mean that I stop viewing human life as somehow more *not killable* than other animal life (Derrida, 2008).

To be 'killable' is to be in a social location where one can be killed without sanction. Killability refers to social status, and not the material act of being killed (one can be *not killable* and yet be killed). The killability of animals, i.e. the fact that they can, in general, be killed (whether intentionally, unintentionally, or as collateral damage) without it being considered 'criminal' has been the subject of contemplation (Schrader et al., 2017). By contrast, humans are not killable – if they are killed, then the act of killing is, in general, subject to investigation, and often sanction. Much of the more-than-human turn has been focused on challenging the killability of animals. The approach of re-animalisation turns this on the head, to instead dismantle the special status of humankind as '*not killable*'.

Take, for instance, the basic life activity of feeding. While the ways in which human societies have institutionalised the breeding, rearing and killing of animals for food have received critical attention, the assumption that humans are not and ought not to be food for other animals has remained mostly unquestioned. After her encounter with a crocodile, Plumwood (2012, p. 91) writes about the revelation that she could be, and almost was, crocodile food, identifying this as a crucial moment for ethical contemplation: 'human exceptionalism positions us as the eaters of others who are never themselves eaten'.

The non-killability of humankind is such a deeply entrenched norm that the idea that people can be food is almost unthinkable. For instance, the term 'man-eater' that is applied to wild animals that kill and eat humans signals the zoöpolitically exceptionalist idea that it is not normal for people to be food for animals. Wildlife histories and presents are full of narratives about and investigations on *why* particular individual animals become man-eaters – they are old; they are injured; they have been forced out of the forest into 'human' habitations (Baynes-Rock & Thomas, 2017; Masurkar, 2021). 'Man-eaters', and those who are mistaken for them, are systematically hunted down and killed or put into captivity, even if bestowed with conservation 'protections'. That some animals may feed on humans just like they feed on other animals is outside the realm of acceptability. The search for some special reason why an animal may kill and eat a human, and its subsequent extermination, are premised on the assumption there is something uniquely intolerable and abnormal about people being killed for animal food.

Re-animalisation would entail dismantling this assumption and the zoöpolitical exceptionalism that underpins it. If humans can kill and eat other animals, then the reverse should be an integral part of more-than-human relations. Re-animalisation goes beyond decisions to dedicate one's bodily wastes or body after death for permaculture; it is not just about becoming food after excretion or death, but about being *killable* for food. And food for not just charismatic large animals, but also for the many miniscule creatures, pests or pathogens, for example, that feed or live off humans, at times injuring or killing them (humans) in the process.

The non-killability of humans produces societal responses of management and extermination of other life-forms, big or small, that use humans for food – and even those who eat what is considered human food (e.g. 'crop-raiders', agricultural 'pests') (Beisel, 2010; Buller, 2008; Dempsey, 2010). Re-animalisation would mean eschewing such responses that seek to eradicate or otherwise manipulate entire species or populations because they feed on humans, and instead learn to live as one among other animals. Any act of self-protection would remain at the level of the individual or family and the immediate (like seen in other animals), without the arsenal of technoscience – and not at societal, institutionalised and long-term scales. Navigating the realities of *also being food* might well offer clearer understandings of the precarious balance between respectful use and exploitation.

Redistributing earthly risks

Dismantling the taken-for granted non-killability of humankind will generate fresh questions of equity. Non-killability manifests with variation across lines of socio-economic privilege. The developmental response to this is to enhance the non-killability of those who are socially marginalised, usually by emphasising their 'human-ness'. Dominant notions of humanity and human wellbeing require inequities *within* humanity to be addressed by bringing zoöpolitically exceptionalist norms of human wellbeing to everyone everywhere. They require the 'upliftment' of those who are *less* insulated from nature to meet the standards of those who are *more* insulated.

Re-animalisation would entail inverting this approach to inequities and injustices. It would be focused on re-locating within nature those humans who lead the most insulated lives. Instead of displacing marginal people in trying to 'uplift' them, the goal would be to learn their everyday practices (intentional and incidental) to live gently and tread lightly on the planet. Instead of tackling social inequities through practices of 'improvement' that cause socio-ecological and animal injustices, the task would be to redistribute the dangers that are inherent to life on Earth so that they are equally borne by all those, human and nonhuman, that inhabit the planet.

The degrowth movement in some ways tries to do this by focusing on the economies and lifestyles of the 'developed', instead of trying to 'develop' the poor (Demaria et al., 2013). Re-animalisation pushes these ideas further and deeper to disturb the zoöpolitical exceptionalism that supports mainstream human lives by redistributing the risks of earthly living instead of expanding the reach of more-than-animal norms. The material and conceptual onus for this shift in approach would lie with the non-poor, those who lead lives of privilege and insulation. The initial inspiration and lessons for how to live more in tune with the rest of Earth would be taken not from distanced romanticised Others, but from spatially proximate marginalised human and nonhuman neighbours and co-dwellers (e.g. Lynch, 2019). Thus, when it comes to rethinking humans as *also food*, the emphasis will not be on tigers and villagers in Central India, but on the urban elite, bedbugs and mosquitoes in New York City and Mumbai.

These are difficult thought experiments, for they are very far from how we have been schooled to think about ourselves and the other beings that share our species identity. They are even far removed from how we engage with preferred nonhuman Others. Yet, as Kallis (2019, p. 101) argues, social and political change would remain impossible 'if we begin with the premise that they are not [possible]' (p. 101). If developmental aspirations of material insulation from nature have been achieved in some form or the other, there is no reason why re-animalisation should remain in the realm of the 'unthinkable', and why it should not become 'a credible alternative to what exists, and the credible to the achievable' (Escobar, 2020, p. 131).

Conclusion

I will conclude with a set of issues for further conceptual and empirical enquiry. The very idea of re-animalisation is bound to generate problems given the material and political force that the idea of dehumanisation has. For one, the negative coding of the 'animal' and the concomitant privileging of the 'human' mean that the idea of 'animalisation' is seen as deeply problematic, as is the suggestion that nonhuman nature and animals can be guides for how human society ought to inhabit Earth. The task then is to show that *becoming and being animal* can be an achievement and not inevitably a demotion of ethico-political status. One aspect of this would be to develop grammars to denounce and combat the material processes associated with 'dehumanisation' without resorting to negative references to 'being animal or animalised', i.e. without being zoöpolitically exceptionalist. It surely is possible to challenge incarceration or torture in and of itself, regardless of who (human or animal) is subject to the same. Another aspect would be to frame narratives and strategies that shift societal imaginations: from the focus on 'shoring up' human and nonhuman lives at the expense of others, to relearning how to be vulnerable and to live as one among many forms of life on Earth. Instead of 'protecting' biodiversity or animals or 'developing' people by sacrificing spatio-temporally or ethically distant Others, more-than-human and social initiatives would concentrate on reconfiguring human lives in ways that are more exposed to and accepting of the risks of earthly living. At the same time, they would highlight how 'animalised' ways of inhabiting Earth can contribute new dimensions to wellbeing. For instance, this can involve exploring and articulating a sense of connectedness where one's wellbeing is tied to the wellbeing of others, human and nonhuman.

Crucially, re-animalisation needs to be carried out with attention to social justice. This entails the redistribution of the risks of living on the planet as a means of addressing social and more-than-human inequities. At the most basic level, this involves divesting the privileged (humans) of their multifarious layers of insulation (from nonhuman nature) as a way of approaching justice. This, obviously, is not easily done, which is where narratives that recode *being animal* as positive become necessary. These are tasks that are simultaneously ontological, epistemological and ethical, and are tasks that are vital for constructing pathways to multispecies justice in a world ruined by progress.

Funding

The research and writing for this paper were supported by the Royal Society of Edinburgh's Sabbatical Research Grant (grant number 65100).

References

Bauer, A. M., & Bhan, M. (2016). Welfare and the politics and the historicity of the Anthropocene. *The South Atlantic Quarterly, 115*(1), 61–87.

Baynes-Rock, M., & Thomas, E. (2017). We are not equals: Socio-cognitive dimensions of lion/human relationships. *Animal Studies Journal, 6*(1), 104–128.

Beisel, U. (2010). Jumping hurdles with mosquitoes? *Environment and Planning D: Society and Space, 28*, 46–49.

Bennett, C., Thomas, R., Williams, M., Zalasiewicz, J., Edgeworth, M., Miller, H., Coles, B., Burton, E. J., & Marume, U. (2018). The broiler chicken as a signal of a human reconfigured biosphere. *Royal Society, 5*(12). https://doi.org/10.1098/rsos.180325

Bhuyan, A. (2021, January 14). How Covaxin trial participants in Bhopal were misled. *The Wire.* https://science.thewire.in/health/peoples-hospital-bhopal-covaxin-clinical-trials-exploitation-ethics-ground-report/

Biermann, C., & Mansfield, B. (2014). Biodiversity, purity, and death: Conservation biology as biopolitics. *Environment and Planning D: Society and Space, 32*(2), 257–273.

Buller, H. (2008). Safe from the wolf: Biosecurity, biodiversity, and competing philosophies of nature. *Environment and Planning A, 40*, 1583–1597.

Celermajer, D., Chatterjee, S., Cochrane, A., Fishel, S., Neimanis, A., O'Brien, A., Reid, S., Srinivasan, K., Schlosberg, D., & Waldow, A. (2020). Justice through a multispecies lens. *Contemporary Political Theory, 19*, 475–512. https://doi.org/10.1057/s41296-020-00386-5

Country, B., Suchet-Pearson, S., Wright, S., Lloyd, K., Tofa, M., Sweeney, J., Burarrwanga, L., Ganambarr, R., Ganambarr-Stubbs, M., Ganambarr, B., & Maymuru, D. (2019). Goŋ Gurtha: Enacting response-abilities as situated co-becoming. *Environment and Planning D: Society and Space, 37*(4), 682–702. https://doi.org/10.1177/0263775818799749

de la Cadena, M. (2015). *Earth beings: Ecologies of practice across Andean worlds.* Duke University Press.

Demaria, F., Schneider, F., Sekulova, F., & Martinez-Alier, J. (2013). What is degrowth? From an activist slogan to a social movement. *Environmental Values, 22*, 191–215.

Dempsey, J. (2010). Tracking grizzly bears in British Columbia's environmental politics. *Environment and Planning A, 42*, 1138–1156.

Derrida, J. (2008). *The animal that therefore I am.* Fordham University Press.

Descartes, R. (1991). *The philosophical writings of Descartes: Volume III: The correspondence* (J. Cottingham, R. Stoothoff, D. Murdoch, & A. Kenny, Trans.). Cambridge University Press.

Emel, J., & Neo, H. (2015). *Political ecologies of meat.* Routledge.

Escobar, A. (1995). *Encountering development: The making and unmaking of the Third World.* Princeton University Press.

Escobar, A. (2020). *Pluriversal politics: The real and the possible.* Duke University Press.

European Animal Research Association. (2020). *How animals are helping in COVID-19 research: A global overview.* www.eara.eu/post/how-animals-are-helping-in-covid-19-research-a-global-overview

Harvey, D. (2014). *Seventeen contradictions and the end of capitalism.* Profile Books.

Haynes, R. P. (2011). Competing conceptions of animal welfare and their ethical implications for the treatment of non-human animals. *Acta Biotheoretica, 59*, 105–120.

Kallis, G. (2019). *Limits: Why Malthus was wrong and why environmentalists should care.* Stanford Briefs, an imprint of Stanford University Press.

Kalu, B. (2020). COVID-19 in Nigeria: A disease of hunger. *The Lancet Respiratory Medicine, 8*(6), 556–557. https://doi.org/10.1016/S2213-2600(20)30220-4

Kimmerer, R. (2013). *Braiding sweetgrass: Indigenous wisdom, scientific knowledge and the teachings of plants* (1st ed.). Milkweed Editions.

Kothari, A., Salleh, A., Escobar, A., Demaria, F., & Acosta, A. (Eds.). (2019). *Pluriverse: A post-development dictionary.* Tulika Books and Authorsupfront.

Laastad, S. (2020). Nature as a subject of rights? National discourses on Ecuador's constitutional rights of nature. *Forum for Development Studies, 47*(3), 401–425. https://doi.org/10.1080/08039410.2019.1654544

Li, T. M. (2007). *The will to improve: Governmentality, development and the practice of politics.* Duke University Press.

Lynch, H. (2019). Esposito's affirmative biopolitics in multispecies homes. *European Journal of Social Theory, 22*(3), 364–381. https://doi.org/10.1177/1368431018804156

Mansfield, B., & Doyle, M. (2017). Nature: A conversation in three parts. Special forum on intra-disciplinarity. *Annals of the Association of American Geographers, 107*(1), 22–27.

Masurkar, A. (2021). *Sherni* [Drama]. Amazon Prime Video.

McMichael, P. (2012). *Development and social change: A global perspective.* Sage.

Merino, R. (2016). An alternative to 'alternative development'?: Buen vivir and human develop-
    ment in Andean countries. *Oxford Development Studies*, *44*(3), 271–286. https://doi.org/10.1
    080/13600818.2016.1144733
Moore, J. W. (2017). The Capitalocene, Part I: On the nature and origins of our ecological crisis.
    The Journal of Peasant Studies, *44*(3), 594–630. https://doi.org/10.1080/03066150.2016.12
    35036
Peggs, K. (2020). Animal rights movement. In C. Rojek & G. Ritzer (Eds.), *Wiley Blackwell ency-
    clopedia of sociology*. Blackwell.
Plumwood, V. (2002). *Environmental culture: The ecological crisis of reason*. Routledge.
Plumwood, V. (2012). *Eye of the crocodile*. L. Shannon, Ed. Australian National University Press.
Samaddar, R. (2021). *A pandemic and the politics of life*. Women Unlimited, an associate of Kali
    for Women.
Schlosberg, D., & Craven, L. (2019). *Sustainable materialism: Environmental movements and the
    politics of everyday life*. Oxford University Press.
Schrader, A., Johnson, E., Buller, H., Robinson, D., Rundle, S., Sagan, D., Schmitt, S., & Spicer, J.
    (2017). Considering killability: Experiments in unsettling life and death. *Catalyst: Feminism,
    Theory, Technoscience*, *3*(2), 1–15. https://doi.org/10.28968/cftt.v3i2.28849
Scott, J. (2017). *Against the grain: A deep history of the earliest states*. Yale University Press.
Severn Cullis-Suzuki. (2020, January 24). *Green originals*. BBC. www.bbc.co.uk/programmes/
    m000df4k
Shrivastava, A., & Kothari, A. (2012). *Churning the earth: The making of global India*. Viking.
Srinivasan, K., & Kasturirangan, R. (2016). Political ecology, development and human exception-
    alism. *Geoforum*, *75*, 125–128.
Srinivasan, K., & Kasturirangan, R. (2017). Violent love: Conservation and invasive alien species.
    In J. Maher, H. Pierpoint, & P. Beirne (Eds.), *The Palgrave international handbook of animal
    abuse studies* (pp. 433–452). Palgrave Macmillan.
Weis, T. (2007). *The global food economy: The battle for the future of farming*. Zed Books.
World Health Organization & China. (2021). *WHO-convened global study of origins of SARS-
    CoV-2: China part*. www.who.int/publications/i/item/who-convened-global-study-of-ori-
    gins-of-sars-cov-2-china-part

Author biography

Krithika Srinivasan works as Senior Lecturer in Human Geography at the University of Edinburgh.
Her research and teaching interests lie at the intersection of political ecology, human–animal studies,
and post-development politics. Her work draws on research in South Asia to rethink globally established concepts and practices about nature–society relations. Through empirical projects on street
dogs and public health, biodiversity conservation, animal-based food systems and non-elite environ-
mentalisms, her scholarship has focused on reconfiguring approaches to multispecies justice.
Krithika's research and teaching are deeply rooted in long-term field engagement and praxis in India.

MONOGRAPH SERIES

The Sociological Review Monographs
2022, Vol. 70(2) 153–170

Ecological uncivilisation: Precarious world-making after progress

Article reuse guidelines:
sagepub.com/journals-permissions
DOI: 10.1177/00380261221084782
journals.sagepub.com/home/sor

Martin Savransky
Department of Sociology, Goldsmiths, University of London, UK

Abstract

Responding to the proposition that learning to live in the Anthropocene involves learning how to die, this article problematises the modes of world-making upheld in some of the contemporary proposals for the global reorganisation of societies towards just, socio-ecological transitions beyond the techno-fixes of geoengineering, green growth, and their attendant ideals of progress. Specifically, it critically examines one such proposal that, inspired by process philosophy, has proven deeply influential in China's recent shift in ecological (geo)politics: the idea of an 'ecological civilisation' based on principles of ontological relationality, democratic responsibility, and a new alliance between the sciences and the humanities. The article argues that while such a project rejects the substantive values of modern progress, its regulative notion of civilisation retains the modern story of progress as a mode of valuation and therefore reinscribes imperial, colonial values at the heart of ecology. In response, the article suggests that learning to die in the wake of ecological devastation requires making life outside the modern coordinates of progress, which is to say living without the ideal of civilisation. Seeking to expand the political imagination at a time of socio-ecological transformations, it calls for 'ecological uncivilisation' as a permanent experimentation with improbable forms of world-making and methodologies of life that are envisaged thanks to ongoing histories of decolonisation and not in spite of them; that strive to live and die well but not always better.

Keywords

China, civilisation, climate change, political imagination, process philosophy

Corresponding author:
Martin Savransky, Department of Sociology, Goldsmiths, University of London, Lewisham Way, London, SE14 6NW, UK.
Email: m.savransky@gold.ac.uk

The difficulty is just this:– It may be impossible to conceive a reorganisation of society adequate for the removal of some admitted evil without destroying the social organisation and the civilization which depends on it. An allied plea is that there is no known way of removing the evil without the introduction of worse evils of some other type.

Alfred North Whitehead, *Adventures of Ideas* (1967, p. 20)

Introduction: The changing climates of progress

Writing in the Opinion pages of the *New York Times* on what later became the focus of his pithy *Learning to Die in the Anthropocene* (2015), army veteran Roy Scranton recalls a day, two and a half years after his return from Iraq, when, 'safe and lazy back in Fort Sill, Okla., I thought I had made it out' (Scranton, 2013). During the four years of his round in Iraq, he was terrified by the idea of dying. Baghdad, he writes, 'seemed incredibly dangerous, even though statistically I was pretty safe. We got shot and mortared, and I.E.D's [Improvised Explosive Devices] laced every highway, but I had a good armor, we had a great medic, and we were the most powerful military the world had ever seen.' His odds of coming home were, on the whole, good – maybe 'wounded, but probably alive'. Yet none of that assuaged the ineluctable sense, every time he would go out on a mission, that death was the order of the day: 'I looked down the barrel of the future and saw a dark, empty hole' (2013, n.p.). After all, he had become 'a private in the United States Army. This strange, precarious world was my new home. If I survived.' He did survive, in spite of all. And for a while, the fact of finally having left Iraq meant the possibility of leaving that future behind, of returning to a more familiar temporal path. But on that day when it truly began to feel like he had made it out, Scranton (2013) turned on the television only to discover that Hurricane Katrina was hitting New Orleans:

> This time it was the weather that brought shock and awe, but I saw the same chaos and urban collapse I'd seen in Baghdad, the same failure of planning and the same tide of anarchy. The 82nd Airborne hit the ground, took strategic points and patrolled streets now under de facto martial law. My unit was put on alert to prepare for riot control operations. The grim future I'd seen in Baghdad was coming home: not terrorism, not even W.M.D.'s [Weapons of Mass Destruction], but a civilization in collapse, with a crippled infrastructure, unable to recuperate from shocks to its system. And today, with recovery still going on more than a year after Sandy and many critics arguing that the Eastern seaboard is no more prepared for a huge weather event than we were last November, it's clear that future's not going away.

A civilisation in collapse. That, perhaps, is one of the meanings of this time of endings, this time of warming and of melting ice-caps, this time of extinctions and of extreme weather events, of droughts and climate migration, of carbon fuelled capitalism and ecological turmoil – a time otherwise now often marked by the name 'Anthropocene' (see Blok & Jensen, 2019). To think of it as a civilisation in collapse, as the end of that which we have called 'civilisation', is to make perceptible, of course, that no amount of technical fixes will do the trick (Nightingale et al., 2019); that the collapse is *ecological* in its most expansive sense, involving not only environmental ecologies but the ecology of the social, of the mental, of the cultural and of the political as well; that henceforth, as Félix

Guattari (2001, p. 28) put it, 'it is the ways of living on this planet that are in question', those very same ways of ploughing the Earth that not long ago we came to call 'civilisation'. Which is why, beyond scientific reports and techno-fixes, beyond international agreements and climate targets, Scranton (2015, p. 27) makes the powerful proposition that, if 'we want to learn to live in the Anthropocene, we must first learn how to die'.

Learning how to die is not exactly easy. It might be said – as indeed has often been said, from Cicero to Montaigne – that philosophy itself was invented in response to this challenge, as an art in learning how to live and die well (Hadot, 1995). Confronted with the urgency of learning how to die as a soldier in Iraq, Scranton found a source of inspiration in the *Hagakure*, an eighteenth century *bushidō* manual by Yamamoto Tsunetomo, which advised that meditation on inevitable death ought to be a daily performance, leading to a becoming with one's death in one's thoughts and mode of living by learning to accept the transience of one's own life. But if this was a difficult lesson, learned in the midst of flying bullets and ubiquitous IEDs, it was also his own personal lesson. While according to former US President George W. Bush (2001, p. 1361) it was *in order* 'to save civilization itself' that Scranton and others were eventually sent to Iraq, '[t]he rub now', Scranton (2015, p. 21) poignantly observes in an ironic turn of events, 'is that we have to learn to die not as individuals, but as a civilization'.

This compounds the challenge. But as I will argue, this is not simply because 'humans are wired to believe that tomorrow will be much like today' (2015, p. 22). After all, whatever the lethargy in the implementation of the international agreements to which governments around the world have committed themselves, recent years have also seen no shortage of new, bold proposals and manifestos for global world-making projects and socio-ecological transitions emanating from divergent political, geographical and cultural traditions – including the Green New Deal, the Pacto Ecosocial del Sur, and even the Ecomodernist Manifesto, among others. Indeed, save for the intervention of an unforeseeable cataclysmic event that might puncture the fabric of time and bring it to an absolute end, perhaps one of the difficulties of learning to die 'as a civilisation' is that the end of what we call a 'civilisation' is more akin to a slow and protracted process of attrition and exhaustion than a punctuated cessation. As such, learning to die 'as a civilisation' poses a profound challenge to the political imagination: its own ending raises the speculative question of the 'afters' to which death might give way, and of the possible and impossible modes of world-making and forms of sociality that might emerge in its wake. Lured by the question of learning how to die today whilst seeking to expand our imaginations, in this article I critically examine one such speculative call and project of world-making that, in full acknowledgement of the need for an 'after' to *this* capitalist, growth-obsessed and ecocidal civilisation, calls for a radical transformation of the very foundations of human collective life so as to found a new, global 'ecological civilisation' based on principles of sustainability, ontological interdependence and relationality, liberal communitarianism, and a new alliance between the sciences and the humanities (e.g. Clayton & Schwartz, 2019; Cobb & Schwartz, 2018; Gare, 2017).

A number of tangled reasons make the proposal for an 'ecological civilisation' an especially interesting and instructive terrain – at once speculative, political and ecological – on which to explore the challenges to our political imagination that the question of learning how to die in the Anthropocene poses. Though it appears to have early roots in the Soviet eco-Marxist notion of 'ecological culture' taken up by leading government figure Ivan T. Frolov in the 1980s (see Gare, 2021; Huan, 2016), the contemporary form of this proposal has been espoused by a collective of theologians, philosophers, ethicists and activists who for decades have sustained and cultivated a philosophical tradition that more recently has come to influence eco-cultural theory and the social sciences more generally. That is, the tradition of process philosophy associated with the work of Alfred North Whitehead, among others – a philosophical tradition that, in their words, rejects the dogmatic materialism of modern thought and provides a 'broader, more realistic, nondual understanding of reality with implications for how we live' (Cobb & Schwartz, 2018, p. 4; Gare, 2017). And while still marginal in western debates, the notion and project of an 'ecological civilisation' has already become the hallmark of the Chinese government's approach to ecological politics and policy, inscribing the very concept into the Chinese Communist Party's (CCP) constitution in 2012, and developing a whole swathe of far-reaching socio-environmental policies in its name (Geall & Ely, 2018; Wang et al., 2014) – a distinctly authoritarian form of ecological (geo)politics that some have dubbed 'coercive environmentalism' (Charbonnier, 2020; Li & Shapiro, 2020).

Finally, it may go without saying but not without noting that the project of an 'ecological civilisation' is an avowedly *civilisational* proposal, one that claims not simply to accept but to fully embrace the fact that modern industrial civilisation is currently writing the epitaph to its own demise and must be replaced wholesale by a new and better global principle of planetary organisation. In this sense, one would hope that the lessons a critical examination of the project of 'ecological civilisation' yields might also perhaps be of some allegorical value, complicating the political image of thought that pits ecological world-making projects, in their noble and innocent pursuit of the global common good, against forces of power and oppression. For if the slow process of civilisational collapse renders the question of learning how to die, of what modes of world-making might be cultivated in its wake, especially challenging, none find this more intractable, more unimaginable, than the heirs of those who, only in the eighteenth century, *invented* the concept of 'civilisation' as such and did so precisely in order to sum up, in Norbert Elias's (2000, p. 4) classic words, 'everything in which Western society of the last two or three centuries believes itself superior to earlier societies or "more primitive" contemporary ones', everything that was said to constitute 'its special character and what it is proud of: the level of *its* technology, the nature of *its* manners, the development of *its* scientific knowledge or view of the world, and much more'. Indeed, created at the heart of the age of European empires, through the prism of the colonial encounter, as a word both for the process that rendered 'man' civilised *and* for the very culmination of that process, the notion of civilisation 'entered the history of ideas at the same time as the modern sense of the word *progress*', and they 'were destined to maintain a most intimate relationship' that would make it 'essential to determine the precise phases of the civilizing process, the stages of social progress' (Starobinski, 1993, p. 4).

This is why in what follows I make the proposition that learning to die in the Anthropocene might require that one learn to live outside of the modern coordinates of progress. And while, like many others thinking about socio-ecological transitions, proponents of an 'ecological civilisation' are critical of the extractivist, materialistic, growth-oriented and scientistic principles that constitute the substantive values of progress of the modern, capitalist world-system, the very ideal of an ecological *civilisation* has 'progress' – a global, boundless and upwards trajectory towards a future that, guided by a set of universal principles, will be 'better' than the present – built into it as a mode of valuation, thereby reinscribing imperial, colonial values at the heart of their world-making efforts. Which is also to say that learning to die 'as a civilisation' probably requires that one learn to live *without* the concept and ideal of civilisation. In other words, it requires a speculative activation of the political imagination which, rather than replace one civilisational model for another, rather than conjure the progressive horizon of a new global situation that would eventually substitute the current state of affairs, refuses the lure of progress so as to give itself over to an ongoing and unfinished experimentation with more precarious, fragmentary, subjunctive and inchoate forms of sociality on unstable ecological terrain. Inspired by the Dark Mountain Project's (Kingsnorth & Hine, 2009) poetic experiment in 'uncivilisation', in this article I seek to activate our political imagination after progress by proposing *ecological uncivilisation* as a permanent experimentation with improbable forms of world-making and methodologies of life that are articulated thanks to the earth-wide precariousness that calls them into action and not in spite of them; that are envisaged thanks to ongoing histories of decolonisation and not despite them; that strive to live and die well but not always better.

Civilising the Anthropocene? Outline of an ecological civilisation

'The term "ecological civilization"', writes theologian and philosopher John Cobb in the preface to the primer on the matter written by Philip Clayton and Andrew Schwartz (2019, p. 1), 'comes close to being an oxymoron', for the very notion of civilisation 'is partly defined in terms of humans altering their environment in favour of the immediate desires of their species. . . . In this sense, it might seem, a civilization is inherently anti-ecological. How then can we describe the goal for humanity as transitioning to ecological civilization?' The answer to this question is usually couched in terms of a concern over the *form* such human alterations of the environment take, and the overarching philosophical, scientific and political principles by which they abide. Indeed, at the heart of the project for ecological civilisation lies a radical, if relatively uncontroversial, diagnosis: that the underlying causes of the present ecological turmoil are inseparable from the entire configuration of social, cultural, political and economic patterns that comprise modern industrial civilisation as such. 'The massive inequality between the rich and the poor', Clayton and Schwartz (2019, pp. 11–12) write, 'is not separate from an economics of unlimited growth and the depletion of natural resources, extinction of species, or global warming. Contemporary civilization is designed to benefit the privileged elite at the expense of the poor and the environment.'

If 'ecological civilisation' could ultimately be redeemed from the sin of self-contradiction, it is because at its heart is precisely the attempt to lay out the philosophical, scientific and political foundations that could ground a new, global civilisation on thoroughly ecological principles. Key to this societal repatterning is the recognition that the hegemonic philosophical traditions that have come to dominate modern culture and its governing institutions, those that have emanated out of the rise, in the seventeenth century, of a scientific materialism that bifurcated nature into two systems of reality – a realm of experiences, and a realm of the causes of those experiences – have rendered much of the natural and human sciences unable to respond to the consequences of the cultural and economic patterns to which they gave shape, patterns which reduce everyone and everything to predictable instruments of a global capitalist machine, thereby leading to 'the degeneration of culture, the fragmentation of enquiry, the multiplication of disciplines and sub disciplines . . . ignoring each other, and a noise explosion hiding stagnation in intellectual life' (Gare, 2017, p. 147).

In their enthroning of techno-scientific mastery and brute matter as the material of which everything is made, modern natural and human sciences have therefore committed themselves 'to explaining away not only consciousness, but life itself, as nothing but physical and chemical processes, supporting a debased view of humanity and life that legitimates greed as the driving force of the economy and of the evolution of nature, imposing thereby a fundamentally flawed model of reality on humanity' (Gare, 2017, p. 144). It is in order to replace such a flawed model and to lay the ground for 'a new world-orientation', that the proponents of an ecological civilisation argue that we must turn to another, more marginal western philosophical tradition that has rejected the bifurcation of nature and the scientific materialism that sustains it. Such philosophical tradition is none other than that of the process philosophy of Alfred North Whitehead, and more broadly, the longer tradition – stretching back to the thought of F. W. J. Schelling – of 'speculative naturalism' in both philosophy and in the biological and ecological sciences, which would provide the foundations on which to develop an ecological 'paradigm' where 'dualism and monism are replaced with a holism that portrays reality not as a collection of objects, but as a community of subjects – an interconnected whole, within which we are constituted by our relations' (Clayton & Schwartz, 2019, p. 41).

This metaphysical holism of an interconnected community of subjects or organisms would, in the first instance, create the conditions for the development of natural and human sciences, as well as forms of agriculture and farming, that are consistent with the reality of organised complexity and its emergence as described by theoretical ecology, making the ultimate existents of the universe no longer bits of matter in motion but 'creative processes, or durational self-constraining patterns of activity, and configurations of such processes at multiple scales in dynamic interaction' (Gare, 2017, p. 178). As such, contemporary measurements of 'productivity', defined in terms of the volume of yields and hours of human labour, would be replaced by a concern for the 'health' and sustainability of the very creative processes and patterns of coordination through which soils, rivers, oceans, human and nonhuman animals, and the entire community of subjects that compose the biosphere, generate and regenerate themselves. The 'health' of a community of organisms, of the Earth itself, would thus be a function of the 'mutual augmenting of the whole community and the component communities of each other, facilitating their continued successful functioning, their resilience in response to perturbations, new situations and stress, and for ongoing development and creativity to maximize developmental options, and can be measured as such' (Gare, 2017, p. 180). No longer centred around capitalist values of productivity, in other words, such holism would instead measure and govern the 'health' of an ecological community as a function of its capacity for resilience, development and creativity.

But there is more. For a holistic metaphysics of organisational complexity seeking to repattern global social organisation cannot rest content with the very modern capitalist settlement that sought to parse out a separate realm of 'nature' as mere raw material for human consumption and cogitation. A 'paradigm shift', as some of its proponents label it, would also involve a correlative transformation of our philosophical anthropologies, rethinking what it means to be human in the wake of the 'recognition that humans are part of, and dependent upon, a living Earth' (Clayton & Schwartz, 2019, p. 99). Conceiving of the Earth as a community of subjects requires that one take seriously what biosemioticians have been arguing for decades (see Emmeche & Kull, 2011), that processes of sense-making are not the preserve of humans but pervade the entire world to varying degrees, such that every organism shapes itself and the pattern of its activity in response to its surrounding world. Humans, in this respect, constitute a difference not of nature but of degree, developing semiotic processes and capacities that enable them not only to respond to their immediate surroundings but

> . . . to act back on the conditions of their emergence, and this implies the possibility of altering the trajectories of their natural and social communities. If the conditions are maintained for pursuing and disseminating the truth, it can be demonstrated we are not condemned to destroying the conditions of our existence. It is the commitment to truth and the conditions for pursuing it that could provide the ultimate foundation and unity for an environmental movement able to successfully challenge neoliberalism, or rather, managerialist market fundamentalism, and create a new, global civilization. (Gare, 2017, p. 164)

It is from the seeds of this philosophical anthropology that a sketch of a political philosophy makes itself perceptible, seeking to provide the socio-political and institutional architecture for the maintenance of 'conditions for pursuing and disseminating truth' with a view towards the creation of a global socio-ecological organisation 'where the destructive conflicts between tribes, civilizations, and nations will have been overcome' (Gare, 2017, p. 166). Accepting the fate of modern capitalist globalisation whilst lamenting the cultural 'fragmentation' which has derived from it, philosopher Arran Gare (2017, p. 166) and others argue that this will involve 'unifying the whole of humanity in a commitment to advancing the health of the global ecosystem and its subordinate communities'.

Such unification, we are told, would take place through a reformulation of globalisation along a multilayered federalism of 'communities of communities' overseen by international governing bodies, such as the United Nations, that would enable us to 'overcome the parochialism of each civilization and incorporate the major insights from all civilizations' (Gare, 2017, p. 184), thereby institutionalising universal 'recognition of the value of life, including non-human life forms and ecosystems, so that only those practices are allowed to flourish that augment ecosystems' (p. 181). According to Clayton and Schwartz (2019, pp. 106–107), such reformulation would require 'top-down' strategies that devise and implement policies, laws and regulations to 'encourage citizens and corporations to operate in ways that promote long-term sustainability and overall well-being', as well as some 'bottom-up' actions in which 'individual citizens, and local organisations, take on the responsibility of acting on behalf of the vision of long-term sustainability and overall well-being'. The aim, in any case, is clear: to cultivate virtues and modes of creative thinking, guided by a more holistic natural and social philosophy, that can foster 'the new social imaginary of a global ecological civilization, and it is in relation to this that all other aspects of culture should be understood and evaluated, and acted upon' (Gare, 2017, p. 210).

This is of course but a brief outline, a theoretical silhouette drawn from two programmatically significant texts that give shape to the political imagination that an ecological civilisation limns. Whether one finds the proposal attractive or repulsive in theory will surely depend on one's political sensibilities, and on one's own interpretation of the process-philosophical tradition. For reasons that will become evident – if they aren't already – I diverge on both fronts (Savransky, 2016, 2021a). But it is not my intention to engage here in a counter-exegetical exercise. My interest, instead, is pragmatic – a concern for the world-making consequences that well-meaning ideas are capable of unleashing. For the fact is that these proposals no longer remain within the realm of philosophical speculation. As Gare (2010, p. 6) put it in an earlier programmatic text: 'The world should follow the lead of China.'

Progress after progress: The burden of an ecological civilisation

Alongside the significantly growing presence of process philosophy in China (Yang, 2010), 'ecological civilisation' made its debut appearance in 2007 at the CCP's 17th Congress and by 2014 was inscribed in its constitution and at the very heart of the Chinese government's awe-inspiring overhaul of political philosophy and governmental policies designed to make the People's Republic of China, currently the world's largest CO^2 producer and rising superpower, no longer beholden to the single capitalist imperative of economic growth and instead becoming a global leader in 'green development', recently announcing their aim of achieving carbon neutrality by 2060 (Geall & Ely, 2018; Wang et al., 2014).

Seen widely as an attempt to resolve the tensions between environmental protection and economic development through the creation of concrete policies of renewable energy, production, carbon reduction and reforestation, the notion of ecological civilisation in China frames the adoption of 'specific pathways, and has laid out pilots and a set of implementable changes in governance that can help achieve them', while simultaneously heralding 'the potential for a more assertive and confident China to assume a stronger leadership role in global environmental debates' (Geall & Ely, 2018, p. 1191). While paying close attention to the successes of the Chinese state to reduce carbon emissions and dependence on fossil fuels, as well as to implement massive programmes of afforestation – a staggering 25% of the planet's net increase in leaf area from 2000 to 2017 – and environmental conservation, Yifei Li and Judith Shapiro (2020, p. 23) remind us in their critical but remarkably detailed study of the politics of the recent Chinese environmental turn that the decisive pursuit of ecological civilisation in China cannot be disentangled from the increasingly authoritarian and repressive mode of governance that characterises its state-led environmentalism, such that 'in the name of ecological wellbeing, the state exploits the environment as a new form of political capital, harnessing it in the pursuit of authoritarian resilience and durability'.

This new 'environmental authoritarianism', as they call it, includes more than the deployment of geoengineering technologies for blue skies and rain, and policies of 'mandatory behaviour modification' addressed to the middle classes of the wealthy eastern coast, controlled for instance through the deployment of 'trash inspectors' who actively police the appropriate disposal of waste, or through the piloting of 'morality banks' that award villagers credit points for recycling and practising a whole range of other 'virtuous deeds' while subtracting points for '"extravagant" funerals and birthday parties or other "acts of immorality"' (Li & Shapiro, 2020, pp. 69–71). It also involves forced displacements and dispossession of peoples for the sake of dam construction and hydropower development in the rural West, the mandatory 'sedentarisation' of herding nomads (including Uighurs, Kazakhs, Tajiks, Uzbeks and Kirghiz) in the name of 'the win-win goals of poverty alleviation and grasslands restoration', thereby making eco-logical migration 'a centrepiece of China's often elusive pursuit of ecological civiliza-tion' (2020, p. 105).

But there is more still. To the extent that the project of ecological civilisation is also a means of repositioning China geopolitically, the panoply of domestic policies are only compounded by a host of international policies of 'green' investment, development and trade, such as the Belt and Road Initiative (BRI) by reviving the old Silk Road across Central Asia as well as establishing new maritime paths along the costs of South Asia, Africa and the Middle East, and now expanding 'dramatically, both geographically and conceptually, with signatories encompassing about one-fourth of the global economy' and a swathe of programmes that include but go beyond infrastructural development to encompass 'anti-poverty programs, food and health aid, education, including scholar-ships for students from BRI countries to study in China and the stepped-up installation overseas of Confucius Institutes, which promote Chinese language and culture so as to create a friendly constituency of foreigners in China' (Li & Shapiro, 2020, pp. 116–117).

What is interesting about Li and Shapiro's incisive and well-informed examination, however, is that it is not quite a liberal critique of the authoritarian nature of Chinese state-led environmentalism, denouncing the non-environmental effects that such poli-cies have upon ethnic minorities and the poor, and seeking to 'unmask' the hidden agenda of global imperialism behind China's BRI programmes. As they rightly point out, so-called liberal democracies in the West are by no means strangers to coercive operations. Indeed, they were founded upon them (Lowe, 2015). The point they make, rather, is that for all of China's achievements, coercive environmentalism is no guaran-tee, for 'even the environmental successes are not always what they seem' (Li & Shapiro, 2020, p. 23). Famously, the geopolitical influences of the BRI also enable the CCP to perform a form of 'dirty migration' whereby carbon outputs are displaced to other signatory countries, whilst Chinese dams across the Mekong Delta have deleteri-ous implications downstream in Vietnam and Cambodia, 'putting 64 species in danger and . . . limiting water flows on which millions depend' (2020, p. 121). Domestically, their mass afforestation programmes are achieved by planting tree-monocultures that neglect the complex and situated requirements of specific ecological milieus thereby further degrading soils and wildlife habitats, whilst their politics of 'ecological migra-tion' and sedentarisation of nomad collectives not only precipitate social and cultural dislocations but contribute to the parsing of grasslands to individual households which 'results in ecologically worse outcomes than larger-scale grazing units comprised of multiple households' (2020, p. 106). It is thus that Li and Shapiro (2020, p. 197) assert that, '[f]rom ecological civilization to low-carbon urbanism, these admirable terms frame the overall discursive landscape of Chinese state-led environmentalism. Yet, beyond their discursive qualities and propaganda functions, they offer little guide to the workings of the Chinese state.'

This, indeed, is a forceful conclusion. But it does not quite help us learn how to die. For while it provides a damning story of the dangers born of imperfect realisation, such a conclusion tacitly retains within its own indictment the ideal of civilisation as a mode of Anthropocenic world-making and political imagination, thereby reinforcing the habitual political image of an ecological politics for a global common good against forces of power and self-serving operations. Which is to say that what both the proponents and the detractors of the Chinese project of ecological civilisation share is the story of 'civilisation' as a long, universal march of human progress out of savagery through the refinement of culture, modes of conduct, laws and forms of socio-political organisation dating all the way back to the Neolithic revolution, as a 'way of living together with shared values' (Clayton & Schwartz, 2019, p. 16). The problem, however, is that this a quintessentially modern story, the product of a political imagination kindled by those who invented the concept of 'civilisation' in eighteenth century imperial Europe not only as its own self-admiring description in the face of non-European, colonised others, but also as a political and moral judgement, 'the criterion against which barbarity, or non-civilization, is judged and condemned' (Starobinski, 1993, p. 31). Indeed, I suggest Li and Shapiro's examination of the CCP's ecological record should perhaps lead us to the inverse evaluation – that rather than a corruption of the ideal of an ecological civilisation, China's recent environmental (geo)politics constitute *its very embodiment*. After all, the word 'civilisation' may have been invented in the mid-1700s as a term of jurisprudence, to describe the change from criminal to civil court. But this remarkably short-lived acceptation quickly gave way to a rival, non-juridical signified which would replace its technical sense so thoroughly that 'the word quickly ceased to be seen as new' (Starobinski, 1993, p. 2). Such, it turns out, is the birth of 'civilisation' in 1756, as simultaneously the process that rendered humankind civilised and the normative outcome of that process. And the fact is that the normative character that the notion of civilisation acquired at the heart of empire rendered 'civilisation' itself the name for a world-making project that – as historian Brett Bowden (2009, p. 224) nicely puts it in *The Empire of Civilization* – was always 'more uniform than universal'. It conferred upon the civilised the right and the duty – indeed *the burden* – to civilise the uncivilised, which is to say to 'rescue' the savages and barbarians from their primitive state by subjugating, re-educating – and failing that, extinguishing – them into the civilisational path of progress. Rather than a name for cultural and political sophistication, civilisation, to borrow Bruce Mazlish's (2005, p. 116) words, has since its birth always been 'a fighting word, a serious political matter'.

As such, if the manners by which imperial Europe has sought to bend the would-be universal arch of history towards 'civilisation' were those 'of the often violent and everly zealous civilising missions or *mission civilisatrice*, missions that were generally designed to ameliorate – where and when thought possible – the conditions of the world's savages and barbarians, usually through tutelage, training, and conversion to Christianity'

(Bowden, 2009, p. 130), then far from rendering it a hollow concept, the coercive environmentalism of the CCP is well and truly *civilising* indeed: relocating and reshaping minoritarian modes of living through forced ecological migration and sedentarisation, imposing 'standards' of ecological civilisation through BRI developmental programmes, and extending the civilising will to uniformity to the Earth itself by means of geoengineering and monocultural afforestation, among others forms of civilisational operation.[1] Which is to say ensuring that 'only those practices are allowed to flourish' that augment its form of socio-ecological organisation (Gare, 2017, p. 181). This, after all, is the burden of (ecological) civilisation in the face of planetary turmoil: the duty and imperative never to regress 'to the agricultural civilization times when productivity was low and people struggled for subsistence', but to *progress* to a global, 'abundant, quality, and sustainable society of ecological prosperity and steady-state economy within development boundaries' as well as 'within resource and environmental boundaries' (Pan, 2014, p. 209).

In the opening to his classic *History of the Idea of Progress*, Robert Nisbet (1980, p. 9) daringly writes that 'we shall know shortly whether civilization in any form and substance comparable to what we have known . . . in the West is possible without supporting faith in progress that had existed along with this civilization'. Perhaps the answer, 40 years later, is 'no'. Of course, as with many other Anthropocenic world-making projects, the theorists and architects of ecological civilisation are fiercely critical of the market-centred, technocratic, growth-oriented and materialistic principles that constitute the substantive values of progress of the modern capitalist world-system, rightly denouncing them as 'modern magic . . . made possible by fossil fuels' (Clayton & Schwartz, 2019, p. 23). But the rejection of these substantive values never amounts to the abandonment of the faith in progress as a mode of evaluation. Progress, Arran Gare (2017, p. 209) writes, 'will then be defined in terms of ecopoiesis, as augmenting life and the conditions for it, including human life and all the co-evolved lifeforms with which humans are participating in the global ecosystem'. Indeed, the very ideal of an ecological civilisation has 'progress' – a global, boundless and upwards trajectory towards a future that, guided by a set of universal principles, will be 'better' than the present – built into its political imagination, thereby reinscribing imperial, colonial values at the heart of their world-making efforts.

Social life beyond the pale: Fragments of a fragmentary cartography

It is in an effort to activate the political imagination otherwise that I suggest that, if the 'next civilization – the next pattern of social organization – will be an ecological civilization if it is to be at all' (Clayton & Schwartz, 2019, p. 30) then perhaps there needn't be one at all. If learning to live in the Anthropocene involves learning 'die as a civilisation', if it involves giving to this socio-ecological ending the power to transform the possible and impossible modes of world-making and forms of sociality that might emerge in its wake, the trials and tribulations of ecological civilisation rather indicate that we instead need to learn how to live *after progress*, which is to say *without* the concept and ideal of civilisation. In other words, it involves coming to terms with the *ecological* collapse of what we have come to call 'civilisation' – one that implicates not only our habitats but also our habits and political imaginations (Savransky, 2021b). To borrow the words and inspiration from the founders of the Dark Mountain Project (2009), a literary and cultural collective who refuse to partake in the Hobbesian search for security and the fervour for global world-making that would ensure the continuity of progressive forms of life in the Anthropocene so as to give themselves over to a poetic experimentation with other forms of storytelling, of writing, and of thinking and being together after progress: 'We tried ruling the world; we tried acting as God's steward, then we tried ushering in the human revolution, the age of reason and isolation. We failed in all of it, and our failure destroyed more than we were even aware of. The time for civilisation is past. Uncivilisation, which knows its flaws because it has participated in them; which sees unflinchingly and bites down hard as it records – this is the project we must embark on now.'

It is thanks to their call for uncivilised writing, in refusal of the progressive horizons that the hope for a new and better civilisation binds us to, and in an effort to give to the death of what came to be called 'progress' and 'civilisation' the power to transform our political imaginations, that I take interest in projects, practices and methodologies of ecological uncivilisation. The imaginative call for ecological uncivilisation is not an appeal to primitivism, however. It is not a call for a 'return' to a pre-industrial or pre-agricultural condition where people supposedly lived in harmony with nature. For that too is the story of civilisation, the retrofitted backdrop against which 'civilisation' emerges as 'human progress'. And the point is precisely that learning how to die requires that we learn to compose other stories, ones that may implicate us otherwise in the earth-wide condition of precariousness that characterises the present (Tsing, 2015). Not, that is, in order to securitise against it. For the drive for security against the more-than-human milieus in which we are inexorably implicated is at the heart of the modern world-system that has rendered the Earth itself precarious and now desperately strives to make its own impoverished mode of life sufficiently resilient to the very events it has brought about (Chandler et al., 2020). It is the imperative by which one becomes collectively impervious to the need to pose and experiment with the question of what learning to die well might mean today, instead making of the very idea of a better, ecological civilisation our progressive horizon and our uniformising home.

If I take inspiration from the post-environmentalism of the Dark Mountain Project in an attempt to rekindle our imaginations, therefore, it is because, rather than call for primitivism and securitisation, rather than an ode to nihilism or a project of global mobilisation, I read – and join – their efforts in what, in a lucid and wonderfully complementary discussion of their work, Jairus Grove (2019, p. 277) calls 'an evacuation'. That is, an escape from a set of progressive 'practices, organizations, and alliances' which have shaped the modern political imagination and 'have failed almost all of us'. While usually scorned by eco-activists as a form of giving up hope in the struggle for environmental progress on a global scale, the Dark Mountain Project (2009) and other such experiments in storytelling and methodologies of life are above all characterised by the refusal of the option to pile progress after progress, civilisation after civilisation. In their unflinching efforts to write this ending differently, 'to live and die well in this world, regardless of how this world turns out' (Grove, 2019, p. 277), contributors to the Dark Mountain Project (2009) make perceptible that to implicate ourselves otherwise in this condition of earthly precariousness is instead to proffer propositions for something more risky and more interesting than either survival or civilisation, a hope for something more

> . . . [h]umble, questioning, suspicious of the big idea and the easy answer. Walking the boundaries and reopening old conversations. Apart but engaged, its practitioners always willing to get their hands dirty; aware, in fact, that dirt is essential; that keyboards should be tapped by those with soil under their fingernails and wilderness in their heads.

Indeed, what after the Dark Mountain Project I'm calling ecological uncivilisation is a name not for nihilistic resignation, or even for the forms of environmental nationalism in which some of its founders have occasionally indulged, but for a speculative reactivation of the political imagination after progress: experimenting with possible and impossible modes of world-making and forms of sociality on unstable ecological terrain. Calling out this dim possibility just as what we have come to call civilisation writes its own epitaph, ecological uncivilisation is an active refusal to be taken further down the progressive path. It names an endeavour in learning to die by seeking, trying out, composing with others, modes of world-making otherwise: worlds that will never make a globe or aspire to be whole, more-than-human methodologies of life that are neither modern nor civilised but take seriously and intensify the moments of contingency and fragility when stories, forms of sociality and practices unforeseen spring up precariously in and as the process of civilisational collapse.

If contemporary thinkers imagining the philosophical and political outlines of an ecological civilisation appeal to Whitehead's process philosophy as foundation and ground, perhaps a different version of Whitehead's thought pulsates through this possible endeavour to learn to die so as to learn to live an uncivilised life. Less, that is, the systematising Whitehead (1967, p. 274) whose centre of vision would be found in his late proposition that it is in the presence of the five qualities of Truth, Beauty, Adventure, Art and Peace that the kernel of 'a general definition of civilization' may be found, than the one – the same one – who remarks that, though present in civilisation, adventures, those always precarious experiments in world-making and modes of living and dying well, also constitute the very *principles of uncivilisation*, the 'ripples of change' that sooner or later activate the imagination to sidestep the groove of progress, the order of the settled and the civilised, to reach 'beyond the safe limits of the epoch, and beyond the safe limits of learned rules of taste' (1967, p. 279). It is Whitehead (1929, p. 19) the pragmatist, in other words, who would always remind us that whatever the philosophical, political and ecological achievements of a programme of planetary unification, life is a bid for freedom and 'the good life is unstable', such that when an established methodology of life 'has exhausted the novelties within its scope and played upon them up to the incoming of fatigue, one final decision determines the fate of a species. It can stabilize itself, and relapse so as to live', which is to say to refuse the adventure of uncivilisation and 'relapse into the well-attested habit of mere life'. Or it can 'shake itself free' and give itself over to an ongoing and unfinished experimentation, without guarantees, reimagining what living and dying well might mean by seizing upon 'one of the nascent methodologies concealed in the welter of miscellaneous experience beyond the scope of the old dominant way'.

It goes without saying that such forms of uncivilised experimentation and methodologies of life on unstable ecological terrain are not new, they are not themselves a sign of progress. For they have been insisting and persisting all along, not in the systems of nations or through the progress of civilisations but in the interstices as in the rough edges of empires, in the form of what, after James C. Scott (2009, p. 8), we might call multiple zones of refuge, or *shatter zones*: collective and multifarious forms of living and dying made on rugged terrain, 'wherever the expansion of states, empires, slave-trading, and wars, as well as natural disasters, have driven large numbers of people to seek refuge in out-of-the-way places: in Amazonia, in highland Latin America (with the notable exception of the Andes, with their arable highland plateaus and states), in that corridor of highland Africa safe from slave-raiding, in the Balkans and the Caucasus'. Shatter zones are the spaces where uncivilised ecological experiments forge an outside to the progressive coordinates of the colonial project, where an otherwise makes itself felt, where an endeavour to learn to die in order to learn to live gets, perhaps, underway. For what 'drives' such collectives to seek refuge out-in-the-outside is not simply the endurance of state oppression or the event of some other calamitous situation. It is also the very lure of the outside, of becoming 'ungoverned barbarians' who elect, 'as a political choice, to take their distance from the state'. Shatter zones, in other words, are composed by and of those who choose to live beyond the pale, to engage in world-making through and as an ongoing ecology of state evasion, prevention and unmaking. This is also why, if such experiments could be called ecological it is not because they are 'good', or because their practices seek to either retrieve ancient environmental values or to found new principles for an alternative form of civilisation. It is, quite simply, because the complexities of migration, multiethnic cohabitation and subsistence that the gesture of life shaking itself free entails have always been formidable, making perceptible that the composition of an outside is impossible without insisting on the precariousness of one's existence as expressed in the need for the persistence of others, human and more, in order for our collective insistence to be sustained. As such, uncivilised life in the shatter zones means that living and dying well is a function of being in unstable, improvised and inventive relations to others without whom one is not, without whom 'mere life' is the best one can hope for, and not for long.

Where might such experiments in ecological uncivilisation be discerned? Scott's was a study of Zomia, a term that describes the highlands that traverse five Southeast Asian nations and four provinces of China, the largest remaining part of the world where people have not (yet) been fully incorporated into the collective life of states – or forcibly sedentarised into ecological civilisation. As such, it generatively resonates with fugitive, runaway and maroon communities elsewhere, from *Kisama* in Angola at the height of the slave trade, or the *quilombos* of colonial (and contemporary) Brazil, all the way to the precarious exercises in black commonism and autonomous food security in Detroit, and the efforts of political autonomy and self-determination in Rojava, among others. Yet, divergent and marginal as they may be, my sense is that the capacity of such experiments in ecological uncivilisation to transform the political imagination relies in part upon the possibility of nourishing other forms of historical and geographical attention. It depends, that is, upon the possibility of mapping an always fragmentary cartography of uncivilised life and (im)possible forms of sociality outside the coordinates of progress, fragments of which I can only begin to trace here in the briefest of ways. For indeed, as I imagine it, shatter zones are not only composed by place-making attempts in the interstices and outlaw edges of the imperial forma-tions of the Earth. They are also made through a history of minor cultural, philosophi-cal, scientific, spiritual, ecological and political modes of uncivilised experimentation everywhere dedicated to the ongoing and unfinished composition of dissensual modes of coexistence and precarious methodologies for igniting a new taste for life beyond the limits of the civilised judgement of taste. Among others, such forms of precarious world-making would include, for instance, the *fin-de-siècle* emergence of a 'metro-politan anti-colonialism' which, as postcolonial historian Leela Gandhi (2006, p. 9) has superbly traced, brought into connection a motley crew of 'Victorian radicals' – including William James, Swami Vivekananda and Edward Carpenter – who wove together disparate forms of Utopian socialism, spiritual mysticism, pragmatism and continental anarchism to create generative alliances with anti-colonial efforts else-where so as to temporarily precipitate a 'mutation of "internationalism" into a series of countercultural revolutionary practices'.

And indeed, fragments of ecological uncivilisation could also be discerned today, across a whole array of experiments at learning how to die in the Anthropocene so as to make life worth living on a precarious Earth. Among them, one might mention those who, in the wake of Hurricane Katrina – whose sighting on TV, we might recall, prompted Scranton to meditate on civilisational collapse – did indeed endeavour to learn how to undergo a certain death of land-based sociality so as to learn how to live an amphibious swamp life, outfitting homes, trailers, as well as bars and restaurants so that they could float off their foundations without having to give to the ever increased dangers of flood zones the power to determine where and how to live (Wakefield, 2020). On the other side of the Pacific, one might appraise the improvisational prac-tices of a collective of Buddhist, Shintō and Protestant priests who, after the 2011 tsunami that devastated the northeast of Japan and amidst the inability of the state to respond to the experiences of sorrow and grief that the wave left in its wake, set up a mobile cafe to offer spiritual care both to the living and to the dead (Savransky, 2021a); or indeed, the efforts of those in and around Fukushima who, faced with the nuclear explosion that followed the earthquake, engage in projects – from DIY radiation moni-toring and introducing medicinal diets and building communities off the grid – of learning how to die so as to learn how to live well with the multitudinous radionuclides the disaster forever unleashed (Kohso, 2020). And as the colonial toxicity of what we have come to call 'civilisation' now truly pervades the Earth, nascent methodologies of life are also cultivated in community gardens in the environs of Arusha, Tanzania, where an NGO has devoted itself to producing, at the interstices of medicine and agri-culture, therapeutic foods and nutritious medicines to enable those living with chronic medical conditions – as with the toxicity of pesticides and herbicides in food, growth hormones in chickens, tissue cultures injected into banana plants, the aluminium in cooking pots, and the very pharmaceuticals that sustain their lives – to learn how to live and die well by implicating bodies into alternative configurations of people and plants (Langwick, 2018).

Ecological uncivilisation: Reactivating the political imagination after progress

The foods and medicines of the gardens of Arusha do not offer a 'cure', however, and neither can one discern in these experiments and methodologies of life the path to a wholly new and better common world to come, or the prospect of a future in which earth-wide precariousness will have been relegated (yet again) to a bygone past. Ecological co-implication is their (our) precarious condition – not the new name for a categorical imperative or a redemptive project for perpetual peace. If a fragmentary cartography of social life beyond the pale might enable one to learn something about how to die as a civilisation in order to learn how to live, it is not because such experiments prescribe lessons on 'the good life' but precisely because they affirm its radical instability. As such, they make of the need for multiple and divergent, out-of-bounds experiments in nourishing new tastes for life beyond the civilised judgement of taste *itself the lesson*. Rather than lament a historical process of 'cultural fragmentation' and yearn for a cosmopolitan, civilised future 'where the destructive conflicts between tribes, civilizations, and nations will have been overcome' (Gare, 2017, p. 166), therefore, such experiments are active vectors of divergence, profusion and dispersal: shards of ecological uncivilisation where (im)possible forms of sociality are improvised on rugged terrain, against an imperial history of devastation brought about by earth-wide homogenisation – the ecological production of a *world without others* in the name of progress and civilisation (Crosby, 1986). Which is why precarious forms of world-making and uncivilised life guarantee nothing, and they authorise nothing. If they fail to lay the grounds for a new, global civilisation, it is only because experiments in precarious world-making espouse such a failure as their very political vocation (Savransky, 2021a). Which is to say that they refuse, within their own forms of sociality, to assume the burden of the upward march of progress as a mode of valuation that would yet again present the future as a forking path between salvation and damnation, civilisation or ruination.

In the end, in the beginning, such nascent methodologies of life are affirmative bids for freedom, uncivilised attempts to learn how to die so as to learn how live well if not always better. What they might yet engender, what they still make resonate, is the possibility of reactivating the political imagination, of upending modern foundations and loosening progress's grip on our imaginations so as to experiment with the possibility of inhabiting the present otherwise, to wager – against all odds – on the chance of rendering ourselves capable of thinking, improvising and imagining lives and worlds composed outside the receding horizon of progress and the settled formations of what we came to call civilisation. In the end, in their refusal of progress they force us once again to rethink the stakes of struggle. Yet they simultaneously provoke us to imagine the possibility that, on unstable ecological terrains, political work after progress might take an altogether more subjunctive, improvisational and inchoate form. It might require a commitment to an ongoing and divergent insistence rather than to a universal mode of existence, to an experience of fugitive activity in the midst of what has been settled, to a tingling feeling of difference and possibility, to an improbable 'perhaps' whose contours we may not be able to ascertain but in whose hold the composition of dissensual modes of coexistence – human and more – keeps on keeping on, out of bounds in the shatter zone, precariously striving to make life worth living and death worth living for.

Funding

The author received no financial support for the research, authorship, and/or publication of this article.

Note

1. On the introduction of the modern notion of civilisation in China, see Xingtao (2011).

References

Blok, A., & Jensen, C. B. (2019). The Anthropocene event in social theory. *The Sociological Review, 67*(6), 1195–1211.

Bowden, B. (2009). *The empire of civilization*. University of Chicago Press.

Bush, G. W. (2001, November 8). *Address to the nation from Atlanta on Homeland Security*. Public Papers of the Presidents of the United States. www.govinfo.gov/content/pkg/PPP-2001-book2/pdf/PPP-2001-book2-doc-pg1360.pdf

Chandler, D., Grove, K., & Wakefield, S. (2020). *Resilience in the Anthropocene*. Routledge.

Charbonnier, P. (2020). For an ecological realpolitik. *E-flux Journal, 114*, 1–6.

Clayton, P., & Schwartz, A. (2019). *What is ecological civilization? Crisis, hope and the future of the planet*. Process Century Press.

Cobb, J., & Schwartz, A. (2018). *Putting philosophy to work: Toward an ecological civilization*. Process Century Press.

Crosby, A. (1986). *Ecological imperialism: The biological expansion of Europe, 900–1900*. Cambridge University Press.

Elias, N. (2000). *The civilizing process*. Blackwell.

Emmeche, C., & Kull, K. (2011). *Towards a semiotic biology: Life is the action of signs*. Imperial College Press.

Gandhi, L. (2006). *Affective communities: Anticolonial thought, fin-de-siècle radicalism, and the politics of friendship*. Duke University Press.

Gare, A. (2010). Toward an ecological civilization: The science, ethics and politics of eco-poiesis. *Process Studies, 39*(1), 5–38.

Gare, A. (2017). *The philosophical foundations of ecological civilization: A manifesto for the future*. Routledge.

Gare, A. (2021). The eco-socialist roots of ecological civilization. *Capitalism, nature, socialism, 32*(1), 37–55.

Geall, S., & Ely, A. (2018). Narratives and pathways towards an ecological civilization in contemporary China. *The China Quarterly, 236*, 1175–1196.

Grove, J. (2019). *Savage ecology: War and geopolitics at the end of the world*. Duke University Press.

Guattari, F. (2001). *The three ecologies*. Continuum.

Hadot, P. (1995). *Philosophy as a way of life*. Wiley Blackwell.

Huan, Q. (2016). Socialist eco-civilization and social-ecological transformation. *Capitalism, Nature, Socialism, 27*(2), 51–66.

Kingsnorth, P., & Hine, D. (2009). *Uncivilisation: The Dark Mountain manifesto*. https://darkmountain.net/about/manifesto/

Kohso, S. (2020). *Radiation and revolution*. Duke University Press.

Langwick, S. (2018). A politics of habitability: Plants, healing, and sovereignty in a toxic world. *Cultural Anthropology, 33*(3), 415–443.

Li, Y., & Shapiro, J. (2020). *China goes green: Coercive environmentalism for a troubled planet.* Polity.

Lowe, L. (2015). *The intimacies of four continents.* Duke University Press.

Mazlish, B. (2005). *Civilization and its contents.* Stanford University Press.

Nightingale, A., Eriksen, A., Taylor, M., Forsyth, T., Pelling, M., Newsham, A., Boyd, E., Brown, K., Harvey, B., Jones, L., Bezner Kerr, R., Mehta, L., Naess, L., Ockwell, D., Scoones, I., Tanner, T., & Whitfield, S. (2019). Beyond technical fixes: Climate solutions and the great derangement. *Climate and Development, 12*(4), 343–352.

Nisbet, R. (1980). *History of the idea of progress.* Heinemann.

Pan, J. (2014). *China's environmental governing and ecological civilization.* Springer.

Savransky, M. (2016). *The adventure of relevance: An ethics of social inquiry.* Palgrave.

Savransky, M. (2021a). *Around the day in eighty worlds: Politics of the pluriverse.* Duke University Press.

Savransky, M. (2021b). After progress: Notes for an ecology of perhaps. *Ephemera: Theory & Politics in Organisation, 21*(1), 267–281.

Scott, J. (2009). *The art of not being governed: An anarchist history of upland Southeast Asia.* Yale University Press.

Scranton, R. (2013, November 10). Learning how to die in the Anthropocene. *New York Times.* https://opinionator.blogs.nytimes.com/2013/11/10/learning-how-to-die-in-the-anthropocene/

Scranton, R. (2015). *Learning to die in the Anthropocene: Reflections on the end of a civilization.* City Light Books.

Starobinski, J. (1993). *Blessings in disguise; Or, the morality of evil.* Harvard University Press.

Tsing, A. (2015). *The mushroom at the end of the world: On the possibility of life in capitalist ruins.* Princeton University Press.

Wakefield, S. (2020). *Anthropocene back loop.* Open Humanities Press.

Wang, Z., He, H., & Fan, M. (2014). The ecological civilization debate in China. *Monthly Review, 66*(6). https://monthlyreview.org/2014/11/01/the-ecological-civilization-debate-in-china/

Whitehead, A. N. (1929). *The function of reason.* Boston: Beacon Press.

Whitehead, A. N. (1967). *Adventures of ideas.* Free Press.

Xingtao, H. (2011). The formation of modern concepts of 'civilization' and 'culture' and their application during the late Qing and early Republican times. *Journal of Modern Chinese History, 5*(1), 1–26.

Yang, F. (2010). The influence of Whitehead's thought on the Chinese academy. *Process Studies, 39*(2), 342–349.

the
Sociological Review
MONOGRAPH SERIES

Rifted subjects, fractured Earth: 'Progress' as learning to live on a self-transforming planet

The Sociological Review Monographs
2022, Vol. 70(2) 171–187
© The Author(s) 2022

Article reuse guidelines:
sagepub.com/journals-permissions
DOI: 10.1177/00380261221084783
journals.sagepub.com/home/sor

Nigel Clark
Lancaster Environment Centre, Lancaster University, UK

Bron Szerszynski
Department of Sociology, Bowland College, Lancaster University, UK

Abstract
In this article we make a case for an understanding of human difference that attends to the way that social collectives engage with the Earth's own capacity for self-differentiation. This draws us into conversation with recent interpretations of Hegel that see at the heart of his philosophy not a self-aggrandizing human agent set against a passive nature but an inherently fractured subject confronting a no-less intrinsically sundered outer reality. We use the example of traditional open-field cultural burning to show how skilled operators can painstakingly develop responses to ecoclimatic variability, putting this into dialogue with Hegel's reflections on the 'incendiarism' of political revolution as a human expression of the wider self-antagonism of nature. We go on to make connections between Hegel's account of the way that subjects can anticipate their own futurity and Indigenous conceptions of non-linear time, suggesting that the emergence of new earth-oriented practices can be seen as a complex interrelation of past, present and future. We close by suggesting that 'progress' for Hegel is not about the collective subject achieving omniscience and omnipotence, but involves the onerous and harrowing coming to terms with both its own divided identity and its exposure to a discordant external reality.

Keywords
earthly multitudes, fire, Hegel, Indigenous peoples, planetary multiplicity, progress, universality

The crack in everything

In April 2021, plans to test geoengineering techniques in the north of Sweden were derailed. The pilot project, funded by billionaire Bill Gates, was to have involved

Corresponding author:
Nigel Clark, Lancaster Environment Centre, Lancaster University, Lancaster, LA1 4YQ, UK.
Email: n.clark2@lancaster.ac.uk

releasing calcium carbonate into the atmosphere to test its efficacy in reducing incoming solar radiation. However, Indigenous Sámi peoples of northern Fennoscandia, working with Swedish environment groups, raised objections. Traditionally semi-nomadic herders and foragers, the Sámi – like many other Indigenous peoples – have experienced invasion, dispossession and cultural devastation. They also face high levels of disruption of human-ecological systems because of the extreme sensitivity of the Arctic region to climate change (Furberg et al., 2011). In an open letter to the project advisory committee and the Swedish government, Sámi representatives and their co-signatories successfully called for cancellation of the trials, citing the catastrophic potential consequences of solar geoengineering on global weather patterns, and the lack of consultation about the trial with Sámi people or Swedish society generally (Sámi Council, 2021).

Echoing the Sámi and their allies, Earth system governance theorist Frank Biermann insists at once that political regulation of solar geoengineering raises challenges that 'are unsurmountable in today's global political system' and that proposed technologies 'assume a level of understanding of the planetary system that does not exist' (cited in Mazza, 2021). Joining other critics, we discern that would-be geoengineers seem set on flipping threats of global catastrophe into quests for unprecedented leverage over Earth processes, a tactic epitomized by ecofuturist Stewart Brand's recycling of his own half-century old mantra 'we are as gods, we might as well get good at it' (cited in Brockman, 2009).

Such hubristic visions are hardly new to the West. As philosopher Todd McGowan expresses the self-ratifying belief for which Hegel is often seen as the exemplar: '[t]he subject can know the world because the world is the product of the subject's own activity' (2016, p. 3). However, just as we should not be taken aback by resurgent fantasies of turning modernity's unforeseen consequences into opportunities, neither should we be unduly surprised to see the Sámi and their allies contesting the latest stab at extending control over the world's disarray and recalcitrance. Over recent decades, resistance from within and beyond the West to totalizing knowledge claims has been rising sharply. At a time when claims to universality are themselves seen to be implicated in cascading social and environmental crises, it is not only large-scale technological projects but any pronouncements on the planetary predicament that soon find themselves confronting counter-assertions of the partiality and situatedness of all voices (see Lövbrand et al., 2015).

As well as being a globe upon which peoples are unevenly impacted by planetary-scale problems, this is more vociferously than ever 'a world of many worlds', of plural perspectives, visions, cosmologies (de la Cadena & Blaser, 2018; Savransky, 2021). In our own attempt to develop a version of planetary social thought, we have sought to affirm the irreducible plurality of knowledge practices while holding onto the insights of wide-angle lenses on Earth processes (Clark & Szerszynski, 2021). Whereas many social critics censure Anthropocene science and related geoscientific thinking for assuming a univocal perspective on equally unitary Earth systems, we take a different view. Over the last 50 years or so, we argue, the Earth sciences have been moving towards a conception of what we refer to as 'planetary multiplicity': the idea that out of the dense interconnectivity of its constitutive physical systems comes the propensity of our planet to shift between multiple operating states (Clark & Szerszynski, 2021, pp. 8–9, 88–90). While not denying that there are problems concerning how and from where this 'non-self-identity' of the planetary body is apprehended, we suggest that a sense of the multiplicity or self-differentiating tendency of the Earth opens up possibilities for understanding the many differences discernible in our own species.

One way of thinking about human difference, then, is to consider the full spectrum of ways in which social collectives have engaged with the Earth's ongoing capacity, at every scale, to shift, transform, or become other to itself. We use the term 'earthly multitudes' to refer to these groupings and all the techniques, practices and tactics they deploy to live with and make use of planetary multiplicity (Clark & Szerszynski, 2021, pp. 9–11, 54). Such an approach helps us to see humans becoming who and what they are through their interventions in the variegated formations and dynamic processes of the Earth – which we view not as an alternative but as a complement to those modes of critique that put the emphasis on more conventional social, cultural and political variables.

When the Sámi and their allies point both to the social differences that hinder globally unified governance and to the dynamics of an Earth system that defy full predictability, we pick up echoes of our own figuring of earthly multitudes and planetary multiplicity. By contrast with some critical social thought, we prefer not to draw hard lines between the worlds of would-be geoengineers and those of more place-based and embedded collectives, though our sympathies lie firmly with the latter. For all our disapproval of certain proposals, we still conceive of solar radiation management as a mode of grappling with planetary multiplicity and thus as a variation on the theme of earthly multitudes.

So where does this take us regarding Western modernity and its self-understanding? How does thinking through planetary multiplicity and earthly multitudes relate to what is frequently taken to be the core conviction of modernity: the belief that those who wield reason have it in their power to advance into the external world, to make it their own, to enclose and possess all that formerly appeared 'other' – or what McGowan describes, again in reference to Hegel, as 'the megalomania of the subject' (2016, p. 7)? The short and easy answer is that we see our earthly multitudes – whatever their accomplishments – as eluding full command over the materials, powers and processes with which they engage, problematizing any such hubris. But there is a more complicated response, one that troubles the terms of the question itself.

Thus far we have been citing McGowan's précis of standard interpretations of Hegel. What he actually argues, however, is that received readings of Hegel as the champion of a self-aggrandizing subject set on a possessive reconciliation with nature are in desperate need of overhaul. Taking cues from Slavoj Žižek and others, McGowan contends that Hegel ought to be seen as the preeminent theorist of an inherently fractured, non-selfsame subject who confronts a no-less intrinsically sundered and fractious outer reality. It is Hegel, McGowan and Žižek concur, who insists that nature or Being is essentially out of step with itself, that there is an insurmountable disjuncture in the world, just as there are inescapable fault-lines preventing human subjects ever being at one with themselves. As Žižek puts it: 'the point of dialectical analysis is to demonstrate how every phenomenon, everything that happens, fails in its own way, implies a crack, antagonism, imbalance in its very heart' (2012, p. 8). Or in Hegel's own terse formulation, '*everything is inherently contradictory*' (1969, p. 439).

Unearthed from the depths of an earlier modernity, this idea of an internally rifted subject facing a self-divided substantial reality resonates with our own thematizing of the interplay of earthly multitudes and planetary multiplicity. This raises important questions for us. What if the idea of a planetary system that is too dynamic, too prone to self-differentiation to ever be mastered has significant antecedents – predecessors lurking in the very places where we usually descry authority and self-assuredness? What would a more self-divided and nature-sundered vision of modernity mean for our own idea of earthly multitudes? And how might it travel and be set to work in the context of the earth-oriented practices whose origins and lineages far exceed the domain of Western modernity?

The following two sections open up these questions by putting traditions of cultural burning in conversation with commentaries on Hegel's response to the political 'incendiarism' of the French Revolution. Staying with these examples, we then turn to the question of time, and ask what might be learned from moving between a Hegelian sense of retroactive temporality and accounts of earthly multitudes engaging with the volatile temporizations of the Earth itself. Finally, in the context of contemporary environmental challenges, we reflect on this dialogue between a traumatically asynchronous Western modernity and the long, not-always-continuous trajectories of collective engagement with a changeable planet – and consider what this 'dialectical' encounter might mean for rethinking notions of universality and progress. In the process, we seek to make space for conversations with our fellow earth-oriented social actors in ways that reckon with our own European inheritance rather than imagining that others – past, extant or yet-to-come – will gift us with the possibility of brand new beginnings.

Earthly multitudes on a fiery planet

Indigenous Australian fire management expert Victor Steffensen offers recollections of cultural exchanges with the Skolt Sámi of northern Fennoscandia. For all the geographic distance and ecoclimatic difference separating the Sámi from his own Tagalaka people, Steffensen recognized shared experiences of coexisting with plants, animals and spirits, and a common ambition for putting younger generations back in touch with place-based traditional knowledges decimated by colonial dispossession (2020, pp. 113–118). And just as state-imposed fire suppression has significantly attenuated customary burning practices across much of Australia, so too have official prohibitions negatively impacted the Sámi – who have deep histories of burning boreal landscapes to stimulate winter pasture for reindeer herds (Cogos et al., 2019).

As Indigenous fire experts have long maintained, 'country' that is denied the flames it is accustomed to not only suffers heightened risk of intense, destructive wildfire but also faces reduced ecological diversity, pest infestations and declining soil fertility (Kimmerer & Lake, 2001; Steffensen, 2020). Knowledge of how and when to burn, practitioners insist, can only be learned by trial and experimentation. This takes many generations to acquire, and when people move into different regions or when ecological or climatic conditions change, asserts Aboriginal Indigenous studies scholar Marcia Langton, these practices need to be revised or relearned (1998, pp. 48–50).

From our perspective, open-field burning is one of the most enduring and intriguing activities around which earthly multitudes assemble. Timely application of fire taps into energy and organic matter that has accumulated over time, and in the process skilled operators can modulate the effects of ecoclimatic change. But for us, even extensive setting to work of fossil fuels – however unsustainable it may be – is a variation on the theme of the fire-using earthly multitudes: the combustion of fossilized hydrocarbons both channelling the material-energetic residues of past planetary operating states and cushioning ongoing environmental fluctuation. While we might well consider solar radiation management as a gathering of emergent earthly multitudes oriented to the unwanted consequences of burning fossil fuels, we should also keep in mind that open-field cultural burning itself is capable of re-engineering vast areas of the Earth's surface. For as environmental historian Stephen Pyne contends: '[t]he aboriginal firestick became a lever that, suitably sited, could move whole landscapes, even continents' (2000, p. 4, see also Langton, 1998, p. 24).

However it is deployed, fire retains the capacity to break free, especially when conditions change quickly. Communities with enduring traditions of cultural burning tend to have intricate rituals of knowledge transmission, and although the hearth fire may be shared with strangers, there are often sanctions on sharing flame itself (Pyne, 1997, p. 28). If danger attends the lending of fire to those unfamiliar with local conditions, how much greater is the threat when invasive peoples impose their own knowledge and practice of fire use on regions with very different fire regimes and land management strategies.

As Pyne has documented in detail, modernizing Europeans increasingly removed fire from their own intensely gardened landscapes – a move they could just about get away with because of the perennial dampness and lack of a distinctive fire season in Europe north of the Mediterranean (1997, p. 156). As the intelligentsia of a rapidly urbanizing Europe turned against open-field burning, they came to see uncontained fire as symptomatic of chaos, disorder and waste – especially when it flared during episodes of urban unrest. In the European countryside and in regions across the colonized world with pronounced fire seasons, traditional fire users strongly resisted attempts to suppress their cultural burning repertoires – frequently using fire as a medium both of political protest and landscape management (Clark, 2018; Kuhlken, 1999). Other earthly multitudes who confronted advancing capitalist and colonial 'modernization' hatched their own forms of resistance, including open confrontation and taking knowhow and practices underground.

While there have been many remarkable acts of survival and resurgence, our sense is that, overall, the combined onslaught of sociopolitical and epistemic violence has had devastating impacts on time-honoured collective means of engaging with planetary multiplicity. Regarding fire, there is growing evidence that suppression of traditional forms of open-field burning has had deeply deleterious impacts on biological and ecological diversity in many places (Pyne, 1997, p. 171). And as traditional fire experts know only too well, disastrous megafires like those that have recently raged through New South Wales and California are further manifestations of extended prohibition of cultural burning (Steffensen, 2020, p. 210).

It is tempting to move from such indictments to the generalized claim that Western societies seek to assimilate and control physical processes while a world of others conduct themselves with and through their immersion in the flows of nature. At this point, however, we want to pause and suggest a more complicated reading. Staying with the fire theme, we turn now to that historical juncture where 'incendiarism' flared in the political and cultural centres of Europe as never before. Specifically, this brings us back to Hegel and his reflections on the most tumultuous event of his time: the revolution in France that literary theorist Rebecca Comay describes as 'the burning center' of his philosophy (2011, p. 5). Is this fiery enthrallment of Hegel mere metaphor, we ask – a rise of figurative concern with fire that corresponds to the suppression of 'actual' fire use – or is something else going on here? And if so, what might that something mean for re-staging the conversation between fire-wielding multitudes in different parts of the world?

Incendiary modernity, revolutionary Earth

As both Comay and McGowan would have it, Hegel's writing on the French Revolution ought to disabuse us of any sense that his convictions lay in the progressive reason-led ascent of the self-determining subject. Neither should his reflections on post-revolutionary terror simply be taken as an exposé of freedom's betrayal or as a recoiling from radicalism run amok, they argue. Rather, for Hegel, the overthrow of the *Ancien Régime* is but one of the many untimely, unthinkable events that comprise historical experience, and its self-destructive sequel is an unsurprising playing out of the new dilemmas or contradictions that arise as soon as old authority figures are dispensed with (Comay, 2011, pp. 58–67; McGowan, 2019, p. 201). The challenge posed by revolutionary activity, then, is for collective human agency to come to terms with its own 'fury of destruction' (Hegel, cited in Comay, 2011, p. 67), in order that the world-shattering forces that have been unleashed can be harnessed for further transformation, rather than careering into exhaustion or self-annihilation. As Comay sums up the Hegelian project, '[t]he task of Spirit will be to reconstruct an existence amid the debris of empire' (2011, p. 59).

It is philosopher Michael Marder, surveying the same blasted terrain, who commends us to read Hegel's engagements with revolutionary modernity alongside his reflections on the physical element of fire (2015, p. 49). There is, Marder suggests, a common logic, a shared structural dynamic that goes well beyond metaphor. Fire, in Hegel's dialectical vision, is the exemplar of nature's inherent self-antagonism: '[i]n the wood's endeavor to consume the air through fire, it fights against itself and against its own source' (Hegel, 1953, p. 34). In this way, fire's power of negativity encapsulates nature's own self-movement – albeit not to the same extent as animal life, because fire soon consumes itself whereas animals never cease to move and change (Marder, 2015, pp. 52–53). Human collective agency, epitomized by revolutionary insurrection, constitutes a further leap in mobilization propelled by an inherently out-of-step or antagonistic existence. But as Hegel has it, in the case of human agents, unlike that of raging fire or roaming animality, there is the possibility of deciphering and grasping the contradictory conditions that impel them. And in this way, human subjects have at least the potential to divert their dangerous powers away from runaway, self-immolation and towards a fraught and juddering self-determination (Marder, 2015, pp. 51–55).

No one is suggesting that we comb the Hegelian corpus for practical tips in deploying fire, whether to burn biotic overgrowth or to torch our masters' mansions. Marder's probing of the essential continuity between elemental fire and revolutionary fervour runs deeper than this. It brings us back to the argument made by McGowan and Žižek that the centrepiece of Hegelian thought is not the tale of triumphant nature-assimilating histori-cal development, but the insistence on the ineluctable sundering and self-division of both the social and natural domains. As Hegel asserts in *The Science of Logic*, '[i]t shows an excessive tenderness for the world to remove contradiction from it and then to transfer the contradiction to spirit, to reason, where it is allowed to remain unresolved . . . the so-called world . . . is never and nowhere without contradiction' (1969, pp. 237–238). Fire, in this light, will continue raging through forests and conflict will keep wrenching society apart, because neither realm has ever been or ever will be an organic whole or plenitude. For Hegel, then, society and nature are by no means categorically separate or opposed. They are bound together through the *internal* disjuncture they share, meaning that separation, discontinuity, rupture is primarily located *within* the social and *within* the natural rather than *between* them. And it is only through thoroughly acknowledging the contradiction in *both* these manifestations of worldly existence that human history has any chance of building back better out of the ruins of repeated catastrophe.

While Hegel's musings on social revolution have received more attention, it is vital to recall that he and his contemporaries were also in thrall to the idea that the Earth itself repeatedly passed through world-shattering upheavals. Growing familiarity with differ-entiated rock strata bearing the remains of entire worlds of extinct animals and plants prompted Hegel and fellow geological enthusiasts to think in terms of an immensely drawn-out Earth history shaken by 'a series of tremendous revolutions' (1970, p. 283). In our own approach, the late eighteenth-early nineteenth-century thematization of 'revolu-tions of the Earth' is a precursor of the notion of planetary multiplicity: an early glimpse of our planet's propensity to fall out of step with itself, to reorganize its component parts into new orders. But it is only over the last half century or so that the Earth sciences have been able to piece together the processes behind these dynamics, and more recently still that we have witnessed sustained philosophical and social enquiry into the consequences of such changes for human existence (Clark & Szerszynski, 2021, pp. 23–32).

Hegel did not fully merge his thinking on the elemental dissonance of fire with his speculations on a revolutionary Earth. He lacked the evidence we now have that fire 'appears more profusely during times of rapid and extreme climatic change', and that epochal Earth history is characterized by very different patterns and types of wildfire (Pyne, 1994, p. 890). Moreover, obsessed as he was with philosophical or conceptual 'reconciliation' with the contrariness of Being, it is hard to imagine Hegel taking genuine interest in the way that different collectives grapple with the changing environments, whether with fire or by other means.

The problem, it hardly needs to be said, goes much deeper than this. Foreclosing on his own most cherished value of universalism (see McGowan, 2020, pp. 19, 22), Hegel derogated peoples outside of Europe – and especially in Africa – as too absorbed in the transience of the natural world to reflect upon their own existence. In this way, more than simply expressing the Eurocentrism of his day, Hegel emerged as one of the architects of European modernity's equation of sociocultural and geographical difference from Europe with developmental backwardness (Clark & Szerszynski, 2021, pp. 110–114).

Much has been said, deservedly, about the implications of Hegel's schema for the entrenchment of racial ideologies, and the role they played in European colonialism.

While it may not be intuitive, one way to deal with this troubling inheritance, we are suggesting, is to push deeper into Hegel's notion of an inherently non-self-coincident physical world – allowing for Hegelian thought to generate an excess, to overreach its own system (see Žižek, 2012, p. 6). This calls for a sustained consideration of the inherent self-differentiation of the natural world, in all its gritty materiality and elemental uncertainty, as the inescapable condition of *all* human existence. And this, for us, permits a certain reclaiming of Hegel's two-sided unsettling of self and world in ways that refuse his own developmental ranking of humankind – and put all earth-bound social beings on the same interminably shaky footing.

While we are intrigued to find traces in the intellectual core of an earlier European modernity of an articulation between a self-divided nature and equally equivocating social identities and mobilization, the troubling issue of a unidirectional and teleological framing remains (see Lundy, 2016). In the following section, we turn in more detail to the question of temporality in order to interrogate the developmental aspect of Hegelian thought and to further explore the potential for bringing Hegel's 'out-of-step' subjects and world into conversation with our own concept of earth-oriented multitudes tussling with the tempos of planetary variability.

Temporalities of the Earth and its multitudes

Anthropogenic climate change is a discontinuous event, a return to circulation of carbon sequestered under distant and very different Earth-system conditions. In another delayed outburst, global warming-exacerbated megafires in New South Wales, California, Alberta and elsewhere explosively release biotic energy that has built up following attenuation of Indigenous cultural burning. And although the planet cannot spool back its own geological history, there are certainly convergences with aspects of past eras that occur as planetary conditions change. It is for this reason that Earth scientists are investigating the fire regimes of the warm, wet, high-carbon dioxide conditions of the Paleocene-Eocene thermal maximum – which occurred some 55 million years ago – as a proxy for near-future climate change (Denis et al., 2017).

So too can the praxis of past earthly multitudes gain new traction when Earth systems pulse and shift. As fire regimes enter novel states, traditional burning practices – precisely because they were forged to deal with conditions of variability – may become even more vital than they were previously (Steffensen, 2020, pp. 211–213). This is also a temporally convoluted process, as long-standing fire-centred land management is likely to have promoted fire-tolerant or fire-loving species, in this way selecting for its own future relevance (Pyne, 2001, p. 25).

With his problematic assumptions about non-European peoples remaining mired in unfavourable natural conditions, Hegel was never going to appreciate the complex temporalities of Indigenous or traditional fire-use (see Hegel, 2001, pp. 110–113). But as we have been suggesting, what Hegel does offer us is a singular thematization of time at odds with itself in both the subject and object worlds. In Hegel's schema, an event as genuinely novel as the French Revolution (with the supplement of Haiti, as recent commentators rightly insist) is always to some extent out of time (Comay, 2011, p. 438). By dint of its radical rupture with the past, such an occurrence can never be at home in its own historical moment; the best that rebellious social agents can hope for is that they begin to generate conditions that may one day prove hospitable to their own deepest yearnings and striving. By this reasoning, an action may or may not seed the conditions that will retrospectively establish its very eventfulness. As Žižek reads Hegel: 'the meaning of my acts does not depend on me, on my intentions, it is decided afterwards, retroactively' (2012, p. 321).

The paradox that propels Hegel's project, contends Žižek, is the intuition that 'what escapes our grasp is . . . *the very birth of the New*' (2012, p. 273). Nothing, it would seem, could be further from the stereotypical Hegel who plots out the continuous ascent of a self-overcoming intellect or world spirit. But as we have seen, this is the very reading of Hegel that Žižek, McGowan and Comay, among others, have sought to subvert through their disclosure of a far more troublesome snarl of agency, fallibility and thwarted possibility in the Hegelian dialectic. And it is here that Catherine Malabou's radical rethinking of Hegel's notion of time opened the way. In her 1996 monograph, *The Future of Hegel*, Malabou set out to overturn the prevailing mid-twentieth-century view of Hegelian history as an effectively closed loop with no opening for the truly novel, for any real futurity (2005, pp. 4–5). In its place, she discerned a much more convoluted interplay between that which can be known or anticipated and those events that erupt contingently (2005, pp. 74–75, 133).

It is only retrospectively, as Malabou parses Hegel, that it becomes apparent that a certain gesture, a modification, an improvisation has passed from singularity to habituation and durability (2005, p. 74). As Malabou elaborates, the process by which contingencies selectively settle into necessities is constantly occurring in the realms of both substance (or nature) and subject. There is newness, futurity, history in both domains. But according to the logic we encountered in the previous section, whereas in the realm of nonhuman nature this becoming through self-differentiation remains relatively enthralled to chance, in the case of human subjects it is possible to consciously intervene, albeit speculatively, in the movements between accident and essence. What Malabou brings to the fore, then, is 'the operation of synthetic temporalizing in Hegel's thought, which means it is the structure of anticipation through which subjectivity projects itself in advance of itself, and thereby participates in the process of its own determination' (2005, p. 18). As Hegel puts it, the substance-subject 'sees itself coming' (cited in Malabou, 2005, p. 18). Again, as we have previously seen, Hegel's suturing of substance and subject is crucial here, for human collective agents temporize, or generate their own futurity, by working with and through the contingencies and the self-differentiation of the natural world (Malabou, 2005, p. 133).

Just as the natural and the social share an inherent self-dividedness, so too are Hegel's 'Old' and 'New' both configured as dissonant, out of step – this being the key to his attempt to break out of any sense of the New organically or teleologically emerging from the Old. It cannot be overstressed that this rupture with 'a continuous process of organic growth' means that the emergence of the New, even or especially should human agents attain some degree of retractive self-determination, is a painful and wrenching one (Žižek, 2012, pp. 272–273). It entails a tearing apart, a violence afflicting previously existing forms and structures – though always with the proviso that such changes only occur because the past itself is always already a site of violent dislocation. Or as we might extrapolate from this insight in the context of the current planetary predicament: it is only possible that (some) kinds of human agency can – violently – push the Earth system into a novel operating state because our planet is itself constituted by a multiplicity of potential states. And, because the social forces driving this disturbance, we need to add, are themselves constitutively stricken and conflictual.

It is understandable that earthly multitudes who are struggling to preserve, restore and develop vital repertoires – especially in the wake of colonialism – put the stress on the violence and volatility of social subjugation. But those who give voice to time-honoured practices have also cautioned against assumptions of originary wholeness or plenitude. 'Everything ancient was once new', observes Indigenous Hawaiian Pacific Studies scholar Emalani Case (2021) – a reminder that what is too easily designated 'traditional' knowledge was at one point novel, improvisatory and experimental. As we suggested in the previous section, earth-oriented practices like cultural burning must be recalibrated when planetary processes fluctuate or shift. And astute earthly multitudes know this, both in retrospect and looking forward. As Anishinaabe scholar-activist Kyle Whyte (2018) recounts, his and other Indigenous peoples experience time as an enspiralling of past and present, in which ancestors grapple with the variability of their environments so as to gift livable worlds to their descendants, while descendants learn from both the successes and shortfalls of these ancestors to keep the spiral turning.

As Comay observes of Hegel's interrogation of the temporal perplexities of the French Revolution, any sense of a linear, causal arc of history is blown apart not simply by the radical break of revolutionary events but by the subsequent resurfacing, reprocessing, re-living of its constitutive experiences. 'Time is not just contracted, arrested, or interrupted', she reflects: 'it is twisted and reversed' (2011, p. 42). If we are to commend Hegel for trying to blast open the idea of a unidirectional developmental continuum, however, we should also credit Kyle Whyte's modelling of Indigenous temporization with outdoing the dialectic at its own game. For as Whyte elaborates: '[e]xperiences of spiraling time . . . may be lived through narratives of cyclicality, reversal, dream-like scenarios, simultaneity, counter-factuality, irregular rhythms, ironic un-cyclicality, slipstream, parodies of linear pragmatism, eternality, among many others' (2018, p. 229).

Hegel and Whyte's unlikely *pas de deux* helps us to envision our earthly multitudes not only as accommodations to ongoing planetary variance, and as the incubators of knowledge, skills and tactics that may acquire new relevance when the Earth itself becomes otherwise, but as the progenitors of actions that are forever at risk of overreaching their own time and place – and unleashing their own world-shattering effects. The hominin 'capture' of fire dramatically increases the capacity of our genus to ride out climatic fluctuations and threshold transitions, even more so when human flame finds its way to vast stocks of concentrated subterranean biomass (Clark & Yusoff, 2014). But as the return to circulation of sequestered energy transforms global climate, shifting wildfire regimes react back upon the very infrastructures of fossil-fuelled social life: forest fire is both sparked by and destroys electrical networks in California, bushfires in New South Wales ignite coal seams in open-cast mines (Clark & Rickards, in press). And as small woodland fires spiral into uncontrollable megafires, even the metropolitan authorities who once sought to prohibit open-field cultural burning increasingly recognize the need for skilled application of fire to living landscapes. At the same time, climate engineers desperate to extract and sequester atmospheric carbon turn to ancient techniques of enriching soil through long-term deposition of charred phytomass (Leach et al., 2012).

Far more than a merely figurative echo between revolutionary incendiarism and the fiery endeavours of earthly multitudes, what we are getting at here is the need to make sense of change or newness itself as a selective realization of multiple possibilities that inhere in the past. As Žižek riffs off Hegel: 'the New we are dealing with is not primarily the future New, but *the New of the past itself*, of the thwarted, blocked, or betrayed possibilities ("alternative realities") which have disappeared in the actualization of the past' (2012, p. 323). Likewise, our own conceptualization of earthly multitudes, fiery or otherwise, acknowledges that immensely varied repertoires for engaging with planetary dynamism have been stalled, repressed, diverted, expropriated. What we have in mind, then, is not a simple rewinding of history, but a counter-factual exploration of the profusion of earth-oriented practices that might be revisited, elaborated upon, developed in novel directions, as the conditions of the Earth itself are transformed. And a big part of this entails bearing witness to the ways that many contemporary earthly multitudes – like the cultural burners we have described – are indeed seeking to revitalize and repurpose skills and tactics that they have inherited from their forebears.

As Comay insists, the structure of experience posited by Hegel in his tussling with the temporization of French revolutionary freedom and terror is essentially traumatic: each attempt to revive and realize the potentials of radical sociopolitical change generates further contradictions and renewed violence (2011, pp. 4–5). Critical thinkers hardly need reminding of the pervasive and recurrent violence inflicted upon a world of other ways of knowing and being by Western colonial powers and by the generalized imposition of capitalist socioeconomic relations. Neither should we forget that much of what has been overwritten and attenuated, likewise much of what has endured and is being reinvigorated, is itself oriented to the risks of inhabiting inherently volatile environments (Whyte, 2018). And even in the absence of oppressive external social forces, a changeable planet retains its potential to overwhelm customary strategies dealing with variability. This too can be traumatic.

Again, in considering wounding 'untimeliness', recent commentaries on Hegelian historical non-synchronicity invite conversation with the fraught temporal experiences of resurgent earthly multitudes. While Whyte and others implicate Western narrations of ecological catastrophe with the successive waves of devastation wrought over centuries by colonizing powers on Indigenous socio-ecological formations, Steffensen depicts a kind of anticipatory grief experienced by Australian Aboriginal cultural burning experts as they witnessed the build-up towards the destructive fires that erupted in southeast Australia in late 2019. 'The whole country was tinderbox', he recounts, 'and I knew that bad fires were going to come' (2020, p. 209). And so Steffensen and fellow bearers of traditional fire-management expertise found themselves at once grieving over the attenuation of thousands of years of skilled burning practice and living amidst imminent social and ecological devastation. 'Transforming past into future', intones Comay, 'anxiety teaches us how to mourn in advance' (2011, p. 90). Or as Malabou puts it, the very retroactive structure of a Hegelian reworking of the past, its combination of preserving and letting go of the old, 'can be interpreted as the labour of speculative mourning' (2005, p. 146).

For Hegel, the 'explosive antagonism' of the French Revolution, in Comay's words, 'marks a traumatic fold in the order of experience' (2011, pp. 59, 42), while for Steffensen, uncared-for country is a 'time bomb' that enfolds grief for interrupted tradition with the anticipation of a world 'exploding into fire storms' (2020, pp. 56, 210). Without wishing to collapse these two expressions of historical untimeliness into each other, we want to trouble readings of Western modernity that too easily presume its universal faith in a progressive continuum and then proceed to use this assumption to impose insuperable divisions between the temporal experience of the West and its others. While widespread contemporary anxiety over ecoclimatic catastrophe suggests an escalating sense of time out-of-joint, an intention of our own notion of earthly multitudes is to propose that human collectives have *always* grappled with the discontinuity and equivocation of their physical worlds. In the final section, we circle back on the idea of a foundational non-self-identity shared by the human subject and its wider world, and we ask how this might help us think about the fate of the notions of universality and progress at the current geohistorical juncture.

Wounded universality and non-linear progress

'[E]very epoch is a discordant mix of divergent rhythms, unequal durations, and variable speeds', pronounces Comay, reflecting on Hegel's view of revolutionary incendiarism (2011, p. 40). 'Real fires . . . burn in eccentric rhythms', observes Pyne. 'They integrate not only seasonal and phenological cycles, but events that are unexpected, stochastic, irrepeatable and irreversible' (1998, p. 30). Just as Hegel extrapolated from the French Revolution to the wider question of how to collectively make history, so too can we generalize from fire to an encompassing vision of inhabiting a dynamic, self-differentiating planet.

Whatever our own judgement might be on their efficacy or their ethics, *all* human collectives, we argue, must find ways to accommodate themselves to the immanent variability of their physical worlds. This is the context in which we affirm the move away from readings of Hegel that equate 'reconciliation' or 'absolute knowledge' with mastering every possibility in advance. In the reworked Hegelian lexicon we have been drawing on, these related terms refer not to some final attainment of subjective omniscience, but to the collective subject's onerous and harrowing coming-to-terms with both its own divided identity and its exposure to a discordant external reality (McGowan, 2019, p. 42). As Žižek tells it, there is a pronounced element of *Entlassen* or letting be in absolute knowing: 'Hegel not only tolerates but demands that we allow the irreducible otherness of nature remain other' (2020, p. 8). Or, as McGowan updates the Hegelian dialectic of dislocated social subject confronting dissonant nature for the era of global environmental upheaval: '[t]he climate crisis . . . is the point of absence of every social order. What every society shares today is the environmental catastrophe we cannot master' (2020, p. 200).

It is important to keep in mind that Hegel's nature is unassimilable by this logic not merely because it is unreachably alien to *us*, but because its inherent transience prevents it from being at-home with *itself*. This resonates with the way that we conceive of our earthly multitudes as unceasingly open, provisional and incomplete in their relation to the immanent changeability of our planet. As with McGowan's point above about all societies experiencing vulnerability to climate crisis, our own schema of ultimately insuperable collective exposure to planetary multiplicity draws us into the issue of universality that has been such a flashpoint in the social science encounter with the Anthropocene hypothesis (Clark & Szerszynski, 2021, pp. 35–38, 49–52).

In contrast to the blanket disavowal of the universal that characterizes much contemporary social and philosophical enquiry, resurgent Hegelian scholarship has tended to affirm the inextricability of notions of particularity and universality in Hegel's thought. For the theorists we have been referencing, Hegel is indeed one of the progenitors of the idea that all assertions of universality expose or generate unassimilable particularities (Comay, 2011, pp. 119–120; Žižek, 2012, p. 523), and that each particular falls short of full self-identity (McGowan, 2020, p. 45). By this reasoning, what Hegel is committed to is a universality not of shared positive knowledge or goals, but of impurity, incompleteness, non-belonging and contingency (see Žižek, 2012, p. 175). As subjects, we meet with others in this way across and through the rift of our fallible being and our mutual experience of the sundering of the world. So far from the attainment of universal intelligibility and empowerment, contends Comay, '[a]bsolute knowing is just the subject's identification with the woundedness that it is' (2011, p. 130).

While the 'multi' in our earthly multitudes refers to the non-generalizable aspect of working or playing with specific constellations of materials, processes and forces, it also attests to the universal exposure of earth-oriented practitioners to the inconstancies – at every scale – of the planetary fabrics into which they weave themselves. If those who deploy open-field fire skilfully appreciate that different situations require different fires, so too are they bound by mutual recognition that *every* burning comes with its own risks, its potential to flare into something more or other than desired (see Bowman et al., 2016, p. 8). We would add that every earthly multitude embodies and is animated by something of the excessiveness of the planetary powers it has joined forces with, such that this spark of volatility smoulders within as well as without (Clark & Szerszynski, 2021, pp. 46–49).

As we read it, the Hegel-inflected universalism of Comay or McGowan does not so much erect a common platform of global social injustice or human frailty as it summons Western collectives to interrogate the challenge that self-division poses for their identities while acknowledging that others will have their own version of riftedness and fallibility – including those injuries inflicted or exacerbated by the former. Not only does this imply facing up to the untimeliness of all encounters – the inevitable failures of mutual recognition (Comay, 2011, p. 126) – it also means accepting that our other-directed projects and imaginings will not bring wholeness to us, them or the world. 'It is only through recognizing that the other is not a solution that one envisions a world of equality', concludes McGowan (2019, p. 230).

If this approach to the Hegelian pursuit of reconciliation compels us to work relentlessly with our own inheritance, so too would one hope that it respects the right of others to review the achievements of their forebears and find them wanting in certain respects – as Whyte (2018), for example, is willing to do. On the other hand, such a task seems to render much more general the question about how to become a good ancestor that is most familiar from Indigenous discourses (Kimmerer, 2013, p. 9; Whyte, 2018, p. 229). It is here, we would hazard, that a revitalized Hegel converses most vividly with our earthly multitudes. For the idea of an Earth out-of-step with itself underscores that even the most time-tested and hard-won practices might be rendered untimely by unforeseeable planetary transformation, just as it reminds us that suppressed or disfavoured knowledge and skills may irrupt into relevance as their worldly context undergoes reconfiguration. Within this temporal spiral, ancestors and descendants, past and future earthly multitudes, reinvent each other, just as the Earth constantly rediscovers and repurposes its own deeply layered productions.

For all our enthusiasm with the idea of Hegel inducting a dynamically self-differentiating nature into the inner sanctum of modern European thought, however, we question the need to put so much rhetorical stress on 'contradiction', 'antagonism', the 'against itself' when the focus is not strictly on social conflict. In this sense we find ourselves more drawn toward terms such as 'out of step', 'nonsynchronous', 'partial' and 'imperfect' used by recent commentators – which temper Hegel's more aggressive and martial idiom. By the same token, while allowing that trauma, grief and wounding accompany extreme experiences of environmental variation, we want to leave room for engaging with change in more opportune and favourable ways. Even if there is to be no final harmonization of any earth-oriented practice with the planetary variability and volatility, there is much to affirm in the way so many earthly multitudes have learnt to work with and through this inconstancy. With skilful intervention, as we have seen, fire is neither a fully compliant nor an utterly intractable force but can become a medium of satisfying or even exultant experimentation. 'They were beautiful fires,' recalls Steffensen of well-timed cultural burns, 'each one lit up in the right place' (2020, p. 81) – a sentiment shared by many who work and play knowledgeably with the stuff of their worlds. For those whose memory of changeable land and sky runs deep, life-threatening transformation can be viewed as more of a gathering-in or rejuvenation of the world in anticipation of renewed gifting than as an act of violence or animosity. 'Even a wounded world holds us, giving us moments of wonder and joy', vouches botanist and member of the Potawatomi nation, Robin Wall Kimmerer (2013, p. 327). And in the eyes of some earthly multitudes such an affirmation of the fundamental generosity of existence is extended to the way that the Earth experiences its own disturbances or upheavals. In Kimmerer's words: '[t]he grasses remember the nights they were consumed by fire, lighting the way back with a conflagration of love between species' (2013, p. 248).

What light, then, can our consideration of cultural burning shed on the contestation over geoengineering with which we opened? In ways that resonate with other examples of careful and adept earthly multitudes, cultural burning is a profoundly place-based project that at the same time contributes to an increasingly global acceptance of the importance of 'pyrodiversity' and the power of well-deployed fire to mitigate some of the impacts of changing Earth systems (see Bowman et al., 2016, p. 8). Or as we might say, it is contingency flaring into necessity. This is at once a cultivation of collective selves and a remaking of the world – albeit one that Hegel himself would not have recognized as an exemplification of what he called reason and freedom. Aerosol-based solar radiation management, by contrast, is not only premised on 'a level of understanding of the planetary system that does not exist', it assumes an understanding that *cannot* exist, because the planet is not self-same or present to itself.

For us, the value of a retroactive reading of Hegel is not that it provides a quick fix for separating geoengineering from more modest, localized material-energetic interventions, but that it focuses attention on dilemmas common to all who work with the 'rough edges of the world' (see Ingold, 2013, p. 73). An appreciation of worldly inconstancy and inherent limits to intelligibility, we suggest, guides the more time-tested earthly multitudes. And in this sense, what is most concerning about certain kinds of geoengineering proposal is less their experimental and interventionist impetus than their unwillingness to learn from a world of vastly more experienced, nuanced and judicious attempts to 'engineer' worlds and selves.

As McGowan (2019, p. 245) has it, Hegel understood progress as 'the movement from more easily resolved social contradictions to more intractable ones' – these thornier challenges including the derangement intrinsic to material reality itself. If that is not the 'progress' of replacing cultural burning with fossil fuels or stratospheric aerosol injection or even fields of solar panels, neither is it the abandonment of all hope in the human subject becoming more aware of itself and its world. More than simply learning from experience, the cultivation of reason and the crafting of livable worlds are a matter of confronting the excess in every accommodation to an inherently excessive Earth. That 'everything ancient was once new' is a vital intuition which applies as much to the Earth as it does to any human collective, as relevant to planetary multiplicity as it is to earthly multitudes. With all genuine newness, for substance as for subject, comes both the erasure of arrangements that once were and the unleashing of potentials whose full trajectory is unknowable. And it is by working with and through this predicament that earthly multitudes can hope, at least provisionally, to advance their cognitive and practical traction on the world.

Funding

The authors received no financial support for the research, authorship, and/or publication of this article.

References

Bowman, D., Perry, G., Higgins, S., Johnson, C., Fuhlendorf, S., & Murphy, B. (2016). Pyrodiversity is the coupling of biodiversity and fire regimes in food webs. *Philosophical Transactions of the Royal Society B, 371*, 20150169. http://dx.doi.org/10.1098/rstb.2015.0169

Brockman, J. (2009). *We are as gods and have to get good at it.* http://www.edge.org/conversation/stewart_brand-we-are-as-gods-and-have-to-get-good-at-it

Case, E. (2021). *Everything ancient was once new: Indigenous persistence from Hawai'i to Kahiki.* University of Hawai'i Press.

Clark, N. (2018). Fire: Pyropolitics for a planet of fire. In K. Peters, P. Steinberg, & E. Stratford (Eds.), *Territory beyond terra* (pp. 69–85). Rowman & Littlefield.

Clark, N., & Rickards, L. (in press). An Anthropocene species of trouble? Negative synergies between Earth system change and geological destratification. *The Anthropocene Review.*

Clark, N., & Szerszynski, B. (2021). *Planetary social thought: The Anthropocene challenge to the social sciences.* Polity.

Clark, N., & Yusoff, K. (2014). Combustion and society: A fire-centred history of energy use. *Theory, Culture & Society, 31*(5), 203–226.

Cogos, S., Östlund, L., & Roturier, S. (2019). Forest fire and indigenous Sami land use: Place names, fire dynamics, and ecosystem change in northern Scandinavia. *Human Ecology, 47*, 51–64.

Comay, R. (2011). *Mourning sickness: Hegel and the French Revolution.* Stanford University Press.

de la Cadena, M., & Blaser, M. (Eds.). (2018). *A world of many worlds.* Duke University Press.

Denis, E., Pedentchouk, N., Schouten, S., Pagani, M., & Freeman, K. (2017). Fire and ecosystem change in the Arctic across the Paleocene-Eocene thermal maximum. *Earth and Planetary Science Letters, 467,* 149–156.

Furberg, M., Evengård, B., & Nilsson, M. (2011). Facing the limit of resilience: Perceptions of climate change among reindeer herding Sami in Sweden. *Global Health Action, 4*(1), 8417. doi:10.3402/gha.v4i0.8417

Hegel, G. W. F. (1953). *Reason in history, a general introduction to the philosophy of history.* Liberal Arts Press.

Hegel, G. W. F. (1969). *Science of logic.* Humanity Books.

Hegel, G. W. F. (1970). *Hegel's philosophy of nature: Being part two of the encyclopaedia of the philosophical sciences (1830)* (A. V. Miller, Trans.). Clarendon Press.

Hegel, G. W. F. (2001). *The philosophy of history* (J. Sibree, Trans.). Batoche Books.

Ingold, T. (2013). *Making: Anthropology, archaeology, art and architecture.* Routledge.

Kimmerer, R. W. (2013). *Braiding sweetgrass: Indigenous wisdom, scientific knowledge, and the teachings of plants.* Milkweed Editions.

Kimmerer, R. W., & Lake, F. K. (2001). The role of Indigenous burning in land management. *Journal of Forestry, 99*(11), 36–41.

Kuhlken, R. (1999). Settin' the woods on fire: Rural incendiarism as protest. *The Geographical Review, 89*(3), 343–363.

Langton, M. (1998). *Burning questions: Emerging environmental issues for Indigenous peoples in Northern Australia.* Centre for Indigenous Natural and Cultural Resource Management, Northern Territory University.

Leach, M., Fairhead, J., & Fraser, J. (2012). Green grabs and biochar: Revaluing African soils and farming in the new carbon economy. *Journal of Peasant Studies, 39*(2), 285–307.

Lövbrand, E., Beck, S., Chilvers, J., Forsyth, T., Hedrén, J., Hulme, M., Lidskog, R., & Vasileiadou, E. (2015). Who speaks for the future of Earth? How critical social science can extend the conversation on the Anthropocene. *Global Environmental Change, 32,* 211–218.

Lundy, C. (2016). The necessity and contingency of universal history: Deleuze and Guattari contra Hegel. *Journal of the Philosophy of History, 10,* 51–75.

Malabou, C. (2005). *The future of Hegel: Plasticity, temporality and dialectic.* Routledge.

Marder, M. (2015). *Pyropolitics: When the world is blaze.* Rowman & Littlefield.

Mazza, P. (2021). Saami indigenous back down Gates-funded geoengineering experiment. *The Raven.* https://theraven.substack.com/p/saami-indigenous-back-down-gates

McGowan, T. (2016). The insubstantiality of substance, or why we should read Hegel's Philosophy of Nature. *International Journal of Zizek Studies, 8*(1), 1–19.

McGowan, T. (2019). *Emancipation after Hegel: Achieving a contradictory revolution.* Columbia University Press.

McGowan, T. (2020). *Universality and identity politics.* Columbia University Press.

Pyne, S. (1994). Maintaining focus: An introduction to anthropogenic fire. *Chemosphere, 29*(5), 889–911.

Pyne, S. (1997). *Vestal fire.* University of Washington Press.

Pyne, S. (1998). *Burning bush: A fire history of Australia.* Henry Holt.

Pyne, S. (2000). Where have all the fires gone? *Fire Management Today, 60*(3), 4–6.

Pyne, S. (2001). *Fire: A brief history.* University of Washington Press.

Sámi Council. (2021). *Regarding SCoPEx plans for test flights at the Swedish Space Corporation in Kiruna.* www.saamicouncil.net/news-archive/open-letter-requesting-cancellation-of-plans-for-geoengineering

Savransky, M. (2021). *Around the day in eighty worlds: Politics of the pluriverse*. Duke University Press.

Steffensen, V. (2020). *Fire country: How Indigenous fire management could help save Australia*. Hardie Grant Travel

Whyte, K. (2018). Indigenous science (fiction) for the Anthropocene: Ancestral dystopias and fantasies of climate change crises. *Environment and Planning E: Nature and Space*, *1*(1–2), 224–242.

Žižek, S. (2012). *Less than nothing: Hegel and the shadow of dialectical materialism*. Verso.

Žižek, S. (2020). The greening of Hegel. *The Philosophical Salon*. https://thephilosophicalsalon.com/the-greening-of-hegel/

Author biographies

Nigel Clark is Professor of Human Geography at the Lancaster Environment Centre, Lancaster University, UK. He is the author of *Inhuman Nature* (2011) and (with Bronislaw Szerszynski) *Planetary Social Thought: The Anthropocene Challenge to the Social Sciences* (2021). In 2017 he co-edited (with Kathryn Yusoff) the *Theory, Culture & Society* special issue on 'Geosocial Formations and the Anthropocene'.

Bron Szerszynski is Professor of Sociology at Lancaster University. He is author of *Nature, Technology and the Sacred* (2005) and (with Nigel Clark) of *Planetary Social Thought* (2021), and co-editor of *Risk, Environment and Modernity* (1996), *Re-Ordering Nature* (2003), *Nature Performed* (2003) and *Technofutures* (2015).

MONOGRAPH SERIES

The Sociological Review Monographs
2022, Vol. 70(2) 188–201
© The Author(s) 2022
Article reuse guidelines:
sagepub.com/journals-permissions
DOI: 10.1177/00380261221084794
journals.sagepub.com/home/sor

An ecology of trust? Consenting to a pluralist universe

Didier Debaise
Fonds National de la Recherche Scientifique (FNRS), Belgium; Université Libre de Bruxelles, Belgium

Isabelle Stengers
Université Libre de Bruxelles, Belgium

Abstract

The idea of 'progress' was undoubtedly at the heart of the experience of the Moderns, guiding at the same time their thought, the values that they gave themselves, the hopes that animated them and of innumerable justifications that they found for all the processes of dispossession, disqualification and dismemberment that they implemented. Starting with William James's diagnosis of the hold the idea of 'progress' has over us, and following his proposition that this idea is at work in the world itself, in the ecological and social ravages that it guides and justifies, this article aims to analyse the political and speculative effects of the notion of progress and to propose, through what we call an 'ecology of trust', other ways of collectively composing our modes of existence.

Keywords

James, Guattari, Haraway, involution, pragmatism, progress

Introduction

What does it mean to think 'after progress'? Would we be at a historical moment of rupture, leaving behind us what would be nothing more than an outdated set of illusions and erroneous habits of thought? Would we be in the era of 'post-progress' as we used to speak of a 'post-modern' thought? We think that the 'turns', the 'posts' of the

Corresponding author:
Didier Debaise, Université Libre de Bruxelles, CP133/02, Avenue F. D. Roosevelt, 50, Brussels, 1050, Belgium.
Email: didier.debaise@ulb.be

academic-media temporality continue to participate in the hold that the notion of progress has still on us. One does not overcome a hold, one must heal from it.

A hold must first be diagnosed, and it is in the thought of William James that we have found resources that may be precious because, like any diagnosis worthy of the name, it does not look for a 'true' cause, but creates the ground where the hypothesis of a cure can be formulated.

James's diagnosis is at the heart of the first part of this article. We are particularly interested in the 'horror of becoming a dupe' that James locates at the heart of modern experience. This horror, he shows, communicates with a fear that has nothing to do with some healthy caution. It has a passionate dimension. Under its sway it is the whole world that becomes suspicious, tempting, likely to lead us to what is not a mistake, but rather a real sin. Those who know they are threatened by sin must become insensitive to temptation. What we have called progress requires this insensitivity. But this fear also raises an ontological question: what universe or world does it contribute to create? It is a pragmatics of the notion of 'progress' that unfolds in these questions and that we will try to implement throughout this first part: how do such notions, such postures, such feelings, affect us and the environments in which we live?

It is following James's diagnosis that we will be able, in the second part of this article, to follow the ways in which paths to a cure may be attempted. It is once again in James that we will find elements indicating that such paths might aim at a regeneration of what we will call an 'ecology of trust'. It is not a matter of establishing a general theory of trust, but of inheriting a heterogeneous plurality of fragile, non-triumphalist suggestions that range from science to activism.

The horror of becoming a dupe

William James characterized the rationality claimed by his contemporaries, those we are now used to calling 'the Moderns', as expressing first and foremost 'horror of becoming a dupe'. Their founding myth would be that of a past defined by false ideas, irrational attachments, subjective interpretations, unfounded beliefs. Their inexorable duty would be to free, by all means necessary, they themselves and all other peoples still prisoners of this past. They would have to suspect and submit to the test everything, including the very stuff of the universe, prone to delude and lead them astray at any moment. The Moderns would be those who would never stop breaking with what, judged to be deceptive or seductive, exposes them to what, for them, is synonymous with perdition.

The sanctification of methods of verification, of bifurcations of all kinds (belief and knowledge, subjective and objective, real and apparent, etc.) coincides with immense processes of disqualification of knowledge that have made one of us say that 'We live in a veritable cemetery for destroyed practices and collective knowledges' (Stengers, 2015, p. 98). What will enable us to resist a universe that can delude us at any moment? What method could protect us from those, charlatans, impostors, who are waiting for the slightest opportunity to deceive us? How can we educate a public that never ceases to fall under the spell of irrational forces against which it is powerless? For Moderns, the guideline seems to be an immoderate taste for any idea, theory, or method identifying truth as disenchantment and hurt, as destroying any reason to believe in ourselves or this world.

James noted in *The Will to Believe* the psycho-social dimensions of this stance: 'he who says "Better go without belief forever than believe a lie!" merely shows his own preponderant private horror of becoming a dupe' (James, 1979, p. 25). This would be the great ritornello of modern thought with its dramas and heroic figures: 'Believe nothing, keep your mind in suspense forever, rather than by closing it on insufficient evidence incur the awful risk of believing lies' (James, 1979, p. 24). We would have the duty to resist this awful, even sinful, risk at any price. We would be bound to forsake the hope and quest of truth itself.

Moderns would then be defined by what, James insists, is a choice. 'Believe truth! Shun error! – these, we see, are two materially different laws; and by choosing between them we may end by coloring differently our whole intellectual life. We may regard the chase for truth as paramount, and the avoidance of error as secondary; or we may, on the other hand, treat the avoidance of error as more imperative, and let truth take its chance' (James, 1979, p. 24). The intense, almost religious, importance that the Moderns give to the notion of 'progress' lies in keeping with the imperative of avoiding error, the imperative of mistrust.

By making time a homogeneous advance, to be imposed on all, and which would not cease to break with its previous forms, progress proceeds as a true machine for disqualifying the past, condemning all those who, in one way or another, still remain attached to it, or give in to the temptations of 'regression'. By defining nature as that which has inspired suspect feelings of admiration and respect, progress turns it into what is to be mastered, exploited and dominated without scruples. By considering knowledge an operation of rupture with common sense, interests, attachments and opinion, progress gives to those who obey the imperative of mistrust the heroic feeling of belonging to the few in possession of unattached knowledge, to the few who alone can fight against this universe of deception.

The thinning of the world

James's diagnosis not only makes the 'horror of becoming a dupe' the central element of the relationships – embodied in the notion of progress – that Moderns have with their own story (childhood that must be brought to maturity), their environments (nature from which one must sternly distance oneself) and with others (those who still believe, where we know), it also gives a dramatic reach to its performative power. For James, the question of dupery entails consequences that are both existential and ontological, which he expresses in a passage from *A Pluralistic Universe*: 'Philosophies are intimate parts of the universe, they express something of its own thought of itself. A philosophy may indeed be a most momentous reaction of the universe upon itself. It may, as I said, possess and handle itself differently in consequence of us philosophers, with our theories, being here; it may trust itself or mistrust itself the more, and, by doing the one or the other, deserve more the trust or the mistrust. What mistrusts itself deserves mistrust' (James, 1977, p. 143). So it is not only the mistrust Moderns entertain towards their world that makes them see the danger everywhere. This world could well become effectively fearsome as a result of the way they treat it.

This follows from one of the great maxims of the Jamesian pragmatism that is too little emphasized. It is only through an act of abstraction, secondary and always retrospective, that we can dissociate ideas and things, representations and experience, theories and the universe. We must ask for each theory, each idea, what it does, i.e. how it transforms the universe to which it is added. And in particular for the notion of 'progress'. We can obviously establish its components (linear time, rupture with the natural environment, objectivity of knowledge, etc.), but the essential question might be how it contributes to the manner in which the universe may 'possess and handle itself'. Behind James's pathos ('the horror of becoming a dupe', running 'the awful risk of believing lies', etc.) there is therefore a real ontological question: what universe is being created through and with our mistrust?

For James, the epistemological and ontological answer to this question can be called 'thinning'. We might say that the density of modes of existence, the plurality of relations which we can entertain with the beings that make up our world and which they entertain between them, the heterogeneity of our knowledge, this 'overabundance of reality' were the target of a leitmotiv: the capricious, reckless, reality was to give way to the uniform course of a nature which would then reliably reward rational knowledge and serve human ends – the Baconian view of progress.

For James, if there is a test that we can put to our ideas, it would be this one: do they result in a thinning of our conditions of existence and thought or in a thickening? This test is more decisive, more constitutive, more essential than the tests of truth, adequacy and coherence, which are taken as primordial, but which in a certain way presuppose it. It was on the occasion of a tribute to the thought of G. Fechner that James proposed this distinction.

Drawing his portrait, he writes: 'He was in fact a philosopher in the "great" sense, although he cared so much less than most philosophers care for abstractions of the "thin" order. For him the abstract lived in the concrete' (James, 1977, p. 70). It is therefore at the level of abstractions that the distinction is made: there are abstractions whose effect is a thinning of what they target, as if they only find their reason and their effectiveness in the subtraction of the qualities of concrete things, of their ways of valuing their environment, of the manifold relationships they weave with others. There are, on the contrary, abstractions that thicken things, enhance unnoticed dimensions, highlight the fragile and event-driven nature of their existence.

Let us take, as an example of a thinning abstraction, the seemingly legitimate question: 'What does this depend on?' Feeling dependent, or feeling that something depends on you, are concrete, painful or transformative experiences. But this question, when asked by a scientist, is accompanied by the clause ceteris paribus ('all else being equal'): anything that could complicate the dependency relationship must be able to be put in brackets so that this relationship can be defined. Whatever is being questioned must be able to be abstracted from its world. The notion of dependence is therefore one of those abstract notions, which seem obvious and self-evident, but whose field of actual relevance is extremely selective. Typically, it is in the laboratory that one encounters phenomena defined in terms of variables that can vary independently of each other so that each can be related to the effect its variation produces, the others being kept constant. But this has not prevented the notion of dependence from becoming an all-purpose abstraction. Thus, in many models in the so-called social and human sciences, including when they are systemic, the clause ceteris paribus is accepted as what a science must be allowed to suppose in order for science to be possible at all. This in turn implies an attitude of methodological mistrust towards anything that could thicken the situation, for example the 'terrible' possibility that the 'subjects' are not indifferent to the intent of the questions they have to answer in the name of science but actively define themselves in relation with the thick situation.

Anna Tsing introduced the correlative notion of scalability, which also makes a being's indifference to its world crucial. For engineers, the operation of a computing device is reliable if it can withstand a change in scale (an increase in the number of users or categories to be managed, for example). As she writes, 'Scalability is the ability of a project to change scales smoothly without any change in project frames. A scalable business, for example, does not change its organization as it expands' (Tsing, 2015, p. 38). Scalability here does not respond to a methodological imperative, but to a practical concern – to render scalable or to maintain scalability has nothing abstract about it. Ensuring that an operation will not be sensitive to circumstances is an actual, hard work, thinning down of the world. It 'banishes meaningful diversity, that is, diversity that might change things' (Tsing, 2015, p. 38). It is the same concern that prevails in industrial organization. And it is also, from the plantations whose cruel invention Anna Tsing recalls, to industrial agriculture, the project that has allowed the production of intrinsically dependent beings: plants selected for monoculture, which cannot live without inputs, fertilizers and pesticides, but which will have the same characteristics wherever they grow. In all cases, it allowed one thin value to become the only objective measure of what becomes a 'product'. 'By envisioning more and more of the world through the lens of the plantation, investors devised all kinds of new commodities. Eventually, they posited that everything on earth – and beyond – might be scalable, and thus exchangeable at market values' (Tsing, 2015, p. 40). Moderns did not just posit nature as uniform, they largely render it so.

But effectively abstracting beings, depriving them of their capacity to participate in the thickness of their world also means robbing them of their own dynamics – monocultures are fragile, vulnerable to epidemics; students who have been led to identify the knowledges that could have sustained and empowered them with instruments of success are ready to accept their authority without understanding them, in an unreliable or irresponsible way. Thinned down worlds are worlds we have good reasons to mistrust and fear.

The thesis that the operations of abstractions that thin down the world contribute to making an impoverished and vulnerable, and therefore also fearsome world, finds its direct echo in what Félix Guattari called a triple ecological disaster. Taking up Bateson's famous 'There is an ecology of bad ideas, just as there is an ecology of weeds' as the epigraph of his *Three Ecologies*, he gave the ecological question a transversal power that seems to us indispensable for thinking 'after progress'. For what has been called progress has for its correlate invasive ecologies, imposing themselves and spreading thanks to the desertification of the ravaged landscapes in which they proliferate.

In *The Three Ecologies* Guattari describes a triple disaster that can be related with what James taught us to call the 'politics of mistrust', reducing environments to a simple resource, using scalable categories that make ways of living, of attaching, of valuing equivalent or insignificant. Presenting these disasters as ecological ravages allows him to characterize as inseparable the devastation of ecosystems by an extractivist logic, the 'erosion of subjectivities' (Guattari, 2000, p. 31) by their confinement in the categories of the individuals and their psychologizing functions, and the destruction of collective subjectivity by a generalized competition at all levels between individuals.

Guattari's analysis thus makes a decisive break with the questioning of progress on the basis of the 'nuisances' that it causes: only categories of another kind, transversal, aesthetico-existential ones (Guattari, 2000, p. 56), may characterize what is required to ward off the triple devastation that threatens life on Earth. Guattari called for a transversal catalytic bringing into being what he named 'existential territories'[1] capable of processually opening up individual and group subjectivities. 'The reconquest of a degree of creative autonomy in one particular domain encourages conquests in other domains – the catalyst for a gradual reforging and renewal of humanity's confidence in itself starting at the most miniscule level' (Guattari, 2000, p. 69).

Consenting to the thickness of the world

It is therefore appropriate to start with what might seem miniscule indeed, in view of the scale of the disaster. If there is one science that has contributed prodigiously to the thinning of life, it is biology dominated by the neo-Darwinian vulgate. According to the latter, a single principle suffices to explain the abundant diversity of life: the blind competition between specific individual lineages. Each living organism would be what it is because its lineage has survived the competition. However, following the now widely recognized pioneering work of Lynn Margulis (Margulis & Sagan, 1995), today's biologists affirm that if the Earth is fertile, full of diverse ways of living, it is due to the invention of interdependent relationships. From the smallest cell in our bodies to the tangle of ecosystems we call nature, no isolatable living thing as such can be credited with what makes it capable of living. As Tsing writes: 'Bacteria made our oxygen atmosphere, and plants help maintain it. Plants live on land because fungi made soil by digesting rocks. As these examples suggest, world-making projects can overlap, allowing room for more than one species. Humans, too, have always been involved in multi-species world making' (Tsing, 2015, p. 22). All of them are what William James called 'social organisms', originating from and participating in mutualist ecologies. An individual is what it is only with others, thanks to others but also at the risk of others.

Biologist Scott F. Gilbert writes: 'Nature may be selecting "relationships" rather than individuals or genomes. What we usually consider to be an "individual" may be a multi-species group that is under selection' (Gilbert et al., 2010, p. 673). Which means that the question of what a living being is capable of has become an open question, all the more so as interdependence can be generative, opening up the group and the beings who participate in it to new possibilities. Biology should thus explore how beings are liable to transform, or even metamorphose, thanks to the relationships they entertain with others. The policy of explanation by dependence (on selection, on genes, today on the genome, even on the proteome) has thus abstracted away what might be a crucial element in the history of terrestrial life.

Interdependence is of course an abstraction, but it is an abstraction that thickens the world. Correlatively, it implies the resurgence of a supposedly proto-scientific practice, that of natural histories, irreducibly empirical histories. Nothing is 'natural' any longer in nature, in the sense of being explainable by general laws in the light of which biologists could ignore the anecdotal and identify the deceptive. On the contrary, biologists must learn to allow themselves to be intrigued, to never assume that they know in advance what is liable to participate in a way of life or transform it. In other words, the biology of interdependence requires that biologists consent to what could resemble a 'regression' towards empiricism, towards a characterization of cases that does not aspire to lead up to a definition of interdependence in general.

It is here where we encounter a central theme of William James's philosophy, the theme of 'consent'. The term must be understood in its most literal sense: *consentire* (feel with or together). It is not a passive agreement but a both wilful and transformative acceptance. Indeed for James to consent first means to *not* reject a perspective or an idea, or an object that is 'difficult' – for scientists, for instance, a perspective which would make them vulnerable to the accusation of regression – but, on the contrary, to deliberately sustain it: 'Sustained in this way by a resolute effort of attention, the difficult object erelong begins to call up its own congeners and associates and ends by changing the disposition of the man's consciousness altogether. . . . Consent to the idea's undivided presence, this is effort's sole achievement' (James, 1950, p. 564).

Biologists who today consent to the idea of interdependence consent to be transformed by what they are dealing with so that what they are dealing with becomes something other than a new field for thinning abstractions in the name of scientific progress. They situate themselves 'after progress'.

We can associate this type of consent with the concept of involution proposed by Deleuze and Guattari (1992, pp. 238–239) thanks to the transversal concept of 'involutionary momentum' subsequently crafted by Carla Hustak and Natasha Myers. They found in Darwin's book on orchids fertilized by insects, often considered anecdotal – not advancing science – the testimony of the passion that possessed Darwin when he studied the 'involutive' relationship that develops between orchids and the wasps induced to try and copulate with them; Darwin also let himself be intrigued, then captivated, by the orchid. Hustak and Myers write: 'we read Darwin against the grain of his evolutionary logics. We are interested in the moments of perplexity, excess, and affective pull, moments when he got caught up in the energetic momentum that ingathers organisms in complex ecological relations' (Hustak & Myers, 2012, p. 82).

Involution, according to Deleuze and Guattari, is always situated 'between' two heterogeneous beings; contrary to Darwinian evolution which concerns lineage and filiation, it is a matter of alliance. The attraction that the orchid exerts on the wasp is not reducible to a hijacking of the hereditary link between sexual excitation and reproduction. The wasp is not duped, it enjoys. As for Darwin, who also enjoys, he has not 'regressed', he has consented to open himself up to affects officially excluded by the logic derived from the lineage of scientists aiming at objectivity. He has consented to let himself be affected by the orchid. And the change of practice of biologists who have consented to abandon the notion of dependence is 'involutionary' too, because, instead of competing for the right definition of interdependence, they are thickening this notion, multiplying its modalities, and, in so doing, restoring to the history of life a proliferating inventiveness that defies our abstract, scalable, categories.

Cultivating trust?

Interdependence is a risk; it can be fragile, because what or whom a being counts on can be lacking for many reasons, the main one today being modern modes of intervention, i.e. progress. But this risk does not generally communicate with mistrust or the horror of becoming a dupe. If thinned down worlds are worlds which we have good reasons to fear and mistrust, thicker worlds require a culture of attention. Correlatively, the risk of trust, when it bears on interdependence, is not between two individuals, but must take on a meaning that is collectively experienced as such. This is why we ask here the question of a culture of trust.

Cultivating trust is part of an ecological regeneration whose affective, existential and ethical dimensions must be understood in terms that may be called pragmatic, because their truth lies in their verification, in the creation of links that have no other justification than what they make possible. They are not bonds of reciprocity, affirming a recognition of the other, but mutualist bonds, that is to say, binding heterogeneous beings who need each other but each for its own reasons. William James evokes a form of 'precursive faith' that allows independent parties to cooperate, to form a 'social organism'. Such an organism 'is what it is because each member proceeds to his own duty with a trust that the other members will simultaneously do theirs. . . . A government, an army, a commercial system, a ship, a college, an athletic team, all exist on this condition, without which not only is nothing achieved, but nothing is even attempted' (James, 1979, p. 29). James takes a deliberately negative example: the looting of a train. How can one not at first sight be surprised that a small number of looters can hold a train full of passengers under control? Why don't they defend themselves, why don't they reverse the relationship since the balance of power is, seen from the outside, favourable to them? What makes the difference is that the looters 'can count on one another, while each passenger fears that if he makes a movement of resistance, he will be shot before anyone else backs him up. If we believed that the whole car-full would rise at once with us, we should each severally rise, and train-robbing would never even be attempted' (James, 1979, p. 29). There are, he concludes, cases 'where faith in a fact can help create the fact'.[2]

Interdependence can be generative. It is in these terms that we will pose the question of a culture of trust. That such a culture offers no guarantee, that it is not 'good in itself', the example chosen by James, the train-looting, but also that of the other institutions he cites, where a closed group or even clique culture often prevails, are enough to bear witness to this. But it should also be remembered that the examples taken by James belong to modern, individualistic societies. These institutions are what has survived the eradication of collective practices which were customary everywhere on earth and which involved the cultivation of the kind of trust that 'making things together' or 'commoning' practices require – a precursive trust but also, Martin Savransky notes, a recursive one since 'the trust of our held-out hand is a trust in another hand's trust, a trust in another hand's trust in our trust in theirs' (Savransky, 2021, p. 101).

A new generation of activists is now sweeping away academic dissertations on the relationship between Humans and Nature by proclaiming 'We do not defend nature, we are the nature defending itself.' This cry situates itself 'after progress', in the sense that it can only be heard as a response to the triple ecological disaster diagnosed by Guattari, the destruction, deliberate or not, of the interdependent relationships between humans and their environments and within the environments themselves. And it does not resonate in a vacuum. From collective vegetable gardens to Zones to Defend, initiatives are multiplying where a culture of interdependence is being relearned. This apprenticeship can be said to be involutionary because, in order to take root in experience, the lived meaning of interdependence requires from each a deliberate effort to consent, demanding that they set aside the right for each to 'decide for themselves' that modern people experience as their freedom.

We propose to call 'generative apparatuses'[3] collectively designed modes of assemblage that both presuppose and induce their participants' precursive trust in the capacity to make sense in common about situations that concern them. Some of these, such as the African palaver, have survived colonization. As for the contemporary US activists' consensus-making process, it has also older roots since it was inspired by the Quaker way of gathering 'Clearness committees' around concerns or questions experienced by community members. Such apparatuses exemplify the transformative efficacy the regeneration of an 'ecology of trust' might demand. Their aim is not to generate unanimous feelings but the involution of conflicting stances, each setting aside the claim to be the right one, and consenting to let the sense that others express something which also matters affect their own positioning. If an agreement is obtained, it will be an event that belongs to no one but may be received with gratitude, because it will have been generated with others, because of others, and at the risk of others.

Generative apparatuses break with the ideal of scalability and with the set of abstractions that thin the world. They are situational and enrooted. This is not to say that they divide and particularize, but that the communications they can generate will demand involutionary alliances, recalling Félix Guattari's catalytic reconquest, a processual creation of interlacing without confusion and without a pre-given definition of common interest and meaning.

In other words, to try to think 'after progress', in the perspective that we defend, is to think after the production of 'thin' individuals, who certainly know that they are dependent – nothing is more dependent than a modern individual – but suffer these dependencies as unfortunately necessary limitations to their freedom. But it is not dreaming of a reconciliation of Humans with Humans and with Nature. Just as ecological interdependencies do not meet any general definition, the ways in which humans can make themselves capable of cultivating and repopulating the areas of experience that modernity has devastated will not unify them. But they will cause them to diverge in ways that can become solidary, opening up a culture of partial connections[4] that demand to be ongoingly taken up again and nurtured.

In this sense, no unitary category should pretend to give us the 'right' perspective on the pluriverse in the making, be it that of a new materialism, of new ontologies or epistemologies that claim to be 'more-than-human'. Knowing that matter is active or accepting ourselves as 'more-than-human' does not mean that we experience it, and it will probably not be of much interest to those peoples who have managed to maintain a culture of relationships with the world they inhabit and belong to.

Perhaps, on the other hand, a deliberate and attentive use of what linguists call the middle voice could be relevant here, because the opposition between the active voice, which defines the syntactic subject of a statement as active, and the passive voice, which defines it as the object of action, is not suitable for involutionary becoming that is always 'between' heterogeneous terms. Letting oneself be touched by, solicited by, affected by, forced to feel and think by, and recognizing that we have been made capable of this thanks to something other than ourselves, belongs to the middle voice. We need to culti-vate a fabric of sociality that transforms our claims into practical stories of becoming with each other, thanks to each other and at the risk of each other.

But perhaps we also need to accept a test that speaks directly to our fear and horror of becoming a dupe: the question of the 'Other-than-human beings'.

Consenting to pluralism

The notion of 'progress' enclosed us alone in a thinned down, that is to say, disenchanted world. Today, we are beginning to conceive that the world could be populated by ways of feeling and making sense, both human and non-human, in which we participate and which require care and attention. But consenting to hear this requirement does not mean feeling at home in a re-enchanted world.

Feeling at home in a pluralist universe is an enticing prospect, maybe the ultimate trick of the relentless universalism which made the 'uniform course of nature' so dear to us. This is why we wish to evoke here, from far away, what, with Marisol de la Cadena (2015), we will call 'Other-than-human' beings. If there is a one question that the horror of becoming a dupe has ripped through, it is that of those 'Other-than-humans' reduced to primitive beliefs, to the catch-all of the supernatural, to the illusions that still bind col-lectives incapable of facing what remains, despite everything – human solitude. We may well become able to feel the dense network of mutual relations maintained by the trees of a forest, but what of the experience of feeling looked at by the forest, of being aware of it as an attentive and clear-sighted presence, who knows us and can shame us? Are we able not to just tolerate it as 'purely cultural'?

Seriously asking the question of 'Other-than-humans' seems to us necessary at a time when thinking 'after progress' demands from us a consent to make room. This does not mean 'ontological liberalism', because the proposal to put on the same foot-ing, to recognize as equally existing everything that makes sense for humans, may irritate philosophers, but eschews the pragmatic test: what does this question of the 'Other-than humans' require of us, and not of humans in general? For it is we who have transformed the question 'does it really exist?', which can make sense in laboratories, into a general judgement operator. The involution we have associated with the Jamesian consent requires in this case the effort of putting aside our filiation haunted by the easy option of tolerance and of refusing as well to enter into abstract polemics about the existence that we would recognize of unicorns, for instance, or other centaurs that we encounter in contemporary scholastic discussions. For whom does the existence of unicorns actually matter? Who knows how to address them, what they ask, what name they answer to? Are there peoples who honour them and know how to sustain the rela-tionship they demand?

Involution takes place between heterogeneous terms, not in the brains of sarcastic phi-losophers, but between visitors and people who know how to relate with Other-than-human beings. And it demands that we, modern visitors, recognize the limited character of the panoply of attitudes we may be tempted to adopt: ironical or voyeuristic distance, tolerant interpretation in terms of subjective cultural beliefs, or else mimetic leap that always risks exoticizing what one aims to share. Using the middle voice we would propose that visitors might learn to let themselves be touched – not touched by Other-than-humans, but by the way in which they create obligations for 'their' people. This is what we would call a pragmatic proposition, refusing to go beyond the effects but focusing on the culture of these effects. Refusing, that is, the position of the good will settlers – the tolerance of those who know that they know better, even if they remain discreet about it. But also the voracity of spiritual tourists who think they can freely appropriate what they feel attracted by.

If biologists have allowed us to say that nothing is 'natural' in nature, that the living, on any scale, enter into relationships that could be said to be artificial in that they do not contradict general laws but deprive them of their power to explain and define, we must say here that the category of supernatural is as misplaced as that of natural. Other-than-humans do not ask to be recognized as 'supernatural' – as we know, it is the missionaries who understood them that way. They do not even ask that we believe that they 'really exist', if that means existing in a public way that every properly equipped human should be able to witness. As Donna Haraway firmly points out, 'animism cannot be donned like a magic cape by visitors' (Haraway, 2016, p. 89).

In other words, the Jamesian 'pluriverse in the making' does not respect the humanist adage par excellence: 'I am human and nothing that is human is foreign to me'. And it is no longer a question of accepting the need to learn how to weave relationships between divergent practical cultures, or to learn the arts of a composition that continue the dynamics of generative interdependence that have made the Earth fertile. We need to accept an involution of such a (secular) materialism into an 'animism' that Haraway, quoting Eduardo Viveiros de Castro, calls a 'sensible materialism' (Haraway, 2016, p. 88). And this means that, while we can say 'we are all "more than human"' to the extent that we can consent to a relationship of interdependence with our kins and symbionts, we cannot say 'we are all animists' when the relation with Other-than-human beings is concerned. Those beings make their own choices about who they will enter into relation with, including recruiting those they choose, be they willing or not. The pluriverse is thus streaked with relations that are recalcitrant to composition. Any precursive trust is misplaced here. Consenting to pluralism means accepting that we do not know.

Not to know does not mean to ignore. It asks for an apprenticeship that specifically concerns those who named themselves humans, an involution of our settled oppositions between what is and what is not possible. Consenting to sensible materialism demands, Haraway writes, 'a certain suspension of ontologies and epistemologies, holding them lightly, in favor of more venturesome, experimental natural histories' (Haraway, 2016, p. 88). To hold lightly and not to reject – this may evoke the two complementary ways that Niels Bohr associated with how blind persons can explore their environment with a stick. Holding it tight implies imposing active questions on that environment – does this resist pressure, i.e. in our case, does it satisfy the criteria for what 'really' exists? Holding it lightly means consenting to render oneself sensitive to what is being explored, including the 'gaps' that signal the partial nature of the connection (see M. de la Cadena, note 4 below). It is consenting to give it the power to touch us, but denying ourselves the power to define it, to categorize it, that is to say, to detach what touches us from the world that has cultivated the art of welcoming it. But we must then resist the fear that could lead our hand to tighten its grip on the stick, to restore the world where we are alone.

In his *Varieties of Religious Experience*, William James proceeds with a lightly held stick. He does not dispute that, held firmly, the stick of our interpretive categories leads to the conclusion that we have no reason to accept as 'true' what saints, mystics and ecstatic people report having seen or heard or perceived. What remains, however, is their experience itself, that of entering into a relationship with 'something greater'. And James asks that we let ourselves be touched by the fruits of this relationship, that we recognize that the saints, whatever their limitations and excesses, are 'the great torch-bearers, the tip of the wedge, the clearers of the darkness' (1985, p. 285). The charity they practised to the extreme has been, he writes, 'a genuinely creative social force, tending to make real a degree of virtue which it alone is ready to assume as possible' (p. 285). We have to recognize that 'without that over-trust in human worth which they show, the rest of us would lie in spiritual stagnancy' (p. 285).

However, this contact with 'something greater' has fruits which may well also inspire fear. Of course, the usual easy answer is to separate the 'true' saints from the fanatics, to whom we would be free to apply our interpretive categories. But why do we ask that the relationship with an Other-than-human entity should make us better? Peoples who have resisted the hold of universalist faiths know well that the relationship with these Others is not without risk, that they do not respond to our idea of benevolence. Above all, they must be appeased and can, if we forget that they are Others, turn into devouring powers. What if Alfred N. Whitehead was right about what Plato named Ideas giving us what we named our soul? In this case, we did not recognize those Other-than-humans who made us their people, and thus do not know how to relate with them. The fact that we are ready to kill (really or academically) in the name of Ideas then verifies Whitehead's warning about the Furies, 'the horrors lurking within [Ideas'] imperfect realization' (Whitehead, 1967, p. 148).

Be it as it may, the testimonies of religious experience that touched William James, as well as his own need for a God who would give meaning to human life as a real battle in which we are called to take part (James, 1979, p. 55), could indicate what we have to question in order to position ourselves 'after progress'. Why do we need that the experience of Others inhabiting this world should carry a call that turns those who respond to it into 'clearers of darkness', or that awakens us from our 'stagnancy'? Are not our worlds crying loud enough? Why not cultivate care, reverence or respect for the obligations associated with Others (including maybe our own Ideas) without lending them a privileged relationship with salvation? As Gilles Deleuze and Félix Guattari wrote, 'It may be that believing in this world, in this life, becomes our most difficult task, or the task of a mode of existence still to be discovered on our plane of immanence today' (Deleuze & Guattari, 1994, p. 75). Involution.

Funding

The author received no financial support for the research, authorship, and/or publication of this article.

Notes

1. 'Existential territories' are part of Félix Guattari's metamodelization of the production of subjectivity developed in *Chaosmosis*. It is their implosion which articulates the triple ecological disaster (Guattari, 1995, p. 55).

2. This is what happened on 9/11 when the passengers of flight UA93, which had been diverted in the direction of Washington DC, learned by phone calls of the New York suicide attacks. Consenting to the fact that they had nothing to lose, they collectively attempted to take control of the plane. The plane crashed but the planned attack had failed.
3. The term apparatus, which is the usual translation of the French *dispositif*, often designates disciplinary apparatuses as analysed by Michel Foucault. We use the same term in order to pragmatically accentuate the involved contrast and complicate the critique of apparatuses as such. Each cultivation practice has its apparatuses and they deserve 'critical appreciation' not knee-jerk judgement.
4. Telling about her relationship with her Andean friend and co-worker Nazario Turpo, Marisol de la Cadena writes: 'Our worlds were not necessarily commensurable, *but* this did not mean we could not communicate. Indeed, we could, insofar as I accepted that I was going to leave something behind, as with any translation – or even better, that our mutual understanding was also going to be full of gaps that would be different for each of us, and would constantly show up, interrupting but not preventing our communication' (de la Cadena, 2015, p. xxv).

References

de la Cadena, M. (2015). *Earth beings*. Duke University Press.
Deleuze, G., & Guattari, F. (1992). *A thousand plateaus*. Athlone Press.
Deleuze, G., & Guattari, F. (1994). *What is philosophy?* Verso.
Gilbert, S. F., McDonald, E., Boyle, N., Buttino, N., Gyi, L., Mai, M., Prakash, N., & Robinson, J. (2010). Symbiosis as a source of selectable epigenetic variation: Taking the heat for the big guy. *Philosophical Transactions of the Royal Society B*, *365*, 671–678. doi:10.1098/rstb.2009.0245
Guattari, F. (1995). *Chaosmosis: An ethico-aesthetic paradigm*. Indiana University Press.
Guattari, F. (2000). *The three ecologies*. Athlone Press (Original work published 1989).
Haraway, D. J. (2016). *Staying with the trouble: Making kin in the chthulucene*. Duke University Press.
Hustak, C., & Myers, N. (2012). Involutionary momentum: Affective ecologies and the sciences of plant/insect encounters. *Differences*, *23*(3), 74–118. doi:10.1215/10407391-1892907
James, W. (1950). *The principles of psychology* (Vol. 2). Dover Publications.
James, W. (1977). *A pluralistic universe*. Harvard University Press.
James, W. (1979). *The will to believe*. Harvard University Press.
James, W. (1985). *The varieties of religious experience*. Harvard University Press.
Margulis, L., & Sagan, D. (1995). *What is life?* Simon & Schuster.
Savransky, M. (2021). *Around the day in eighty worlds*. Duke University Press.
Stengers, I. (2015). *In catastrophic times: Resisting the coming barbarism*. Open Humanities Press.
Tsing, A. (2015). *The mushroom at the end of the world*. Princeton University Press.
Whitehead, A. N. (1967). *Adventures of ideas*. The Free Press.

Author biographies

Didier Debaise is a permanent researcher at the Fonds National de la Recherche Scientifique (FNRS) and Professor of Philosophy at the Free University of Brussels (ULB). His main areas of research are contemporary forms of speculative philosophy, theories of events, and links between American pragmatism and the French contemporary philosophy. He has written three books on Whitehead's philosophy (*Un empirisme spéculatif, Le vocabulaire de Whitehead* and *L'appât des possibles*). Two of his books appeared in English: *Nature as Event* (Duke University Press) and *A*

Speculative Empiricism (Edinburgh University Press). He is currently working on a new book, *Pragmatique de la terre.*

Isabelle Stengers is philosopher, Professor Emerita of the Université Libre de Bruxelles. She is concerned by the questions of scientific practices and related to the philosophy of Deleuze, Whitehead and James as well as to the anthropology of Latour and the SF thinking adventure of Haraway. Among her books published in English translation are: *Order out of Chaos* with Ilya Prigogine, *The Invention of Modern Science, Cosmopolitics I* and *II, Capitalist Sorcery* with Philippe Pignarre, *Thinking with Whitehead, In Catastrophic Times* and *Another Science is Possible.*